Why Do I Feel This Way?

What Your Feelings Are Trying to Tell You

2d Edition

DINA L. WILCOX

Copyright © 2024 Dina L. Wilcox.

All rights reserved. No part of this book may be reproduced, stored, or transmitted by any means—whether auditory, graphic, mechanical, or electronic—without written permission of both publisher and author, except in the case of brief excerpts used in critical articles and reviews. Unauthorized reproduction of any part of this work is illegal and is punishable by law.

ISBN: 979-8-89419-397-7 (sc)
ISBN: 979-8-89419-398-4 (hc)
ISBN: 979-8-89419-399-1 (e)

Because of the dynamic nature of the Internet, any web addresses or links contained in this book may have changed since publication and may no longer be valid. The views expressed in this work are solely those of the author and do not necessarily reflect the views of the publisher, and the publisher hereby disclaims any responsibility for them.

One Galleria Blvd., Suite 1900, Metairie, LA 70001
(504) 702-6708

Contents

Introduction to the Second Edition 1
Dear Reader 5
Acknowledgments, with thanks. 19
Chapter 1 Where the Story Begins 23
Chapter 2 My Voice, Your Voice. 41
Chapter 3 We Are What We Feel 61
Chapter 4 Fear Weekend: Thinking Fear to Death. 86
Chapter 5 Of Adventures, Detours and Distractions:
            "I Just Want Someone to Love" 114
Chapter 6 In Search of the Elusive Memory 139
Chapter 7 Telling. 177
Chapter 8 Raising Healthy Voices 208
Chapter 9 Say It Isn't So. 234
Appendix A: Exercises for the Brain. .267
The Collage Exercise. 269
Bibliography 271

Introduction to the Second Edition

Dear Reader,

As is often the case with second editions, this one became necessary because a few things have changed since you might have read this book last. That's true, not so much for the objective facts proven by scientific research, but much more in my own thinking about how I see the research through my own filters. Here's one good example of how my thoughts have changed, as it pertains to one point in particular.

In my opening letter to you in 2013, I referred to our brains as the "place inside us" where our "feelings, emotions and intuition, fear, love, memories, inner voices and consciousness reside. Today, I would have to change *where* I believe they "reside" and even how they operate. In this edition, I begin a new conversation about these, this way:

> We don't know much about where our feelings and emotions—like fear and love—"reside," exactly. Science can only track the lights of them in our brains after they have been activated. Electromagnetically, they can be seen traveling across the channels of our brains; however, no one yet knows where they were created from, nor how they got into our brains to be processed. While the path they travel can seem, itself, to be miraculous, it doesn't tell us very much about what feelings are, either. Nor, for that matter,

does it tell us how feelings got to be so powerful. Did they just appear on earth one day, full-blown (you might ask), to change the entire landscape of everything it means to be a human?

In my second book, *Consciousness, Reality, and Making Love*, I gathered the evidence that suggests our feelings and voices and consciousnesses all reside elsewhere; they are likely to be parts of a separate, non-physical sensory system we have, and have yet to realize. We know our sight, hearing, tasting, smelling and touching are vitally important tools to help us maneuver our physical lives, but we seem to have overlooked, or minimized what I call our *non-physical senses*, the ones we cannot see but know with absolute certainty are very powerful in our lives: our imaginations, intuitions, feelings and emotions, dreams and even our consciousnesses.

My own research since 2012 has convinced me we do have a second, non-physical sensory system—we were born with them fully in tact—and while they cannot be seen, surely, they cannot be ignored. Your common sense, and you're having of these senses tells you the truth of this, and, just by being human you know how important they are as tools to everything that occurs in your life. Even if we wanted to ignore them (as we often do; dreams are a good example of this), we must acknowledge they very often run the show we call *"my life"*. They impact us, and we would do well to follow where their signals are trying to lead us. Together, they make up who we are, how we will live our lives and how we and others will know us.

What it comes down to is this: in a beautifully synchronistic Universe, how could we believe there would not be a system of tools for all our feelings and their companion characteristics? Would we expect *"Mother"* Nature to give us such powerful aspects without the tools with which to successfully utilize them? You hardly need to be told that your feelings tell you how you are reacting to some person, place or event that has just occurred in your life. If you fail to get the message from your feelings, you run the risk of walking blindly into your next adventure.

It is for these reasons you are now able to hold in your hands *"Why Do I Feel This Way?"* in its Second Edition. I want to welcome you (back) for an update, and, if you are meeting this book for the first time, I want to thank you for giving it a chance. There are additions to the text as it appeared originally, and the quotations from scientists have been removed; as a dedicated nonscientist, I write for others like myself. You will not find scientific jargon in this book, nor—you may be relieved to discover—any mathematical equations. What you will find, for instance, is a conversation about intuition that has been expanded from the first edition to include the wide-held belief that our intuition is, in fact, our inner voice. Again, we speculate, but we don't know much about intuition, just that we are learning the ways we can know it is really important to us.

In 2012, I told you of a voice that suddenly started talking directly to me about the ways I was *being* with my feelings. I told you it said, "*You have to go through what hurt you, and not around it anymore.... can do that.... won't have to alone....my strength to lean on.*" That voice, which sounded as if it was coming from both inside and out of me at the same time, came to help me in the darkest days after my husband died. I believed at the time that it was the voice of my feelings. Today, however, my relationship with that voice has changed dramatically. I now know it is the voice of what many people call their "Higher Selves," the part of each of us who is always looking out for our wellbeing.

In the first edition of this book, when you met my voice, I just referred to her as *her*; to me, *she* is still just *her*, but she is distinguished from my intuition in several ways. Unlike intuition, this voice is not a running monologue in my head. Rather, *she* challenges me, actively loves me and wants always to guide me in the best direction I can go to accomplish what I have set my sights on. I can ask *her* for guidance and, when I do so, I always get the answers I need.

There's another *non-physical sense* that is critically important. I think it very likely that, one day, science will discover consciousness is made of the energy of the Universe, which we currently know as "*dark matter*". In the meantime, scientists are still debating the broad spectrum of whether it is a figment of our imagination or will one day prove to be just another brain function. In your behalf, I was certain, you dear reader, would want to know if a big change like that was even a possibility, and that's another reason for this second edition.

We'll be talking about consciousness because it is one of the keys to understanding what it means to be a human.

Whether you are returning, or you have discovered my book for the first time, I am specifically grateful to you for doing so. My goal for my books is to convince you that *human is an extraordinary thing to be*. I do hope you'll contact me at my completely new website, dinawilcox.com.

Since the first publication, in 2012, many hundreds of wonderful people have chosen to add beautiful quotations and images of flowers and other items. I want to thank all of you who have done so, for you have filled my heart with joy. This book is dedicated to all of you.

Thanks for reading!

Dina
August 10, 2020

I celebrate myself, and sing myself,
and what I assume you shall assume,
for every atom belonging to me as good belongs to you

Walt Whitman, *Song of Myself*[1]

Dear Reader,

That quote from the poet Walt Whitman may seem presumptuous as a starting point for introducing myself. Yet this book, in its way, is about what you and I have most in common, so I admit I have made certain assumptions about you. I have had to, you see, in order to write this to you.

This book is about deeply personal things, like our feelings, emotions and intuition, fear, love, memories, inner voices and consciousnesses—things we all have—and one of the places inside us from which they operate. They are the *responses* we have to everything we experience in our lives, and regardless of what we might think about them individually, they exist, first and foremost, to serve us. In fact, the history of human brains—every atom of them, as Whitman suggests—has been the story of fine-tuning our parts to enhance our chances for maintaining perfect wellbeing. Since long before we humans started writing our own stories, our brains were set on an evolutionary course that would enhance our ability to manage our own selves, so that our species would thrive and survive. As you might imagine, many things have changed in response to our changing needs.

Scientists have said nature chooses to keep those things that have worked best over time. The result, so far, has been this: even counting any individual differences in human physiology, we almost all have brains that process our responses in pretty much the same way. This is true regardless of who we are or where in the world we live.

---

[1] Walt Whitman, "Song of Myself," *Complete Poetry and Selected Prose*, p. 25.

I do not assume that you, as I, will find comfort in this great sameness we share. Many people seem determined to prove their individuality in a world filled with so many *others;* this is one of the subjects we'll consider in the last two chapters of this book. My purpose in these pages is to show you that these things we have in common do not detract from each person's extraordinary uniqueness; rather, they are the foundation, the starting point, if you will, of the individual contributions every one of us makes to the whole of humanity—whether we intend to or not.

What I have assumed is that you are very familiar with your particular kinds of responses. You may be confident you know everything you need to know about your feelings and fears, and what your version of love feels like. Certainly you know you are the only one who holds your memories. After all, that's your life you're living, and no one else can live it from inside you, the way you do.

For some time now, scientists who study brains with imaging machines—which enable them to watch brain-parts light up as their owners feel and think and act—have been offering new information about how our responses work, and many of them have speculated about why they might work as they do. I believe you and I, as non-scientists, are the primary users of this information, because things like our feelings and fears and memories directly impact the choices and decisions we're making all the time. If we are going to live our lives deliberately, and not as victims of circumstances, we have a need to know at least some of what science is revealing about how we do that, so we can keep taking care of ourselves.

Some of what I've learned I have put into this book to share with you because I have assumed you are curious about yourself, as I am of myself. You might even want to know what your brain could tell you about yourself if it could talk to you directly. Perhaps you wonder how it manages the many bits and pieces of information you are confronted by every moment of your life. I certainly have wondered, especially those times when I'm feeling exhausted or getting a headache from an overload of incoming information. I was surprised to learn my brain seems to be amazingly clear about what's going on in there, even when I am feeling far from clear.

I have also assumed you might not be reading much neuroscience, because much of what has been written, even for us non-scientists, can be very technical and difficult to follow. You won't be finding any of that in this book. Here, feelings and emotions, memories, love, fear and our other responses to life are described in plain language, and they are incorporated as parts of an ongoing series of stories. The stories are mine, taken from a particular period of my life, when I conducted unscientific experiments to figure out what my brain was doing with all the feelings I was having, all the time. If you want to read more of the science, I've listed everything I have referenced in a Bibliography at the end of this book.

Perhaps you've heard the cliché that says life is what happens when you think you have everything under control. Suddenly there's an event that forces you to look at your humanity in a different way than you automatically do. Maybe you'll decide to reorder your priorities; you might move into a bigger picture, perhaps go undercover for a while before you re-emerge for all the world to see you as the truly amazing person you have always dreamed of becoming. For some people, that big a life-change is often triggered by a serious illness or an accident, either to themselves or to someone they love. Here, you can ponder making a big change simply because you want to.

My story started, as it does in chapter 1, with two people meeting to fall in love. Two years later, Art was diagnosed with the infection of HIVirus, just as we were planning to be married. Instead of the joyful life I had been holding in my mind's eye, I was, instead, forced to watch while the disease held him in its grip for three tumultuous years, during which my life changed many times over and then once more and for all time.

After he died, I discovered I had become an angry and suspicious woman—I was unrecognizable to the woman I had been before, and all my rage and suspicion were directed at me. I couldn't trust my own feelings; they were too powerful for my comfort, too conflicting—to state it simply, I didn't want to feel the way I did but I didn't know how to stop feeling that way. I tried to deny my feelings, to pretend I was just fine living inside of whatever life had *dished up* for me. As you will read in chapter 1, I even tried to outrun an imaginary clock I pretended was governing my feelings. I showed them my best stubborn resistance, until I finally had to admit I was failing miserably at it, just as I suspected I had failed at keeping my husband alive. In my despair, I had come to believe I was unreliable and powerless to change or effect anything.

Then a curious thing happened, which you'll read about in chapter 2. Just when I had convinced myself I had done everything wrong and could never trust myself again, I heard a voice speak to me. It seemed to be coming from both inside and out of me at the same time. It told me I had to go "through" my feelings and not around them anymore. Although I had never heard such a voice before, I trusted it instinctively, and I promised I would do what it advised. The rest of the stories in this book are about the 10-year journey the voice sent me on, a period which I sometimes called "mining my own self."

Now, I am certain that voice was being used by my brain to tell me what I needed to do in my own behalf, because I was at my lowest point and could not help myself. Over the next 10 years, as I worked with a support group, and then, later, with a counsellor, to *mine* my feelings, as they said, I was also reading what science was revealing about my brain. That was helping me understand how it might have been possible for my brain to tell me something I was not consciously aware of knowing.

From the science, I also learned that the purpose of every feeling is to tell me about itself, to give me the one simple truth it holds that I would need to think about if and when I wanted to respond to it. That seemed logical, because my brain is organized to help me thrive, and when I understand what I am feeling I can use that knowledge to act in my own best interests. I was learning that my chances of thriving can be greatly enhanced when I am living my life deliberately.

What does it mean to live deliberately? It means living with intentionality, with the intention to use all the tools at my disposal to make good and smart choices and decisions in my behalf. It also means allowing myself to trust that, as a human, I have some pretty amazing tools to help me live well in the long run.

It would not be an exaggeration to say that one of your most important responses to life is your feelings. Feelings are your touchstones for knowing yourself, because so much of what you know comes from your feelings. Yet, I am assuming you, as I, know many people who are not comfortable with their feelings. Perhaps *you* have wondered more than once why a hurt feeling you were having was making you feel even worse than you already did. Sometimes, understanding what your feelings are trying to tell you can be like walking into your darkened living room during the darkest night. You move slowly and cautiously until you find the light switch that will show you where the furniture is so you can avoid tripping over it. You may be cautious about your feelings because you don't want to *knock* anything over or disturb what you fear you may not be able to set straight again.

Today, I find comfort in knowing all our relationships with our feelings start out in pretty much the same way. Feelings are one major way we all respond to what our five senses are revealing to us. But, far from neutralizing us into some bland sameness, each of us will always respond to our feelings in our own unique way. That's because, even though our feelings all do the same things, in every body there is only one person who has the precise combination of experiences and thoughts who is going to have to decide how they will react. Whatever action you take, or do not take on the basis of how you feel is processed and determined through the filters of your own, individual perceptions; it is colored by your memories, your longings and so many more characteristics that are yours alone. No one can ever feel your feelings exactly as you do, and what you feel about them makes you the extraordinary individual human you are on all the earth.

When you know this about your feelings, you can begin to see how powerful you are, naturally. On the other hand, perhaps it is precisely because that kind of power comes so naturally to us that we can easily become overwhelmed by it. Instead of letting nature take its course, you may work hard to deny your power. You might even allow others to convince you that you are not powerful. Like plugging a huge spotlight into a tiny table lamp, you might use your *amps* to keep your brightest lights low, or dim. You may say you wish more than anything that you were powerful, yet you might be denying your feelings and the expression of your true natural power under a belief that says you must protect yourself from such feelings. You might be concerned, or even fearful that, if you are too powerful you will no longer be accepted in the relationships you have in your life. In the last chapter of this book, we'll imagine what the world could look like if we were able to live powerfully, naturally, and peacefully together.

This book is all about you, and me

Although I am not a scientist, I have always been curious to know what goes on inside me. If I discover I am lying to myself, I can be relentless about getting to the truth and understanding why I would do that. I used to joke that knowing myself was my first full-time job, the one I could never quit. About 20 years ago, that need to know led me to start reading neuroscience books. I wanted to know what my brain might have to tell me about how my life looks from its perspective.

One of the most interesting things I've learned is that most of what our brains do they do automatically. We get thirsty so we drink; we jump at the sudden sound of a truck backfiring; we feel cold or hot so we cover or uncover ourselves. While we may be thinking about what we are going to drink or wear, or be talking about how startled we all were at the sound of the truck, we don't have to think about doing these things in response. Our brains will force us to do what we are "hard-wired" to do: stay alive.

In fact, many of your responses happen automatically to ensure you will take the best care of yourself, keep yourself safe, and quickly, if necessary. Since your brain's primary function is to keep you alive, and you need certain things to facilitate your survival, the basic things have always been built in to ensure they will happen whether you are paying attention or not. As you will read in chapter 3, though, even with those things you will do automatically, your feelings will often give you every opportunity to think about and decide how you are going to act on them.

Before you can truly decide to take any action that will be in your best interests, you must first understand what you believe your best interests to be. You probably know you do that by thinking, but did you know that you can also use all your "responders" to help you think about the decisions and choices you will eventually make? That's *why* you have so many different kinds of responses. In chapters 4-7, you will see how your feelings—along with your memories, intuition, thoughts, emotions and even your fears—are all there to assist you in making your all-important choices and decisions.

In chapter 4, you'll read about an unscientific experiment I conducted over what I call my "Fear Weekend," in which I made a discovery about a fear that I didn't even know I was feeling. You will also read that I discovered, at the end of my weekend that, although some fears are easier than others to overcome, there is a practice we can follow to break even our most fearful fears down and simply blow them away. I still use this method, every time I find fear in myself.

Over the course of that weekend, my inner voice came back to visit after a long period of silence, and *she* had much to say about my fear. Writing in my journal, I began to notice I was expressing thoughts I had been unaware of having—which was a sure sign my voice was checking in to be heard. It was also during this weekend that I came to think of the voice as the interpreter of my fears and, by my definition, my feelings. That helped me realize I could manage a lot more about my life than I knew, and how I could do it.

For this reason, chapter 4 will revisit inner voices in depth, enabling you to think about your voice, both as I have imagined mine and as I have heard from others who have spoken about their internal voices. You might be surprised to know I have found evidence of what I call our inner voices in sources as disparate as neuroscience, philosophy and metaphysics. Some of these sources are also listed in the Bibliography at the back of the book.

In chapter 5, we'll take on the subject of love. I'll tell you a story of an experience I had that only became an unscientific experiment retroactively, long after it was over. It's a familiar story of trying to love someone who is incapable of accepting and giving love. I'll tell you now that I very nearly lost myself before my inner voice showed up this time. When she did come, *she* asked the simplest question and it changed, not only my course of action, but enabled me to leave a hurtful relationship and, finally, put to rest the suspicion I had long been carrying around after Art's death: that I did not deserve to be loved.

Chapter 6 will take a close look at what happens to all those things we think we have safely filed away in our memory banks. It, too, has an unscientific experiment, one that showed me how our memories—even those we don't know we have—make a contribution to living our lives deliberately. Although I'm not assuming anything here, this experiment might inspire you to begin thinking about opening your own imaginary unscientific laboratory.

The memory of fear

Everyone has fear. Even those of us who insist they are never afraid of anything. Fear is one of those responses that is hard-wired into our brains to ensure we act quickly in our own behalf when threats and danger leap out at us. As our brains became more sophisticated, to keep up with all the changes in humans' lives over eons of time, fear has changed, too. At some point in time, we stopped needing it to be just an automatic response mechanism, and we started to think about it. You may have experienced, in your own life, fear that is quite powerful, even overwhelming, when you think about it.

As I was researching and writing this book, I interviewed Dr. Joseph LeDoux at New York University's Center for Neural Science. Dr. LeDoux introduced the concept of "emotional memory" in the early 1990s, as a means to distinguish between the two kinds of memories he was identifying in his lab (you'll read about these in chapter 6).[2] In particular, Dr. LeDoux told me that his work is involved with the "learning and storage of emotional fear memory."[3]

As he explained it, he studies the ways the brain "detects and responds to emotionally arousing stimuli," that is, the way "emotional learning occurs and emotional memories are formed, and how our

---

[2] Joseph LeDoux, The Emotional Brain: *The Mysterious Underpinnings of Emotional Life*, p. 9.
[3] LeDoux, Music and the brain, literally," in *Frontiers of Human Neuroscience*, Volume 5, Article 49, pp. 1-3, June 2011.

conscious emotional feelings emerge from unconscious processes."[4] He told me that "we have to accept that the initiation of our fears is not always under our control. Something happens to us from the outside or from the inside—a random thought, or something occurs to your mind and the whole system is activated. You have a thought and in one case it's going to the amygdala [the fear processor in your brain] to turn it on and in the other case you want it to go to the amygdala to turn it off but it doesn't want to. [We] don't know why that would be the case, except, probably, [we are] highly oversimplifying what a thought is."[5]

From this statement, you might begin to see how complex our brains are, and therefore, how complex we humans are. While many things are happening automatically in our brains to process our fears, Dr. LeDoux seemed confident that we ourselves have an important role to play in managing our fears, by applying our consciousnesses, that is by thinking.

Not surprisingly, he cautioned that: "Habits are hard to change. I think habits can be broken," he said, "it's not easy, but they can be."[6] As you read both about fear and memories in this book, you can listen for the ways my own experience reinforced this message from Dr. LeDoux. In fact, I had asked him specifically about fear because I had discovered, during my "Fear Weekend", that I was the key component for dissolving some of the fears that used to stop me from going after the things I want in my life.

Happily, for us non-scientists, Joseph LeDoux is also a wonderful musician. He plays with a band of neuroscientists, called The Amygdaloids, who are on a mission to teach college students and the rest of us about our brains. You can learn more about and follow this band and their music at their website: www.amygdaloids.com.

---

[4]   LeDoux, The Emotional Brain, *ante*.
[5]   LeDoux, recorded interview notes, January 25, 2011.
[6]   *Ibid*.

Looking beyond our individual selves

When you get to chapter 7, the conversation will begin to branch out from concentrating on us as individuals to looking at how we live together in communities, including strangers living together in the same world. We'll consider things we do and do not say to each other, and the secrets we keep from one another, even with the best of intentions. I'll tell you about the secret Art left me with, and how, after he died, it took on a life of its own. It became so powerful that, finally, it forced me to tell what I had promised years before I would never reveal to anyone.

In the telling, I found the door to my own freedom, and as I walked through it, I learned our brains are wired to cause natural connections to form between and among us. In fact, the simplest act of talking is one of the most powerful ways we can promote the survival of our species. From there, in chapter 8, I'll tell you about some of the specific responses and activities that have evolved in us for nothing so much as creating and supporting connections, and how these are important between us. Some of them will surprise you; others will be very familiar. Together, they'll give you a great overview of how your brain maximizes your survival by making life fun along the way.

In the last chapter, I'm going to take everything that came before and invite you to join me in an unscientific experiment which will only require your imagination. We'll take a brand-new look at what we think of as reality. We'll do extraordinary thinking about how we have come to define our realities and ask if it is possible for us to choose, instead, some other kind of reality, one that, perhaps, we could all agree would be more to our liking.

Along with your imagination, the last chapter will also call upon something I have mentioned in a few of these paragraphs so far, but you will not have to do anything in preparation for using it. It's your consciousness, and it will show up, automatically, wherever you are. Consciousness is a powerful tool when you're thinking: you deliberate, decide and then choose what to do or what to think about whatever is on your mind. Consciously, you can even decide what to believe about something as big as a new reality. While thinking is also something you do automatically, what you think about is uniquely made up of who you are and what you perceive and experience in your life. Some people have used their consciousnesses to create amazing inventions they have put into the world, ovens that cook roast beef to perfection and the printing press and computers that have made it possible for you to hold this book in your hands, for a few examples. Others have applied their consciousnesses toward helping them go along, taking what comes, as if there were another force outside them that is really in charge of how they live.

There has been, for many years, much debate among scientists about what consciousness really is and where it is generated inside us. There's good news here for us non-scientists: we do not have to participate in this debate. We can be satisfied to know that, when we wake up after the sleep our bodies need, we are conscious again: of how cold we are, how hungry, perhaps plans we made for the new day ahead and, ultimately, about anything and everything that is *out there* for us to *take on*. We can luxuriate in our consciousness, apply it to everything we perceive as well as anything we dream, with nothing at all to stop or prevent us from doing so. Consciousness is automatic, and it, like dreaming, and imagining, is available to us at all times.

With consciousness, each of us has the capability to live deliberately, with the intention of realizing our heart's desires and loving our lives. We can reflect on those things we may misperceive as being more powerful than we are, and we can change the course of our lives as often as we want. I believe discovering what is truly in our best interests is the grand surprise we shall find at the end of the adventure I call *thinking it through*, and in chapter 9 we can think our reality through with nothing more than our conversations. After reading that chapter, you may even want to take it with you out into the world and invite others to conduct this experiment with you.

You might as well know now, I assume you are a very powerful person—whether you think so or not—and writing this book to share both my own stories and what I have learned about our brains has motivated me to share these thoughts that have been on my mind for a long time.

Finally, to help you get into shape for hearing and getting to know your own inner voice, you'll find a couple of exercises in the appendix. One is just for fun—with a serious purpose—and you can do it alone or with your friends. It might get you laughing as you envision clearing your head in order to hear the sound of your inner voice, and laughter is a wonderful response for bringing about connections among people. The second exercise is for creating collages. These are a great way to give your brain—and your inner voice—a chance to show you, in images, what's really on your mind.

Food for thought

As a young girl, I never knew that anyone other than I had secrets they turned to for comfort inside their heads. Now I know we humans live most of our lives inside our heads, in our minds and imaginations, our perceptions and our interpretations of everything our senses take in. This characteristic of every human is, perhaps, the very best reason why it is so important we talk to one another. We are the only *others* on earth who are like us, and each one of us is another's very best natural resource.

In our time on the earth, we have learned our technologies very well. We are sophisticated about our electronics and high-tech communication devices. Yet, too many of us exalt the place of these technologies in our lives at the expense of our human resources. Some use these as tools to hold themselves apart from others even as they exclaim technology affords them the greatest communication potential.

Our brains are revealing that our biological heritage includes a great bias for interdependence: we need each other to survive. It is only when we exercise all the resources we have that we can realize our full potential for being human, perhaps the one thing we take most for granted. Without knowing what, and who, our natural resources are, we can mistakenly think our external technologies are the only sources of our power, and that they complete us as humans.

Now, we don't have to wonder whether or not, in reality, we need each other. Our brains have started to speak to the many scientists who have invited them to the research tables. We have a great opportunity for a grand adventure that will take us toward bringing our lives into balance. We can know about the amazing, complex things that are our natural, human capabilities, the ones that have been developing for all of humans' time on earth. Indeed, they have withstood the tests of time. You and I are perpetually evolving into what works best, and no one can take these things away from us. Getting to know them enables us, at last, to take a deep breath and incorporate *all* our skills, the technological and the natural, in order to move forward as whole human beings in a way nothing else around us can. If not we, then who? Why not now?

Like I said at the outset, this book is all about you, as it is all about me and the things we have most in common as humans. Replace my stories with your own and indulge yourself in a private unscientific discovery of how extraordinary you truly are. Then take yourself out into the world with the *others*, for surely, everything you assume we shall all assume.

See you out there!

D
October 10, 2012

Acknowledgments, with thanks

One of the most important lessons I have learned in my life is that it is natural for humans to want to be acknowledged. I say this without irony. It is human nature, perhaps one of those things that has been hard-wired into our brains, a subject that receives much attention in this book. In fact, there is very little we can accomplish by ourselves, without the assistance and support from others. Acknowledgment, then, is a joy, a small thank-you, in this instance, to the many people who have loved the supported me in my work.

Dr. Justin Moscarello of the New York University Center for Neural Science agreed to be my science editor, to ensure that I have appropriately interpreted the science I describe throughout the book. I thank him for his generous and straightforward reviews of my manuscript and most thoughtful comments, as well as for not showing any judgments or predispositions about working with a non-scientist.

Dr. Joseph LeDoux, who runs the Center for Neural Science was most gracious in sharing his great wealth of information about his own work in fear and memory by granting me an interview. I appreciate that even long after our interview, he continued to offer his generous availability and assistance.

Many non-scientists have given me the benefit of their wisdom and skills, and I acknowledge them with my sincere thanks and appreciation. My good friend and editor, Karen Burd, who listened powerfully, and patiently, as I read each chapter aloud, often in multiple iterations, is a constant source of profound inspiration for me, with her insightful questions and encyclopedic memory of everything she has ever read. I am most grateful to have her in my life.

Thanks, too, to the Fates who sent me my sister, poet and writing teacher Nadell Fishman, along with her thoughtful consideration of my work and great editorial reading. Your close attention to details is nothing short of inspirational. Please know that your comments steered me to what works best in this book.

Anne Penman—who was the facilitator of the Caregiver's Group that fate, and one good friend steered me to—was the first person who taught me not to fall into the trap of believing that where I am at any given moment is the only possibility for my life. Without her extraordinarily loving generosity and patience, which allowed and enabled me to make the long, often painful journey back into myself after my husband, Art, died, I am certain I would still be stuck somewhere else along the road, lamenting all the things I did wrong.

Toward that end, I have also been blessed with the support of many people I have met at conferences and in the Landmark Education community throughout the life, so far, of this project. You know who you are, and you know that your enthusiasm for bringing a book like this into the world has held me up when I doubted myself. For you, thank-you barely suffices. Hence, I am filled with joy to be able to acknowledge you all. Know that it comes with my heart.

D

Love after Love

The time will come
when, with elation,
you will greet yourself arriving
at your own door, in your own mirror,
and each will smile at the other's welcome,
and say, sit here. Eat.
You will love again the stranger who was yourself.
Give wine. Give bread. Give back your heart
to itself, to the stranger who has loved you
all your life, whom you ignored
for another, who knows you by heart.
Take down the love letters from the bookshelf,
the photographs, the desperate notes,
peel your own image from the mirror.
Sit. Feast on your life.

Derek Walcott

1

Where the Story Begins

I was a widow at 44. My 46-year old husband died almost five years after he suddenly appeared in my life, like a comet, unannounced and unexpected. When he landed in my world, I imagined dreams coming true on into forever, but, like the comet, he couldn't stay long. A terrible sense of loss moved in quickly to take his place, and even though it stayed way longer than he had, I could never regret having been there when he first touched down.

It was at an old hippie resort in the Catskill Mountains of New York State—a place that had once been a Communist party camp—on a Friday night at the end of August. I spotted him across the dance-floor when I wandered into the room where the music was playing. He was standing with half his back to me, and all I could see were faded blue jeans and a crisp, white, straight-from-the-office shirt with the sleeves rolled up to reveal tanned forearms. He had sand-colored hair he wore just like other little boys from the Midwest: straight with a side part and short around the bottom. In the spotlight he stood under, the top of his hair, bleached by summer, glistened like the mica embedded in a New York City sidewalk when the sun catches it. I noticed; even his shirt seemed to be shining *dayglo* under the spotlight. I noticed, and I stared longer than was polite. Later, when we passed each other in a narrow hallway and squeezed to get by, I momentarily lost my equilibrium staring into his Caribbean Sea-colored eyes fixed on me as he smiled. Again, I noticed. I was having trouble moving away from this guy.

He asked me to dance the last dance of the night and then walked me to my cabin in the woods. He was smart and funny, and when he took my hand I could feel the air about him of a party going on all the time.

I could hardly wait for the night to end so I could see him again in the morning. Sleep was impossible; my thoughts and feelings were racing. It seemed as if I had known him all my life, as if the star he rode in on dropped him where he landed because I was there and I was there because he was coming. He had an uncanny knack for knowing, within minutes of meeting me, just what I needed to feel cared about, and he made me feel that way. For all the time I would know him, I would treasure this about him. I would watch him over and over again—with our families, our friends, everyone we met together—as he instinctively found just the thing we all needed to feel loved, and when he did, he was in his glory to give it to us. It was his reason for living. He was the perfect partner for me, a little magic for the girl from New York City who was inclined to be skeptical, even cynical, and oh so very analytical. I, cast in the role of the slightly atypical lawyer, reserved and holding back, quiet, shy and serious, became the watcher suddenly thrown into the great passions of life. Art's kind of loving would change me forever.

In the summer of our second year, we were planning to get married. Then he had trouble breathing, and by the time they examined him in the hospital emergency room, somebody—one of many nameless, faceless people on that frightening day who wouldn't notice, wouldn't listen and should have known—was yelling at *me*, demanding I tell him how it could be possible that Art could have been using only six percent of his lung capacity all that day. As if I knew. I had been terrified by having to watch him all that day, the obvious lack of oxygen as he struggled for every breath during the long *"Intake"*, but I had not been so crazed that I couldn't catch the irony of *them* coming to *me* for that answer, as if they hadn't kept him waiting for 16 hours before they even noticed him at all. By the time they were ready to put him into a bed, it was the middle of the night and they were forcing me to leave him there, to go home, alone. I all but made them swear he would still be there in the morning and I would be able to find him.

Pneumonia, they said that day, and because he was a young man and it was 1988 in New York City, they put him in the AIDS Unit. I found him there, asleep, the next morning, hooked up to the skeleton mother who was feeding him breakfast from a clear plastic bag. Breakfast was always our favorite meal out together. I watched them for a few minutes, a little jealous of the intimacy of their scene, and then I turned away and left him to go to work.

He slept for almost all of the first 24 hours and was already feeling better by the time I returned later in the afternoon. The nurses had ordered a second dinner, for me, so I could eat with him, and then they let me spend the night, no questions asked. I soon figured out where we were, and their solicitousness held disturbing reams of confessions about what routinely went on in that ward.

While Art rested after dinner, I walked the halls so I could peer as far into all the other dimly-lit silent rooms as I dared, trying to force them to give up their secrets. Make a note, I told myself; they must keep the lights dim because the virus makes bright lights hurt eyes. I could feel myself panicking with my need to figure out what had just happened to us and what was yet to happen all at the same time. I had to do something, but I didn't know enough, yet, to know what it was. I thought of my walk as a fact-finding tour at the center of the epidemic. While he slept and I walked, I could feel his life, my life and our life change forever.

Over the next two weeks, they did little more than build his strength back up. One afternoon, his young doctor ran up a flight of stairs exhilarated to report the great news that Art didn't have *pneumocystis carinii*—the pneumonia of AIDS—and all the hospital staff who came in contact with him that day celebrated that one young man would be saved.

However, my life had already taken a sharp veer off into the surreal, so I figured until they tested his blood I'd hold off on the celebrating and just keep watching. They didn't do the blood test until the day he was discharged two weeks later, and they sent him home with instructions to rest for another two weeks, when he could call them for the results. Kafka couldn't have written it better.

Dina L. Wilcox

"People Living with AIDS"

On the night we got the diagnosis—our first official night as *"People Living with AIDS"*—Art and I misplaced our ability to think along the same lines for the first time. In the taxicab-ride home from the doctor's office, with his new diagnosis between us, there was no conversation, no holding of hands. We sat at opposite ends of the back seat, each staring intently out our own window. In my racing mind, I was beginning to pare down my list of the people who were dearest to me, who I took for granted I would have to tell because Art would need them to love him. That was the way we always managed illness in my big family, and I grew up knowing everyone could be counted on.

So I was unprepared, on that night, to learn Art had not been so lucky as I. He grew up knowing no one would want him if he got sick. He was determined no one should know, and as he pleaded his case for keeping the secret, his face told me he was ashamed…so ashamed.

Slowly, I came to see he had already equated his illness with the end of loving, and I was uncertain about what to do with that. I promised to keep the secret with him because his eyes were screaming that, since I was going to have to leave him anyway, I should just do it and get it over with fast, and on that night of all nights, he needed to understand I wasn't going anywhere without him. From my perspective, *we* were under attack and we needed to be strong together if we were going to beat this thing. Silently, I tore up my imaginary *"to tell"* list and pushed it out of my mind altogether.

I had a lot of feelings by the time that night came, more than a few I'd frozen in suspension from the two weeks we spent waiting for the test results, and the two weeks in the hospital before that, as well as the two weeks Art had spent getting sicker each day before he finally agreed to go to the emergency room in the first place. I didn't know what to do with such feelings as these. They terrified me. I was afraid to allow them to stay in my mind. For the first time, there were things between us I didn't feel safe telling Art. Standing with my back to him in our bedroom as we ended that night AIDS moved in, and looking straight into the end of the world, I imagined myself cupping all my feelings in my hands, wrapping each one in tissue paper and carefully, so as not to disturb them in any way, explaining to them I would put them into a box I would store way in the back of my closet and no one but me would know it was there. I would mark the box *Later*, and I promised myself I would take it out when I had the time and place to think about those feelings from a safe distance. Later, after the world ended.

I was determined I would have to deny my feelings on that night because I promised AIDS it was in for the fight of its life if it thought it was going to take Art away from me. I could see I was going to need a clear mind for every decision and action I would have to take if I was going to keep him alive. There would be no time or space for the luxury of thinking about such petty things as my hurt feelings. They would just get in the way.

What I hadn't determined was this: I was afraid if I paid any attention at all to how I felt I would fall apart. I would simply explode into more pieces than I would ever be able to find to put myself back together again.

Art lived three more years, during which I learned many new things. I learned I had been raised to revere and blindly trust any professional in a white medical coat, and then I learned—as I watched the dearest doctors and nurses struggle with confounding new variations on old illnesses—how to untangle myself from that early, naïve position. I learned about prejudice and fear and secret-keeping from the inside out. I found these things existed in our new life because, even though you were merely a sick person who was going to die, somehow the word had gotten out your disease was a bad one politically and that gave everyone outside of you the right to judge you as unworthy. I also learned what it means to be a caregiver, working 24 hours a day and hardly being able to find a moment when you can sit quietly and try to calm yourself down enough so you can just think, to figure out anything other than what is the next thing to do. These were terrible, brutalizing things to learn, and they all came with still more feelings I quickly packed away, for *"Later"*.

I had quite a pile of un-felt feelings by then, but they were as nothing in the end. Altogether, they couldn't even compare with the feelings of, finally, being helpless beyond imagination as I watched Art waste away no matter what I did, until he just disappeared. On the morning he died, someone put a chair in the middle of the living room in the cabin we had been renting in the woods near where we had first met—we had moved there six weeks earlier to get him some fresh air to breathe—and I sat in it. As I vaguely noticed my family moving around me in fast motion throughout the day, I sat, not moving at all, looking at my empty hands perfectly still in my lap. Try as I might, I could not make my hands set me straight about why it was they suddenly had nothing at all to do.

In the days that followed, everything that occurred was just something which imposed itself on me. Beautiful spring mornings, for example, required I wash my face, and I resented their bright and sunny disposition overstepping their side of my window. The only thing I wanted to do was sit perfectly still, without moving, so I could hold on to the rapidly disappearing pictures of Art in my mind.

Days

A week later, I opened the law office we had worked so hard to set up in the six weeks since we had left the City for the mountains upstate. We had been so busy, both of us, pretending we were serious about what we were doing—starting a new law firm—when all we were doing was denying what we could not do at all. Now, slowly dragging the great bulk that was my body, I was forced to move into an actual life.

I was determined to do everything *right,* whatever that would require of me. I was all that was left of the Art-and-me we had created together, and I wanted everyone who saw me to think I was bearing my loss well, for his sake. How was I to know I only thought there was a *right way* because I had picked up some foolish notion as a child that you can make the dead person proud by the way you bear your sorrow?

With powerful longing, the only thing I wanted was not to have to think about myself or how much everything hurt. I longed for someone to tell me that, if I could just hang on, all those old, buried feelings raging inside me would dissolve by themselves, just go away and leave me alone. What I most wanted was to be alone, so I could work at not feeling any of what threatened me. How could I have known that was exactly the opposite of what I truly needed?

For weeks, every person I met had a message to give me, and every message seemed to reinforce some great popular wisdom that said my feelings would only get in the way of *"doing it right."* Within a matter of weeks, almost everyone who talked to me said I should be *"moving on"*, as if they had all taken a course together and learned the same lingo. Apparently *"moving on"* is the single-most important piece of advice people have to give you when the person you love the most has died—should I have been suspicious that it might also be the most dangerous piece of advice? It seemed as if everyone was being really careful to avoid asking me anything about how I was feeling.

Over and over again, I was told it would be wrong for me to "hold onto him," and it would be right for me to "get on with my life and let him go," without "dwelling on the past." The past, I presumed, was where the feelings belonged. I could accept that; I just didn't know how to get them out of my present and into the past without having them destroy me in the process. A lot of people offered tips and suggestions about how I "should" do the right thing, reinforcing the urgency of their tips with prescriptions that I remember how young I was—as if that would somehow make it easier for me to do whatever I was supposed to do—"as he would surely want you to." Everybody seemed so certain of their advice that, in no time I was wondering, in a bitter, ironic way, why it was only *I* who seemed not to have been informed of the rules they had all, obviously, somehow gotten a copy of. Where had I been *that* day? As far as I could see, I was the only one around who still needed to know, and I didn't have any idea what the rules were.

All I knew was my feelings were starting to torment me. They felt like enemies preparing for a great battle inside me. I needed to know how to deal with them (because my plan to hide them in the closet obviously was not working), and my need was fast becoming urgent. Days and then months were passing without any relief and, no matter what I tried to make myself think, I couldn't seem to find the *right* thing, the one thing I had wanted, with the best of intentions, to do for Art's sake.

Months

Four months after he died, I had nearly driven myself crazy. Now I was longing to tell somebody everything inside me—the feelings and sorrow and even a growing rage of unmitigated frustration—had all gotten bound into a terrible knot, and I couldn't figure out how to untangle it. I needed help. Desperately, I went to see a therapist whose name I pulled out of the local phone book. When I explained to her my husband had recently died of a heart attack—dead was dead, wasn't it? So how could it matter to her, a total stranger, that I had to keep Art's secret for him instead of telling her the truth?—she explained in great detail how tribal cultures all around the world deal with the wife of a partner after his death. She said the grieving spouse is allowed to go off into the woods, or the jungle by herself for a full year before she will be expected to return to the village and take up her rightful place in the life of the community again.

I saw her a few more times after that, but all I did was not tell her the truth about anything else that had happened to me, so we soon came to the end of any help she could offer me. I felt kind of bad about that—one more thing to blame myself for—because I knew I had left out some pretty salient facts. I comforted myself by thinking she would never have to know I had decided in her behalf that my version was enough for her and way better than my terrible truth. She hadn't made what hurt me feel any better—I hadn't given her much to work with on that score—but she had helped me in one important way. Her village in the jungle analogy implied there was nothing I could do about the way I felt now, and I could expect to feel better at the end of the year. Even more, she had made it sound as if it would be a natural process and would happen without my having to do anything deliberate. I would take that to hold onto even if I couldn't do anything about my raging feelings. I would settle for what I got because it was something, at least, and more than I thought I deserved. The most important thing was I had kept Art's secret safe, and I could continue to do just that while I waited for my normal life to resume.

My normal life. Which one would that be? The one I had before I met Art that was changed forever by our loving? The one I counted on having with him, only without him? How would I do *that*? And how would I recognize feeling normal when I couldn't allow myself to feel anything at all because, once I opened *that* door, too many piled-up feelings were going to come crashing down on me, and that was the one thing I couldn't allow to happen?

I told myself maybe I didn't need to have all the answers. The therapist was an expert. She obviously knew more about grieving than I, and she had spoken honestly with me even if I had not returned the favor. She had offered that I would feel better after a year, and that meant I had eight whole months to get there. It seemed a long shot, at best, given the way I felt after the first four months, but I decided I had no other choice but to hold on to it, and wait.

Years

As I ticked off the months to the end of my first year without Art, I knew I wasn't feeling any better. I could feel panic threatening at my outside borders. I was afraid to talk to anyone about that, though, because the one thing you learn very quickly when your person dies is you do not want to burden anyone with your sorrow, especially as time goes by. That's a sure sign you're not *doing it right*.

At the one-year deadline, I thought I actually felt a little worse. It would be quite some time before I would learn feeling worse is the natural result of the protective coating—the shock of his death—dissolving. All I knew was that time was passing all right, but the magic healing I had always heard it promised seemed nowhere in sight. Immediately, I moved into thinking that, if there was a formula for the situation I was in, I had obviously blown my shot at discovering what it was.

In fact, many more years than I could even have imagined would have to pass before I would be able to consider that I had been struggling to recover, not only from Art's disappearance from my life, but also from the insinuation of things like the AIDS epidemic itself and even the powerful experience of caregiving. As I had told the therapist eight months before, everything had gotten tangled up together and I couldn't separate anything out from anything else. I had meant it; it had been the one thing about which I had told her the simple truth. But I could not have known I would only become clear about what was all tangled up inside me *after* I started to do something about it. Until, and unless, I could allow myself to take that mountain apart, none of the advice the therapist or anyone else had given me could even begin to help me figure out what to do to make my life feel right again.

By the time Art was dead two-and-a-half years, I had convinced myself I was crazy. I looked just like a person who had successfully *moved on*—I had bought a house, I was running my own law practice and my office was just another fixture in the tiny hamlet in which I lived. None of the people I met on a day-to-day basis asked how I was *doing* in the way they used to, and no one gave me any more advice. It seemed as if, in the rule book they all followed, it was all over by then. Most people I met now, I knew, had never even heard I once had a husband who died.

The irony was, I had all the characteristics of a lovely new life, but I wasn't anywhere in it. My old feelings were still in there all right; I could feel them rumbling as if they were arranging a protest rally and were going to break out any minute. I hadn't *moved on* at all, not in the way I would have expected. I had put on a good new coat and everyone loved the look of it, but all I had accomplished was to turn myself into someone who was uniquely not-me, a chameleon whose real life was still buried deep within her waiting for something to happen to it. *I* was waiting for something to happen, and I had become an angry person in the meantime. I resented the new presence of this someone-else-as-me-person. People actually thought she was happy, and I was angry at how easily fooled they were by this phony in my clothing.

Even more than that, I was convinced something must be wrong with me. I had failed at grieving—*could somebody actually do that?* I kept thinking I had known all along I wasn't going to make the one-year deadline for feeling better—there must have been some signal way back at six months that I had missed—and now it was too late for me to go back and try to do it over. I actually fantasized about going back and doing it over so I could get it right. I thought I had done all the right things, what had been expected of me. I had dutifully tried to follow the advice of people who seemed to know better than I what I *should* be feeling and what I *should* be doing, but that wasn't the worst of it. I could think of no reason at all why Art would be proud of the way I had managed his death, and that really made me sad.

I had tried never to think about him. I had taken away all his photographs as fast as my family had taken all his clothes from the cabin. (I had been too stunned by his death even to think about how quickly and proficiently they had packed up everything the very night his body had been taken to the funeral place and made it all disappear as if it had never been there—as if *he* had never been there. It would be years before I would even wonder if they had done me a favor, years before I would meet Henriette, who was still washing, ironing, folding and putting her dead husband's pajamas back into his dresser drawer, to keep them "fresh," she said. I would be grateful, then, so appreciative my family had thought to spare me that, at least, even though it had hurt me so much to have nothing left of Art in his own home.) I had forced myself to stop talking to him under the pretense he had to be somewhere and so he must be able to hear me, right? I had taken to screaming at myself instead, demanding I stop missing him when I found myself thinking about him. I had vehemently denied I felt better if I sneaked a look at a photograph, or if I closed my eyes for just a stolen moment and imagined myself dancing with him, his arms around me. I had done what I thought was expected of me, but there had been no reward for my effort, nor any help to dissolve the painful feelings inside me. I was doing the opposite of getting rid of those old feelings. I was pushing new feelings down in after them all the time.

Try as I might, I just couldn't do anything else. What lay at the bottom of all my worst feelings was the most terrible one. It confounded me just to touch its edges whenever I felt it rumbling in my belly; I didn't want to go anywhere near it. It was the feeling of a day I knew very well was coming, when I would have to turn my back on Art and walk away to a new life because he had died and I had not—

Had I expected I would die, when I was never even sick? Was that why I had so deftly removed myself from this new life I was having? Was I waiting, still, to die? And was I thinking what did it matter how I passed the time while I was waiting?

It didn't matter. *I* didn't matter. For all my feelings there remained a question I could not answer for my own sake, one that no one had ever thought to try and answer in my behalf: Didn't Art deserve better than this? How could I *move on* and simply leave him for a new life?

Even the thought I could do that to him felt like punishing him over and over again for dying.

Today, I can call that survivor's guilt, but then I had no name for it, only the fear and dread of such a day ever coming anywhere near to me. How could I have known what to do with those feelings? They were enormous in my eyes. They blinded me, for years, prevented me from being able to see the plain and simple illogic of worrying about what Art deserved, or of thinking my survival continued to be linked to his and could not be altered in my behalf.

Do we always ask what are we supposed to do with our wedding vows, afterward? I was looking for the link that could still stand between us, but I could not see how only I was both the cause and effect of the looking. I was trying to squeeze causality from coincidence, to find some internal logic that would make comprehensible the inconceivable, that such events could happen with no meaning at all and dead was in fact, under any circumstances, *just dead*. Every time I thought about taking away from Art the only consideration, I had left to give him, I was bereft as if it was the first time.

I felt desperate, caught in the middle of I couldn't do what I believed I had to do and I could never make myself feel better if I couldn't do it. Now, it really was too late. The new person I had become felt empty and sad to me, but she was the one who had survived Art's death. She had become bigger than I was, living in my house and practicing law under my name. It seemed to me I was without remedy. I would never be able to get back to my familiar self again—the woman who had for so long been perfectly clear about who she was.

Long before I ever met Art, she was the only one I knew I could always count on to know *me*, and, as I would discover later, she was the only one I recognized as the person who had loved both Art and me. I had lost her in the turmoil of events, and that was my trap: I would remain stuck there inside the new person who had replaced me, but I would never be able to disappear so she could simply take over from here.

Suddenly, I understood all too clearly the looks on the faces of the old widows I saw, their husbands all dead, for they must surely know what I was learning. I remembered the look, the sound of one woman who said, when we were introduced and she was told my husband had recently died, "I'm sorry for you. I'm sorry for all of you. For what I know and what you have to find out." She had brought me the chill of death for the first time. I was still younger than Art had been when he died, and my life, which felt over, wasn't going to end for a long, long time.

The beginning of being saved

I got lucky. A new friend stepped in to rescue me. "Maybe it would make you feel better if you had some other people to talk with," he offered. I protested: "It's too late, and groups just sit around and feel sorry for themselves, anyway. They never actually get better." And, finally, "I don't need a group. I just have to let more time pass."

He ignored me and made some phone calls. One night he delivered me to a group of men and women he begged me to meet. They had all been in long, traditional marriages and had each lost a wife or husband. They had formed a support group eight years before and had continued to come together every so often to give each other consolation and camaraderie.

On the night I joined them, they respectfully arrived in advance of me and saved me a particularly large, overstuffed chair in the living room of an old house that had been converted to a public library in our town. As I anxiously sank into the chair, one rather stern-looking woman handed me a sheet of paper she called *"The Rules of the Group. These are the rules of the group,"* she said simply, and then she waited, standing in front of my chair, for me to start reading. Somewhat apprehensively, I read Rule No. 1: *"Whatever you are thinking or feeling is exactly the right thing, and nobody who has never stood in your shoes can tell you anything else"*.

When it forced a bark of a bitter laugh out of me the woman, obviously satisfied, moved to her seat in the very wide, oblong *circle* of chairs and couches. I bit my lip hard so I wouldn't cry. She had been waiting for my reaction. As I peeked around, I could see all 10 of them had been waiting.

They were a group of men and women much older than I, who were waiting to talk with me about what they had already learned: that everyone's grief is theirs alone, unique to the relationship they alone have lost. They would tell me there is no such thing as a popular wisdom borne of our communal experiences of the deaths of our loved ones, nor was there any rule book that was hidden only from me. These were the important things there were to tell, the things every one of them before me had had to learn the hard way.

Rule No. 1 said I was the expert. No one had ever said that to me. It implied it was *my* loss. It was *my* grief. *I* was entitled to have it exactly the way I wanted it to be, for *me*, for all it had cost *me* and no one else. What I was feeling had nothing at all to do with anyone else.

It also implied each one of us would have to learn we have a right to do whatever we want to do with our sorrow. That the rule existed at all was a proof of some kind that I could not have been expected to know that in advance. I could have wept with joy to think that, maybe, just maybe, I might not have done everything wrong after all.

They gave me permission, at last, to feel only as I was feeling. I started to cry as the message sank in, and I cried on and off for nearly two hours as the wonderful group rallied around me, each taking a turn and talking about her or his own experience of loss. One man talked about never wanting to move so much as a chair out of place in their home, and a woman spoke of saving one sweater that never lost *his* scent to cry herself to sleep with when she needed to. Then they listened sympathetically as I, at long last, started to talk about my own experience for the first time. With much trepidation, I told them Art died of AIDS, and I held my breath until I was sure they were having no reaction at all. *What did I expect?*

When I was done talking, as people do, we stopped and went into a kitchen crowded with library cartons piled high around kitchen things and a small table with chairs to have the coffee and cake they had brought. We talked for two more hours, laughing and then sharing stories of how lost each of us had been, and about how Rule No. 1 had become the all-important saving grace in each of our lives.

It was a memorable evening. It signaled the beginning of knowing there might be nothing wrong with me. I just hadn't known.

I never saw any of those people again, but they steered me in the direction of the center of my life, where I guessed I might find my right mind. They released me from the cell that had grown up around me, made of the fears and confusion of the last five-and-a-half years, since the day Art was diagnosed with AIDS. From my new vantage point, I was willing to believe I could help me get the rest of the way back to the self I had lost.

It had been such a simple step, really, one well worth taking, and I wanted to remember that: reaching out to others and allowing them to show me what they had already learned by walking the same path I was just starting down. How miraculous it could be, after all, when people were willing to come together to give each other their stories, for all our sakes. I left them hoping I would have a chance to do the same for other people someday.

Even so, I was aware I had received only a very limited freedom from my cell. Much work lay ahead of me. I had joked bitterly about not being able to start over again, but I thought I might just be able to do something like that. I hoped it was not too late. Armed with their love and good wishes, I joined a support group for people who had cared for and lost those they loved to AIDS.

The Caregiver's Group

At my first meeting, I watched and listened to the small band of women who had cared for and lost husbands, brothers and sons to AIDS.* I heard myself in all their stories, and I felt something inside me relax with gratitude to be in the presence of their telling. When Anne, the facilitator, invited me to introduce myself, I said my first name as they all had and then started to talk about Art. Patiently, quietly, they listened as I told them about his ordeal, nodding their understanding. When I stopped talking, Anne asked me gently, "What about you?

---

*   The members of the group would change frequently and, as people would come and go, we would also be joined by men and women who had lost their partners.

Where are you in all of this?" I looked back at her blankly, having no answer. *Where, indeed, was I?*

I was suddenly weeping for having just arrived at the verge of giving up control of all the feelings I had kept locked inside me for so long. Through tears, I told them about imagining myself storing my feelings carefully in tissue paper until I could *deal* with them, *Later.* I explained that hadn't worked because my feelings had become too violent and now I was afraid to let them out. Surprising myself, I even told them how sure I had been at the start of it all that I would be able, at least, to get back to my familiar self—the woman I had known myself to be before I ever met Art—but that must have been my rational mind thinking, when I had no idea what was ahead of me and how much events would change me. Then, sobbing, I told them I had gotten lost to myself because those precious parts of me were tangled up with the feelings of Art's illness and death, and I had allowed everything to pile up inside me because I couldn't bear to think about how much everything hurt me. AIDS had come and wiped out everything, taken everything from me. In its wake, there was left only the fear I had changed so much that I would have to stay lost forever.

Had I intended to tell them all that, even to recall for myself the misery knowing I could no longer feel anything except fear and rage? I had not intended to say all that. I had forbidden myself even to think about what might have happened to the woman I had once been, and it was unlike me ever to have shared with strangers the rest of those words that had suddenly—even violently—torn through me on their way to their freedom. I used a few of the minutes of silence the others allowed me when I stopped speaking to avoid looking at them, to stop shaking and to wipe away the last of my tears. I was stunned by the sound of my own litany of loss.

By the end of that first meeting, I understood what I had spoken were simply my true feelings, right out of my broken heart—when was the last time I had allowed my heart to speak for me?—and I had spoken only because I had felt safe, finally, in that room where the Group met once a week. I wondered if my familiar self was, after all, still there inside me, buried in all that pain, and I dared to ask myself if I would allow the knot inside me to untangle by doing something, at last, about my feelings. For so long, I had been too afraid I would unravel if I so much as touched that knot, but now I knew I was aching to get started. A week suddenly seemed too long before I would be able to talk that way again. My words had left new feelings inside me, eagerness…and hope.

The answer was "Yes"

For most of the early months, the Group talked about nothing as much as the things other people said to us that hurt us nearly too much to bear. It was the common ground on which we were left standing long after our people died. I told them about Rule No. 1, and as we talked and talked still more, we found the courage to free ourselves from the hurt feelings of other people's expectations. It would be quite a while before we would finally start talking about what we expected.

I had started talking at last, and I had much, much to say. After I said all I could about the other people, there was still me. I saw I was still denying myself in order to uphold the imaginary standard of *"moving on"* that I had gotten locked into. It had become automatic behavior to me and would not be so easy to shake. I learned how to ask myself if I could have known to do otherwise, and I could only peek at how, someday, I might have to figure out how I felt about having chosen to honor anything other than my own feelings. Those answers would be a long time coming.

Much of what I had to say, at first, was angry, and my anger was frightening to me. It would spit out furiously, viciously, in words so filled with rage against myself I often thought they would break me apart. I had known for a long time I was angry with myself, but I had never before heard the full extent of my grudges against me. I had become the villain in my own piece, the one who had lost Art, who had failed to save him from dying. I had failed to do the *right* things for his sake. I had only succeeded in making a complete mess of everything that had been so important to me. As the Group listened, they held me with their eyes, telling me it was okay to feel only as I felt; I was doing a good thing for myself even though it hurt. It was the way I watched *them*, each of us in our own turn, as we confronted our worst fears.

I allowed that, because my words were dotted with all the things that comprise my life, they were thrilling, too. They meant there was some place inside me where I still knew myself better than I thought I could ever have a right to again, some place that had been holding my truths until I could bear to hear them coming from my own mouth. They were like crystals deeply embedded in my words of rage, each quiet little truth radiating a warm promise of more to come.

It was glorious, really: the more I talked, the more there was to say. And through all the days of talking, I knew I was, at last, finally somewhere I needed to be. Now I wanted everything.

2

My Voice, Your Voice

One day early on, as I was leaving the Group, I heard a voice. It wasn't the usual stream-of-consciousness voice I knew so well, and it wasn't the sound of my well-versed inner critic—which had been doing quite a lot of talking at that time. This tone was soft as a whisper, and gentle, yet it was very clear and direct. It spoke simply, without any emotion, as if it was merely stating a fact that needed to be said:

> *You have to go through what hurt you, and not around it anymore.... can do that.... won't have to alone....my strength to lean on.*

Then it stopped.

The sudden appearance of such a voice should have been disconcerting, yet I didn't stop to wonder where it came from. Rather, it was the words themselves that stopped and held me. The truth of them was apparent, and so simple that I trusted them instinctively. The voice was telling me what to do, and that I must, now, do it.

More importantly, the voice was telling me there was *something*, at last, that I could do to help myself. In the instant it spoke, I saw that I *had* been talking around what hurt me. I was trying frantically to convince myself I never needed to listen to my feelings. That was true about me, and I didn't need to think about how the voice could have known to tell me that. I also knew that, for all the fear that had me running away from my feelings, I had not even once considered taking on my feelings so boldly as the voice suggested. I had been avoiding even thinking about anything that threatened the delicate emotional balance I had been trying to freeze myself into for so many years.

At once, I felt the voice rescued me, and I didn't ask it anything. It seemed able to speak from inside and out of me at the same time. Its words made me understand what nothing else had, instantly: I would not be free until I plowed through all those buried feelings. My fear of them had stopped me from even entertaining such a thought as that, before.

It had been a few months since I joined the Caregiver's Group, and I knew they would afford me a safe place to do the work the voice instructed. How grateful I was, again, that my friend had not given up his intention to help me, for he had brought me to this Group, too, those people who I now knew I could rely on to be here with me. Although I had no expectation for what might lay ahead of me, I had every expectation it would demand much of me, and I knew that, once I started, I would have to keep going wherever it took me. I would have to stay with it for as long as it took to get everything out. Although that seemed daunting, I was excited to think that, at long last, my dormant life might be starting again.

<hr>

I began quietly. I never mentioned to anyone I was following the advice of a seemingly disembodied voice in my head. I didn't hear the voice again for many months after I started doing its bidding, but I did feel its strength—my own strength returning—actually vibrating inside me. That gave me the courage to find in myself the words that would speak of one buried feeling at a time.

One day, I envisioned myself walking into an empty room that had only a small mountain of black coal in it, and the coal pieces had somehow melted together. I knew my heart was buried inside there—I imagined I had put it there for safe-keeping on the night AIDS moved into my life—and I had only my fingers to work with to free it. When

I grabbed the first piece of coal off the mountain, I saw that it was a feeling. I watched as I held it up to the light with my fingers, turning it over and over as I examined it, and I talked to it until I was satisfied, I knew what I needed to know, and it had no more secrets.

I returned to that room often over the next several years. Each feeling pulled off the little mountain started as discomforting; the way I imagine a grain of sand would feel to an oyster. Sometimes it took days, even weeks to run through a full cycle of understanding one feeling before I could go on to another, and although I frequently complained bitterly, *I just want to be done with this,* I somehow found a patience I had not been willing to give myself in all the years before. I saw at once that each of my denied feelings had important things to tell me about myself, about who I had been when they first arose and why I had been so afraid to acknowledge them. When I stopped misunderstanding and started to know the truth each feeling had for me, I saw myself moving one step closer to recovering, not merely my heart, but the self I had become estranged from.

The process was painful and called up many tears. Yet it was exhilarating, every time, to find myself becoming familiar again.

After a while, I saw a pattern to the work. I could tell when I had pulled a new feeling off the mountain of coal and a new cycle of discovery was beginning. I could even sense when the next feeling was going to be an especially big and powerful one. My throat would fill with tears and I would have trouble speaking. It would happen just that way every time. Of course, I was also on the lookout, always, for the dread of what I still assumed would be the very last feeling: when I would have to turn my back on Art and walk away from him, into a new life without him.

Sometimes I got angry at the truth of a particular feeling. I hated hearing what it had to say about me because it made pretending impossible. Pretending had been painful, but it had come to feel so familiar that it was its own comfort. I thought, then, I might prefer not to know how I felt at all. I argued with myself, reminded myself I had promised, and I renewed the promise I had made to the voice: I will try to get out of my own way and let the truth of the feelings out. I even cheered for them as I pulled them off the little mountain and into my eager hands. I wanted them away, all of them, and I told myself each one would make me brave for the one that was going to come after it. That was my heart in there, the way back to myself, and I knew, finally, that what I needed more than anything was me.

I was doing *this*, for *me*. Gradually, I was becoming able to distinguish my experience from Art's, my life from his. I was determined to recover every feeling that had been mine. Wasn't I, even at long last, only doing what I had promised I would do when I packed them into that imaginary box I had stored in the back of my closet, marked *"Later"*? I began to see that I had known for years I would have to take all those feelings out of both my present and any future I could ever hope to have. They did not belong there. They would only continue to be obstacles unless I moved them into the past. In time, I would even begin to see that, although I had been so sure I had done everything wrong, what I had actually done was everything I could think of at the time to take good care of and protect myself. How grateful I was that the voice had spoken.

Days, months and then two years passed, and I was still *mining* my feelings in that little mountain of coal. There seemed no end to how much of what I experienced I had ignored and denied. I seemed to have disallowed any feelings about anything other than the narrowest version of what was happening to me. But I had been very careful in choosing my plan: I had kept it narrow to clear my mind for the work of keeping Art alive. Instead of cowardly, I began to see my strength. By the time I reduced the coal mountain to a little hill on the floor, I had gained a new confidence and was ready to free my heart.

The second time I heard the voice

One morning, I woke to a startling winter sun. It was January 1st, almost six years after Art died and almost three years after I had joined the Group. I woke feeling agitated, as if some powerful dream had left its imprint on me even though I couldn't recall it.

It was a blindingly beautiful morning, the kind that only January and northern mountains can offer: bright sunshine and heaps of fresh, soft and clean, sparkling snow everywhere. Looking out at it, I wanted to run into it and roll in it. It was the perfect place to take my distress, and as I dressed to take my Jeep out into the mountains that surrounded my house, I was already thinking out loud. The Group always joked about our cars being the best therapists.

At first, my thoughts rambled as I drove. Because the words were a familiar litany against the great beauty of my surroundings, I barely paid attention to what I was saying.

Then something changed. Suddenly I became aware I was talking to an imaginary companion who sat alongside me. I had conjured her up before but never pretended she was anything more than a sounding board for me. Yet now, here I was, acknowledging she had been through a terrible ordeal. I told her I was sympathetic to the sadness and pain she had been struggling with for so long, and I knew I had avoided and ignored her. I had even been contemptuous of her sorrow. I wanted her to know I was aware of all the neglect I had heaped on her, too. Sadly, I said I knew she needed to be loved and cared for, and nurtured back to good health after all she had been through, her loss.

I caught my breath when I heard myself say "your loss," but what came out of my mouth next was even more startling. "I want you to know I'm proud that you've been courageous, to wake up every morning and act as if life will be better, even as I have stood on the sidelines snickering that it won't be." Who was I talking to? I told her I wanted to stop punishing her and stop being so angry.

This wasn't about some *she* sitting next to me on the seat like a cardboard cut-out of a human being who could absorb my rage and sobs without reacting. This was about *me*. I was talking to *me*. I was ready, finally, to feel compassion, not for her, but for *me*, for what *I* had been through, for *my* loss. It had taken me six long years to feel for myself that I was the one. *I* had gotten up every morning and been willing to pretend, to go through the dread-filled motions of a life whose outer edges had been the only place where I could have existed.

It was apparent *I* was finally ready to feel fully my terrible ordeal. *I* had suffered the pain and too much sorrow and anger that I had heaped on top of myself. I was ready, so ready to acknowledge what I could not have before: I deserved to receive my own love.

For all my trying to do the *right* things, all I had achieved in my own behalf was to push me away from myself. I had abandoned me, even before Art died. Now I was ready to claim this, even this not-yet-fully-re-formed life, as my life, to take it back from that woman who was running my law firm and wearing my clothes, who I had put in my place and been willing to pretend she was me. I wanted to make it up to myself for the neglect and my absence, my inattention when what I had needed more than anything was, at least, my own love. I was ready to live fully inside my own life again. Suddenly, I wanted to do that with a passion I hadn't known, until that moment, I was still capable of feeling.

Tears came when it hit me. Sobbing, I had to keep on talking. I had to tell myself all the things I had neglected to say when I woke up not-dead on the first morning after Art died. I needed to tell myself—urgently—and to make sure I heard everything I had to say. I wanted to take good care of me, as good care of me as I had taken of him. I had never compared my pain to his before; the fact that he would die had always made his pain greater than mine. But, somehow, my pain had been judged unworthy, by me. I had stopped myself, forbidden myself even to think about how I felt. That had been so easy to do. What had *I* suffered that compared to his knowing every day he was going to die?

None of that mattered now. The only thing that mattered on this frozen day in January was that I had just found my heart in the little hill of coal, and it was strong and pink and still beating. It was healthy and beautiful, and I was alive. I wanted to feel as strongly for me as I had for Art, and I knew how desperately I had been needing to hear myself say that. I wanted to change the way I treated myself, and I demanded to know what my intentions were. Could I now, finally, count on myself to do that? Before I even finished making my demand, I was already answering myself: *"I am going to have to start living my life"*.

And then, before I saw it coming and just as the choking tears started me gasping my own words out loud, I was trying to explain to Art that, although I had done everything I could think of to avoid this moment—when I would have to turn my back on him and walk away—I saw so clearly I couldn't have prevented it. I wasn't powerful enough. I had simply lived, and that meant I *had* to live.... and, finally, *"I'm sorry, Art, I didn't want this to happen, didn't want this day to come between us, but I just can't live a life filled with terrible sorrow all the time"*.

It was the moment I had been dreading for years, and it came down to a choice that was no choice at all. At the end, I just walked over to the other side of it. There, where I was all I had, I couldn't live without loving myself anymore. I felt so sad to think it must also mean I could not love Art anymore because I had chosen myself over him.

The voice started to speak then. I recognized the same soft whisper inside my head, and I heard it, again, coming wondrously from inside and out of me at the same time. I had been touched to hear my own words of caring and moved by the compassion I could feel for myself, so new for me. Even so, I could not have anticipated the words the voice spoke. I could only accept, once again, that they must have been coming from my own heart:

"You can continue to hold onto your feelings for Art.... give yourself permission to miss him for as long as you want to.... don't have to let him go ...start out in search of something you call the rest of your life. But it is time for you to do just that".

The voice got stronger as it went along. It said I was strong:

"Just look at how strong you are. You have survived your loss".

It assured me, as it had once before, that I wouldn't have to take the next steps alone; it would be with me and I could rely on its strength. This time, though, it added, *"your own great strength"*.

By the time I got home I was exhausted, spent and dried of any more tears. I no longer needed to imagine someone sitting on the seat next to me. The voice became that woman. I knew I would always think of her as *she,* and I knew *she* was inside me. I was content with that. I trusted *her.* Through *her,* I could learn to trust myself again.

Dina L. Wilcox

The Fantasy Woman

Much of what we know about ourselves comes through our feelings. Evolution seems to have arranged it so that what we think about our feelings helps us decide how we want to act on them. For me, the voice is like the stage prompter behind the wings, reminding me that my feelings speak of possibilities. When I hear it speak, I know that choices are available to me. Always, it speaks simply of what my feelings are trying to tell me about myself.

Some years after my January ride in the mountains, the voice came again, not with words, but with an image to my *"mind's eye"*. I saw a woman I had seen for the first time and then night after night when I was 13 years old. Although the woman's presence had been critically important to my young life, I had had no way of knowing, at that time, that it was also bringing me another kind of message, one that would only become relevant to me years later and be just as important to my adult self. I could not have imagined, at 13, that any such message could have come from my own, internal wisdom; I was way too young to know that I could have had wisdom at that age.

At the time, as I imagine it now, it was as if the voice took me by my 13-years old hand to some magical place night after night for the last 15 minutes before I fell asleep. In that place, I watched the woman live as a grown-up version of me. She was a fantasy woman who was perfect in every way, and she loved her life, the life I invented for her as I watched. I am convinced now, that my voice brought me to that place to keep me from falling into the despair caused by the feelings of a shy, invisible teenager.

I was a pretty ordinary teenager. I was so shy that it hurt. Shy—that's the polite word we give to a teenage girl's desperate longing to be invisible. If I was called on by a teacher and no less by classmates in the schoolyard, I flushed crimson, humiliated by my inability to speak. I felt betrayed by all the great words I secretly knew I carried around in my head, the ones I read in all those books, yet could not say to anyone when I needed them the most. Over and over again I was reduced to mumbling, whispering and painfully exposing that self, the one I would gladly have traded for any other girl around.

As neither a beauty nor a scholar, I was so sure that the future—like the painful present—was going to be stocked with an awful abundance of ordinary. During the days, I couldn't even think about my life without loathing it. Everything about me was wrong, just wrong. I stood at the bathroom mirror at least once a day and verbally abused my *"beadly little eyes"*, while I actively hated the kind of hair, I had gotten stuck with. It was never going to be the cheerleader's straight, shiny hair, but something frizzy and curly and what, at the time, the adults around me seemed to love calling *"mousy brown"*. Oh, how I wished I could pass right through 13 and all the other teens as quickly as possible, undetected.

As miserable as I was during the terrible days of ordinary, I got to celebrate a very different me every night. Then, alone in the privacy of the bedroom I shared with my younger sister, I travelled to that magical refuge where the fantasy woman lived. She appeared there every night on cue, soundlessly, and she stayed for as long as I needed her to fall asleep. She made it possible for me to balance the awful feelings of a 13-year old who was sure she would never be able to make her mark on the world she could inherit, and to survive that child's life one day at a time. She was the image of a possibility for a kind of life that I could only long for. Even as it seemed impossible that she could be grown-up me, I was sure I was somewhere inside her. I could feel me there even if I could not see me. She enabled me to dream that I could grow up right there, and that I could feel as complete as I imagined she was.

Truthfully, if I had thought about it at the time, I would surely have thought that all I was doing was making it up, and that it just made me happy to do so. While I can still say that was so—I did, after all, make her up, and it did make me happy to see her there every night—I could not have known that this fantasy came with assistance from a voice I would not meet until I was an adult, or that the voice would bring the fantasy woman back with another message for my grown-up self. I never thought about where she came from or who she was—no one in my real world had ever lived as she did. I only knew that, like a painter, I was completely absorbed in the joy of embellishing every detail of her fabulous life. I ascribed to her every characteristic I wished for myself, and then I stepped back in the dark and watched her live in her world, enchanted at my power to tweak her with simple brushstrokes to perfection along the way. She lived exactly the life I wanted, a life I loved through her, and she seemed so perfect that I never thought about how—or if—I could ever become her.

How could I have known that she was the perfect antidote, the cure for a shy girl who couldn't speak for herself? It didn't matter that I didn't know she was on a mission to make me feel good. She was my fantasy woman, like no woman I ever knew, and she was all mine. She had all the right words at just the right times. She was smart and articulate, and people were so happy to be around her. They were eager to hear what she had to say. They trusted her to speak simple truths, and she had a great reputation for saying exactly what she meant without wasting words. She was everything I was not. Of course, it didn't hurt my 13-year old feelings that she was vivacious and not at all shy. She was glorious to look at—I made sure of that—and she was happy. She made my heart sing with happiness just to see her.

When I was *"mining"* my feelings with the Group all those many years later, my voice sent me that same image of the fantasy woman one more time. As you will read in chapter 4, it took me a little while to recognize her—I had forgotten all about my girlhood fantasies by the time I was a grown woman—and then it took me another little while to figure out why she, of all women, was suddenly appearing in my grown-up mind's eye.

Of course. She must be a message sent to me by my inner voice, and since my voice had sent her, again, it must have been my voice that had sent her that first time all those years ago. Things were starting to make sense. What other way but through my imagination could my voice have reached me with such an important message when I was only 13? That woman had been the salve for my teenage anguish, and now my voice must be trying to encourage me again, using the fantasy woman to show me that I have choices, again; there is a new possibility for me to love the rest of my life.

Little did I know that night after night, as I was carefully adding the details that colored in the pictures of her life, I was also creating that very possibility for the kind of life I would want in my actual future. I made that connection with the help of my voice during my

"Fear Weekend" (Chapter 4), the very weekend when I was coming closer to making a decision about where I wanted to take my life in transition. When I remembered and recalled the fantasy, I knew it was precisely the life I had so carefully crafted for that woman that I most wanted for myself. Even more importantly, I knew that I had been working toward it all along. The fantasy woman had been me all those years before, and now I was ready to become her. I had only needed a little prompting from my voice to see that. That was the kind of help that only my voice could give.

The voice of wisdom

My voice always speaks to me of my feelings. Of course, my thoughts may *see* things differently from my feelings, even though, biologically, thoughts and feelings are closely related. Sometimes, my thinking can be clouded by perceptions, fears, longings or any of the countless other things that drive us humans. My truths can get lost in those clouds, confusing me and making me suspect that my feelings are unreliable. Thinking can bring me too many choices, and distractions. Thinking holds out the promise of grand adventures that will fulfill my heart's desires, not to mention my wishes and fantasies. While I love to daydream, my thoughts can sometimes look better than reality and, being *only* human, I can easily turn to wanting the truth to look more like my fictions.

For the record, feelings are not to be confused with thoughts. Feelings are just what they are, whether we like them or not. You might say feelings are born fully formed. They arise of their own accord, automatically, as we're going about living our lives. They are there to tell us something is happening, or has just happened, and we must pay attention. After mere seconds pass, our brains will take over, so that we can then know what the *something* is and start thinking about what, if anything, we might want to do about it.

The journey from the beginning of a feeling to the brain's thinking about it is instantaneous. Your thoughts are entirely created by you, and they always have an agenda: to initiate, design, plan, and even to provoke other feelings in you. Maybe you've had the experience of your own thoughts triggering feelings of sadness, or anger, or fear.

Perhaps my feelings use my voice in self-defense to communicate with me. Time and again I have discovered that the voice can bring me back to what I imagine is the very center of my life, where I live in a perfect balance and am clear about what is in my own best interests. The voice does it just by defining a feeling I may be uneasy about. From that place, I can choose to act deliberately, to be in charge and not get trapped in the flotsam of my life. Knowing what is simply true for me makes it difficult for me to act as if it's okay to put myself in the path of disappointment, or even harm, out of ignorance or naivete.

It is unlikely many of us have ever been told positive things about hearing voices in our heads. More likely, we've been told if we think we hear a voice, we'd better ignore it, but, even so, there are voices that do appear to be speaking in our heads at different times in our lives. Don't you sometimes hear voices speaking in your dreams? Have you ever started running out to cross a busy street and heard a loud voice shout and stop you in your tracks? Those are parts of you, enhancing—or saving—your life. I believe our inner voices may have come to be a part of our brains precisely to give us access to the unique wisdom that lies within each of us.

The theory of evolution says all kinds of biological systems have evolved in our bodies and brains to support our increasingly complex lives. While I am no scientist, I have experienced just such a mechanism in my inner voice. Following its wisdom—my own, natural wisdom—I am able to know what my feelings are trying to tell me. I am, that is, if I am willing to trust my own, natural process of being a human who has experiences that bring feelings into my life for a purpose.

If there is magic in this, it is surely not mine alone. We all know things about ourselves, the things that are true for us even if they might not be true for anyone else. These things are the ways we define and recognize ourselves. They are the wealth of information that becomes the source of our extraordinary uniqueness.

My voice is uniquely mine and, because I trust it, it's easy for me to offer this: you have a voice that will always be just the same for you, albeit perhaps it may *speak* to you in some different form. Your voice will have precisely the words and images that tell of you, *your truths,* meant for you alone to know. It's likely it has been there all along, quietly living your life right along with you, having all your experiences and waiting until you might need it to communicate your truths to you.

What do I mean by your *truths?* As it is for each of us individually, your truth is the explanation of how you feel, the critical piece of information that enables you to understand yourself so you can decide how you want to act as you go on about the business of being You. Knowing how you feel means you can readily decide what to do about the things on your mind. Each of us has different truths, just as each of us can only feel the ways we alone feel. Knowing this can be more than helpful for making the choices and decisions that will move us or put on hold the actions of our lives.

Experiencing your own, one-of-a-kind inner voice, you can learn to trust what it has to say to you—what you yourself have to say about how you feel, the simple truth of your feelings. Just by allowing yourself to accept that you might have such a voice, you may be freeing your extraordinary human ability to think for yourself. You do not have to agonize over feelings you cannot figure out or become imprisoned by feelings you think you might prefer to ignore and deny.

The ways our voices communicate are different for each of us. My friend Marilyn says she doesn't hear a voice at all. Rather, she reaches a moment in time when she "just knows" the truth inside her. She says she feels it come up from her "deepest self," the "constant" part that is "not messed up with other messages." My friend Michael says he experiences his voice as a feeling, too, a feeling that confirms his thinking. You may experience your voice as my friends do, or you may hear your voice, sometimes, as I hear mine, in words.

Your voice could just as easily show you words. You might see them as you write your thoughts in a journal, as I did while I was thinking things through during my Fear Weekend (chapter 4). Your voice might send images or pictures, either to your *mind's eye* or onto actual canvases as you are creating them, by painting or making collages. You might be a musician or an artist who uses a camera, fabric, clay or another medium, and your voice may choose to use your favorite medium as well. Once you get to know it, you may realize ways it has been communicating with you all along—you just never *heard* it. Perhaps even as you read this, you are already beginning to wonder if maybe *that* was your voice, that one time....

Your voice may also communicate with you through images you are attracted to, even if you do not create them. If you love to read, your voice might provoke some of your best thoughts while you are curled up with a novel or magazine, even a newspaper. Suddenly, there it will be, the thought that *pops into your head* or the picture that appears in your *mind's eye*. A portion of text might suddenly *jump out at you*, offering you a perfect picture of something you may not have remembered seeing in a dream. Or, you may find it in the place your mind wanders off to in your daydreams. You might decide to keep a journal so you can have a physical place to capture what your voice has to *say* at any time. The more you trust it, the more it will speak to you.

Perhaps you are a person who gets strong *gut feelings* without any apparent trigger at all. Suddenly you notice you are perfectly clear about an issue you've been grappling with and you know exactly what you have to do to resolve it—you may even be surprised at what the resolution will be. Or you may be someone who not only remembers but easily understands the meaning of your dreams. Perhaps it is your voice communicating with you through images while you are asleep, or while you are using your wild imagination. You might wake up from sleep knowing the answer to a question, a resolution to a challenge or a dilemma you are trying to figure out while you are wide awake.

If you love to sing or climb mountains, or if you are a basketball star—in your life, your imagination and even in your dreams—your voice can communicate through a song you suddenly notice you're humming, or by the exhilaration you feel after your climb, and you might find it in the thrill you get from seeing yourself floating up to sink a basket that wins a virtual game. Indeed, we have heard many stories of athletes who routinely visualize themselves working at their sport in order to ensure every action they take will be precise, the best it can be.

Regardless of how your voice communicates, it will bring information for you, about you. Just as the answers we are seeking are different for each of us, so too are the messages we receive from our inner voices. Yours might even send a picture to your mind's eye reminding you of something that occurred when you were a child, which you can now understand differently as an adult and use to transform your life in a way you could not have before.

What can keep you from hearing or seeing what your inner voice might have to say? You can choose not to hear or see it. That choice, even made unconsciously, can act as the signal to your voice that you want it to remain still. My voice seems to know—you might say instinctively—there are times when I do not want to hear what it would have to say. Of course, my voice is not separate from anything else going on within me. It's only logical, then, that I get to decide even what advice I might be willing to hear from my own thinking.

Maybe we choose not to hear our voices because we're afraid of the power inherent in being fully responsible for ourselves. Maybe we don't trust our own ability to think our way through to the important answers we need. Or maybe we've been overburdened by the weight of too many external messages from others who would have us believe they are smarter about us than we can be about ourselves. I call these the messages of external experts, and you'll be seeing more about them later on.

Maybe it's simpler than any of these reasons. Maybe your feelings sometimes get caught in the clouds your thinking brain sends up when you are imagining what you want. With my voice doing its job, I can trust myself to make choices and decisions that are based in reality, even if I do think I like my fantasies better. I believe this is what our inner voices do because, as part of us, they must surely participate in the work of enhancing and ensuring our survival. That's what our bodies are all about.

There has been much written about inner voices, and much has kept voices locked in mystical and spiritual domains. That makes it easier for us to discount them. Some writers and other experts would have us believe it is only they who are best-suited to be proper guides, and only they can unlock the treasure that is your inner voice. My experience suggests such external expertise is not necessary, as a matter of fact.

A voice does not swim in the stream of consciousness

You may already be aware of a constant stream of words floating in your head. We register random thoughts as we move through our days, and these words collect in our *"streams of consciousness"* whether we want them to be there or not: *"look at that car stopped in the intersection"*; *"don't forget the appointment at three o'clock"*; *"why am I suddenly humming an advertising jingle for a product I don't even use?"* All these words can feel like one long, meaningless monologue that we carry on for no good reason. Periodically, we might even wish we could just stop it for some peace of mind. Have you ever wished you could *"clear your head?"* You may both wish and be able to, but keep in mind the words you will be discarding will not be the words of your inner voice.

My inner voice has never conveyed a random thought. It does not swim in my stream of consciousness. Nor could it ever be confused with my inner critic, or be found dishing out *"popular wisdom",* those words of advice I am routinely—against my will—left with after countless conversations and product advertisements. I believe our inner voices are concerned only with what we want, need and think and, primarily, with how these things are revealed by our feelings. They can be found in the sounds and images of us striving to understand ourselves and to manage our lives to the best of our ability. Our voices are always paying attention, even when we are not. When we need them to, they can communicate with us in a variety of ways, telling and showing us things that we ourselves may not even be aware we know.

One afternoon not too long ago, I was changing the sheets on my bed. I was thinking, I thought, about nothing in particular. As I bent over to tuck in a corner, my voice suddenly shouted out, *"No generosity of spirit, that one"*, and then it got quiet. I bolted straight upright in surprise. My first thought was that *she* sounded angry, as if *she* was annoyed with me. My second thought was that I hadn't heard from *her* in a long time. In fact, years had gone by since my voice had last spoken to me. Then I thought about what *she* said and I just had to laugh. *She* caught me thinking about something I had not been honest with myself about. I hadn't even realized it was still on my mind—because I had decided that when I banished all further thinking about that particular matter, that was the end of it.

I admitted it. *You're right*, I thought. *That is how I feel about him, and now that I can admit it, maybe I can finally stop thinking about that guy altogether.*

"*That*" guy was someone I had met a short time before, when I joined a gym after moving back to New York City to pursue my dream of becoming my fantasy women. He approached me to say he had never seen me there before, so I must be new at the gym. He welcomed me to the community and then struck up a pleasant conversation. After that, every time he saw me at the gym, although he stopped to chat, it was becoming clear and clearer that we had very little in common. One day he showed up with a different attitude: although he stopped to chat as always, his once friendly demeanor belied a few presumptuous barbs, about how much money I must have and then, sneeringly, how I must be *"brainy—I took you for a real brain right away"*, he said, as if I had offended him by answering his question about the book I was writing. He had been asking me about my book since the very first day we spoke, and I felt hurt by his remarks. I couldn't figure out why he stopped to talk at all if he didn't want to, and I eventually changed my hours at the gym to avoid running into him again.

That didn't stop me from trying to figure out what had occurred between us. I continued to argue with him in imaginary, defensive conversations in which I tried to explain away whatever I pretended I might have done to offend him. I tried to give him the benefit of any doubts I had, even though I couldn't find anything I had done or said to warrant resentment, and the more I thought about it the more I had to admit that I would never be able to know what happened. I felt frustrated, even after I told myself it was time to stop thinking about him for my sake. I just didn't have enough information to reach any kind of conclusion.

When my voice shouted out what was simply true for me—that I thought he had shown no *generosity of spirit,* a way I describe someone who is not willing to risk getting to know another person—my frustration ended abruptly. I realized what I had been trying hard not to notice: I had some pretty strong feelings of my own about *him.* Did I even *like* him? I had wanted to take him at his word, and because my feelings were telling me that I did not, I had chosen to ignore my feelings. As soon as I was able to be honest about how I felt, I stopped needing to think anything about his words, or his action, or whatever might have been his intention. I knew that he simply did not matter to me at all.

Have you ever wanted something different from what reality was bringing you? How did you balance the facts, the feelings, the *wanting* inside you? Perhaps we all act, sometimes, as if we think we can hide bits of information from ourselves without consequences. As if we take for granted that we are made up of a variety of virtual compartments, we think we can *bury* things inside ourselves so we won't have to *know* them. We keep things *locked away* behind imaginary doors in our minds, and we are so sure we can keep them tightly closed, that we shall never have to be exposed to what lies behind them.

Of course, we don't have doors in our brains, just a lot of electromagnetic activity that is generated by chemicals responding to being alive. That's what we have most in common with one another. It's called human nature, even if we use different words to describe it. Maybe we pretend we can hide things from our conscious knowing because we're trying to protect ourselves in any way we can from feelings we anticipate will disappoint or hurt us. Perhaps we think knowing how we feel will force us to change a course we have set for ourselves, and even if we know we should *go* with what we feel, we think we are not ready or willing to do that. We may choose to manipulate the truth instead, to accept the parts we like and ignore the rest. Or, we can decide to deny our feelings so they cannot get in the way of what we want—all because we have decided that what we want is different from what *reality* is offering us, and we like our imaginary version of the truth better.

We might embellish and even make up stories, and then we forget we made them up. We pretend our stories are the truth of what is really going on, and then we proceed to act, not on our reality, but on the stories themselves. We can become so intent on holding onto our stories that we lose sight of the simple truth of what our feelings are telling us, and we can even deny what is actually happening to us. Small wonder, indeed, that a voice might have evolved in our brains to assist us in understanding the simple truths of our feelings. The truth may be simple, but there is little about our human nature that is uncomplicated.

Over time, my voice has taught me not to judge myself harshly for things I do that I may not understand, or appreciate. That's good, because, after all, a human is a complex thing to be in a world filled with choices. *She*—my voice—has taught me to trust myself and always be in my own camp, not to be suspicious of my motives and what I might be too willing to perceive as my failings.

I am often surprised by things *she* says. *She* may say something I am convinced I did not know, and I marvel at how that can be possible. *She* may answer a question I have just asked, and, then again, *she* may just as likely answer a question I haven't yet asked. Sometimes, *she* can even answer a question *she* forces me to recognize I have been trying to avoid thinking about altogether. *Her* messages are strong, always, and their meanings are clear: my feelings are important. They are trying to tell me about myself, and I must allow them to do that in order to act in my own best interests. In *her* unique way, my voice makes me the expert on me.

Knowing about our voices can change the way we feel about ourselves. When I get great advice from my voice, I know it is coming from me, and that tells me I am trusting and loving myself unconditionally. Too often, the words unconditional love and even the notion you might love yourself are reduced to clichés that have been trivialized by popular wisdom. Still, I must ask: what's wrong with loving yourself?

Loving yourself can help you realize the great power you wield naturally, the power to know yourself and to stand up for yourself, to say this is who I am and this is how I choose to make my life. It is the power you can realize from trusting your internal voice, because it is a power that comes from confidence deep inside you that says you are equipped to know and care about yourself.

Aren't you lucky to have yourself to practice loving on? After all, aren't you the one person who stands to lose the most if you do not?

3

We Are What We Feel

As I've said before, sometimes I don't appreciate the way I feel. A feeling can make me uncomfortable, and I wish I didn't have to have it. I may even wish I could convince myself that my life would be easier if I didn't have to have my feelings altogether, but I know too much for that, now. When I feel that discomfort, I know it's time to remind myself that, in their own, quirky ways, my feelings are part of my natural survival system. They are directly related to my ability to live well, and to thrive.

Evolution is believed by many scientists to be a random act or, more correctly, countless random acts that have been occurring in nature since before there was time. Who knows who or where these things come from? Maybe someday scientists will figure it all out, but that's the way it is today and that's the way it will stay for our foreseeable future. Today, the conclusion is that some of the random acts have caused things to become integrated into our bodies—selected, the scientists call that—because those were the things that proved to help humans survive.

Maybe we have messy relationships with our feelings because they started out as random acts. We don't really know if our earliest ancestors had them, but we do know that, when feelings appeared, they were parked right in the hard-wiring of our thinking brains, which evolved sometime after our first and oldest *"reptilian"* brains (that is the oldest part of the brain). Who knows for sure how that all happened?

Whatever the answers, I confess that, more than once, I have had to wonder what feelings are all about. How can I make peace with them, and how am I supposed to live with them?

Here is the basic truth about feelings: We are always going to have them, and working with them will always make our lives better and healthier. The having of them is automatic, and we do not need to make any decisions about whether or not we want them. We don't get to choose whether or not we shall have them. We just have them.

Maybe feelings prove that nature has a sense of humor, because, in the arena of feelings, you can often experience a tension that is much more than uncomfortable. Maybe you've noticed. Whether or not that will ever be proven, it seems certain that nature intends you will have a hard time ignoring your feelings just because you think you might want to—especially, perhaps, when you might want to more than you'd like to admit. If there's a hierarchy among our responses to life, feelings will be pretty high on the list.

Some feelings can generate other feelings about themselves. Have you ever felt overwhelmed by your feelings, or fearful of how angry you were? Have you ever been anxious because you felt depressed? See what I mean? Feelings are quirky. You might expect something so important for your survival would at least be clear about its intention to help you. Wouldn't you?

Have you ever known someone who you thought *"makes too much of her feelings,"* or listened to someone who seemed convinced he doesn't have to give his feelings any mind at all? Some people act as if their feelings only get in the way of their rational, logical thinking and good decision-making, if you let them. Has anyone ever advised you could be tougher and more successful in your life if only you could learn to control your feelings better, perhaps the way he does? Has anyone ever tried to convince you that you are *"too emotional"*, or accused you of being a *"slave to your emotions?"* See what I mean?

Just for the record, feelings and emotions are very closely related; they're interacting all the time, but they are not exactly the same, even though we often use the words interchangeably. While some feelings can sometimes carry the same names as the emotions they are related to—anger, for instance—they do different things.

With some exceptions, the key word that distinguishes feelings from emotions may be *consciousness*. Think of fear, one of our oldest emotions. Fear forces you to fight in your own defense, or to stop *"dead in your tracks"* or to flee to safety, all without your having to think about it and deciding which choice to take. The earliest humans needed something that would operate automatically—their brains couldn't *"think things through if their lives depended on it"*—and when fear evolved, it survived because it managed to help keep people safe in the face of danger and threats.

Of course, it may only be that feelings prove nature has a sense of humor, because, in the arena of feelings, you can often experience a discomfort that can feel much more than uncomfortable. It can feel like a punishment for some action taken in the immediate past. Maybe you've noticed. Have you ever asked yourself, *"What does it say about me that I feel this way?"* Have you ever wondered, *"What would other people think of me if they knew I feel this way"*? Did you ever feel tormented by a feeling you didn't know what to do with?

Whether or not you have pondered or wondered about all of this, it seems certain nature intends you will have a hard time ignoring your feelings just because you think you might want to. Many neuroscientists have written that our feelings may have more to tell us about what it means to be human than any of our other responses to life. You can find some of their books in the Bibliography at the end of the book.

No matter what we might do about them, our feelings live in their own truths. By their very presence they invite us to think about who we are and what we want. They suggest we become aware of what we need, and they urge us to be deliberate about what actions we are willing to take to have our needs met. Feelings themselves might even think we give them an awfully hard time by attributing meanings to them they never intended.

Although we might attach intentions to them, I am certain feelings themselves would say they have no hidden agendas. They're just trying to do their jobs. If there's any misunderstanding between us and our feelings, it's probably because we don't understand what their jobs are and how they're supposed to work to get them done.

To begin, then, feelings and emotions are very closely related, but they are not the same. Our brains process feelings and emotions differently, and by using two distinct parts of themselves.

With some exceptions, the key word that distinguishes feelings from emotions may be consciousness. You don't have to do anything to know that you're having an emotion, because the word itself suggests action—emotion means *"to move away"* in Latin. Think of fear, probably our oldest emotion. Fear forces you to fight in your own defense, or to *"stop dead in your tracks"* or to flee to safety, all without you having to think about which path to take. The earliest humans needed something that would operate automatically—their brains couldn't *think things through if their lives depended on it*—and when fear evolved, it survived because it managed to help keep them safe in the face of danger and threats.

By comparison, feelings trigger conscious thoughts, and for a very good reason. When you're having a feeling, you must decide to do something with it even if you decide to ignore it and do nothing at all. Suddenly you'll realize you're feeling a certain way because you're thinking about it, and thinking, you—and only you—will decide how you will act on what you feel.

As for that discomfort you may think is being generated by your feelings, it's actually not coming from your feelings at all. You may be having conflicting thoughts—thoughts you have created with your thinking brain. For now, you can think of your thinking brain as the part of your brain that loves to offer you a full range of choices for things you could do about any given situation. Sometimes, the more you think about your feelings the more your thoughts can confuse their simple message, until you can hardly remember what you were feeling in the first place. Just put that thought away for now; it will be showing up again later.

These distinctions between emotions and feelings, and even between feelings and thoughts, are good examples of why it's important for nonscientists to know even a little bit about how our brains work. We can use these bits of information to know something important about ourselves, like our feelings help guide us in making choices and decisions. You and your consciousness are the necessary components for every action you will take on the basis of your feelings. If you leave a feeling hanging all by itself, there will be no action, because your feelings, unlike your emotions, do not come with predetermined actions built in. They give you all the power—and the responsibility—in the matter of dealing with them.

Anger is a good example

Here's a simple unscientific experiment you can ponder to see how you might control one particular feeling—anger. Imagine that someone has just said something that landed on you as an insult. His words triggered anger in you, and you got emotional. Instantly, your heartbeats increased in number and intensity; your face got warm and maybe even red. Emotions always trigger physiological reactions in your body. You cannot prevent them, because they are the ways your brain starts to prepare your body to act quickly in response to a situation that might cause you harm.

However, you will not be prompted to respond automatically in any particular way. If the words you heard represented a danger to your life—let's say the speaker was delivering them while coming toward you with a knife—your brain would force your body to take action to keep you safe. You would act involuntarily and so quickly that you wouldn't have any time to think about it.

In this example, although your brain will prepare your body to react to the insulting words you heard, just in case, it will quickly become clear to you that you are not in danger of bodily harm. In your brain, that clarity will mean the emotion of anger was converted into a feeling of anger. This is where your consciousness comes in.

To say that another way, if you did not act automatically, it was because you were not forced to do so. Your brain will have determined your life is not threatened and you do not have to fight or run away. Instead, you will soon be thinking about how angry you feel, and you will begin to contemplate what action, if any, you want to take.

Of course, you won't stop to notice that you are feeling angry, whereas, before, you were having the emotion of anger. Only your brain will know that the threat-to-your-life part is over and you are now having the experience of feeling angry. Nor would it be accurate to imagine one brain-part had to turn off before another could turn on since the moment you first heard the insulting language. Even though we say you have *moved* from the emotion of anger to the feeling of anger, the time that passes will be mere milliseconds during which there will be much communication within your brain, as its multiple systems prepare you to manage your anger appropriately. It is only language that limits us to time.

In any case, however you got to this point, you are now in a new situation, one in which your brain is asking you what you want to do in response to your anger. You are now at the point of all this energy you've been expending: your feelings are for helping you decide whether and how you want to act.

Now could be the perfect moment for your intuition, and maybe even your inner voice, to report for work. They can remind you about some feelings you have about anger. Maybe you swore you would deal differently with anger the next time you had a chance to. Perhaps you picked up some tools at an anger management class. You may be seeing a picture in your mind's eye, or your memories may be recreating something you learned in that class. Maybe you're seeing a happy resolution to this incident, you feeling triumphant at having managed your anger in just the way you always wished you would when you decided to take that class. Your thoughts may be coming and going quickly, and you may have to do some remembering as well, but once you are aware of what you're feeling, you can take all the time you want to for thinking about them.

Thinking about your feelings gives you an extraordinary opportunity to be the most powerful person in your own life, and to live your life deliberately. Not only can you think about how you feel, you can think about it often, or sometimes, as much as you want to before you decide what to do, or not to do. You can understand your feelings, just as you can choose to shut them down and pretend they do not exist. You can decide to stop thinking about them now and pick them up again later. Maybe you want to have a conversation with the person who insulted you, but not until after you have calmed down and decided what you want to say. You can argue with yourself about your feelings, and you can talk about them with other people. You can also write about them in a journal. Best of all, you can use your ability to think about what your feelings are trying to tell you, to help you be the person you want to be in this important moment of your life.

What I didn't do with my feelings

When I was denying my feelings, I lived in fear of what I imagined they might do to me if I gave them a chance to reach me. They had been piling up in the weeks leading to Art's diagnosis and, instead of acknowledging that I simply felt the way I did, I decided to pack them away for a time I called *"Later"* so that I wouldn't have to think about them. They scared me as nothing else ever had before in my life, so it seemed a smart thing to do, to deny how I felt when I was overwhelmed. I tried to soften the impact by promising myself I would deal with them later, when, perhaps, I might better be able to manage how much they hurt. Whatever I thought I was doing, what I learned, later, was that I had only allowed my fear to convince me that I could not trust the feelings of hurt and sadness. All I achieved by denying those feelings was additional years' worth of losing touch with myself and ending up with a box overflowing with denied feelings that gave me no peace at all. They refused to disappear.

It was many years later, when my inner voice gently, but firmly, told me I had to think *through* my feelings, that I was finally able to understand the simplicity of what feelings were all about. Mine were trying to tell me I knew how to take good care of myself: All I had to do was allow myself to feel as I did, and my body, which includes my brain, would have done the rest. After all, my feelings had not come at me from outside myself. They had been generated by my experiences. They *were* me, and I had unwittingly denied them by choosing—pretending—that I had to be afraid of them.

It took me years to figure out the truth about my feelings and to understand what they were trying to tell me. During those years, I came to trust my inner voice, and I learned a little neuroscience along the way, but, I had only put off the inevitable need to uncover the truth of those feelings by myself. When I finally did allow my feelings to tell me what was simply true for me, I understood that they were just doing their job. Not understanding, I had lived in fear of my own feelings, and that fear—a feeling in its own right—was nothing more than something I had created out of whole cloth.

As you will see in chapter 4's discussion of my *"Fear Weekend,"* I eventually discovered that I had created a conflict between my (old) feelings and my (later) feelings. I had been afraid of all those powerful feelings I pretended were to break me apart if I acknowledged them, and I had attempted to deny them altogether to prevent that from happening. When *"Later"* came, it was precisely from those painful feelings that I would find the very self I had been convinced I had lost. More proof—if you need it—that nothing is ever simply this or that where we humans are involved.

Ultimately, I learned that the antidote to my experience was to trust all my feelings unconditionally. Feelings may not ever reflect some independent truth, a universal truth that can be measured objectively and called reality, but they will always reflect what is simply true in the moments I am feeling them. By understanding the purpose they serve in my life, I can recognize what I am feeling and deal with it in any way I want or need to at the time I am having the feeling. After that there is no reason to think anything about them again. This seems, to me, to be a more practical way to relate to feelings. What I learned blazing my own path to a relationship with feelings I had come to think of as my enemies was only that old, denied feelings never go away. They just lie there inside you waiting to be acknowledged; and they can do you a lot of harm while they're waiting.

What's a human to do?

Knowing how your brain manages your feelings, and trusting that your voice can help you understand what your feelings are trying to tell you, you can feel free to allow yourself, simply, to feel as you do. You can trust that you have no need to be uncomfortable about how you feel, or worse, to deny it. Your feelings are just what they are.

For me, knowing that enables me to feel confident that I can trust myself to take good care of myself. I no longer have to think of my feelings as my enemies, as I once did, and the way my friend Henriette did after her husband died.

Henriette's story

Henriette's husband died of AIDS about a year before Art, and when I met her, she was already working with the Caregiver's Group I had just joined. We couldn't have been more different as women in the world. She was younger by almost 20 years, shorter by at least a foot, darker-skinned and much more richly endowed in body than I. Her life experiences—she had come north to the Hudson Valley of New York State with farm workers as a young woman from the south—were as unfamiliar to me as mine must have been to her. She was also raising a four-year-old daughter alone through the painful experience of her husband's death.

For all our differences, our experience as caregivers in the AIDS epidemic rendered Henriette and me just the same. In no time, it seemed, we were traveling hand-in-hand together over the landscapes in our minds' eyes. As we began to spin out the stories of our daily lives of caring for husbands who would die, we found ourselves finishing each other's sentences. There seemed no end to our sameness, the ways we perceived what had happened and what was still happening to us. Even as each of us continued to struggle with our private loss, we came to know each other like the sound of our own beating heart. Most importantly, we both soon realized our relationships with our feelings were very much the same.

Henriette came to the Group one day terribly upset. She had been sick with a flu that had brought diarrhea and weakness for a few days the week before. It had been so bad one night she had gotten scared that maybe all those HIV tests she had been getting over and over again for years had been wrong. She had felt so sick she called her sister-in-law in the middle of the night just to have someone to talk to, to keep herself from feeling alone and afraid.

"But," Henriette said, she would not tell her sister-in-law what was keeping her so afraid. "I knew it wasn't that," she told us. "I couldn't be infected with the AIDS virus after all this time." Even so, she could not stop worrying, could not get the fear out of her head. "I was lying to my sister-in-law because I didn't want her to know the truth, why I was scared," she explained, and I even knew there was no way it could be the truth."

As I quietly watched her sitting across the table from me, it was the fear in her voice that held me, my fear, too. *It's always the same*, I thought. *It's as if your whole house gets infected with AIDS, as if the virus soaked into the woodwork and you're inhaling it, as if you will be tainted with it forever after that.*

How deeply inside myself I understood what my friend was saying. She was feeling afraid of the lie her thoughts were telling her, and she was terrorized by her own feelings of fear. Her feelings had become her enemies and she could find no relief from them. At that time, I had that same fear inside me.

Variations on the theme

An old friend of mine, who had stopped calling me after I finally confessed the terrible secret that Art died of AIDS, called me one day about a year after my confession. She said she was sorry she had stopped calling but she had been convinced I didn't call her again because I had started to show symptoms of the disease, and, she said, "I just couldn't deal with the truth."

Listening to her pronouncement, I felt the dread of fear wrap itself around me, again. *People are waiting for me to show up with AIDS,*

I thought bitterly, even years later, and the thought hardened into cement in the pit of my stomach. *Why couldn't she just accept I was not infected because I said so?*

Not long after that, my uncle called from across the country. He had warned me in the days after Art died that he was going to stop calling because I didn't need him enough. Several years had passed during which we had not spoken at all and, when I finally stopped being angry about what I had perceived as other people's failure to comfort me, I had called and coaxed him back into my life. We had started speaking regularly by telephone after that.

"By the way," he said, suddenly changing the subject just before he hung up. "How often do you have to be tested?"

I misunderstood. We had been talking about my law practice. "Tested for what?" I asked innocently, and only as I asked did I start to *"get it."* Then I started to pray he wouldn't mean what I knew he meant.

"You know...for the HIV?"

My throat stuck. "I don't have to get tested." I barely garbled it out before I reminded myself I didn't want to sound hard after our reconciliation, so I made myself get soft for him. "I used to have to get tested every three months." I whispered, "but I don't have the virus so they told me I don't have to get tested anymore." *Please stop now* I begged him in my thoughts.

"Oh," he said, "because I've heard that it can lay dormant for seven years and then you find out you have it."

Mechanically, I started to count the years I had left since the last time I was tested. "I don't have it." *How can you say this to me?* Four years. *If I get it, I'll call you.*

I tried not to think about it after that, but he aroused the fear in me, and I became obsessed with what he said. Even though I knew I had no reason to doubt, I made myself go through the blood test all over again, as I had done every three months for the three years Art was sick with the virus, and then for another year after that because his doctor had told me I should, just to be sure.

That's the way it is with AIDS. So much fear that no one can tell anymore what the real thing is to be afraid of. If you got caught in the web of the epidemic, you reacted, not for yourself as you might in any other situation, but from the fear of all the prejudice and stigma outside you, the social fear of people you didn't even know, which you internalized in the face of what you absolutely knew to be true.

The first time I had to go to the Department of Health to be tested, I came away shaken and resentful. It was just after Art's diagnosis, and I wasn't in good enough emotional shape to be challenged in any way to begin with. Even so, there was no way I could ever have prepared myself for the ordeal of testing for the virus in those early days. The screener started asking me questions about my sexual practices as if she had a right to know. Then she asked me to tell her about my intimate life with my husband and about his sexuality, questions it tormented me to be asked so close to the day my happy life was wrenched away from me. I was near hysteria as I struggled to keep answering her, and I kept my eye on the door all the while in case I could not stand her prying any longer and would have to run from the room.

Finally, feeling impossibly cornered, I stopped her. I was desperate. "I can't do this," I said, visibly shaking all over. "Can't you please stop asking me all these questions now?" I was pleading.

"It's pretty simple," she said matter-of-factly, without even making eye contact with me. "You either answer the questions or you don't get the test." I was shattered. *Why is she challenging me? Don't I matter at all? Can't she see what her words are doing to me? What kind of a disease is this, anyway?*

After that test, I calmly made a strategy for dealing with the questions in the future, arming myself before I had to be tested again. I gave myself permission to stop listening whenever I needed to and to answer their questions any way I wanted to. I got bolder as I went along—*why not?* I had to be there every three months, but I didn't have to be anybody's victim—and I dared myself to answer more and even more outrageously than I had the time before. The look on my face defied every new tester to *bring it on*, to challenge me the way the first one had. I imagined all the testers meeting together for a drink after work and talking about me, the angry crazy woman from the west side whose husband was dying in the apartment while she was out giving reckless responses to their salacious questions. Nobody seemed interested to know that, if I had become that crazy woman, it was because I had been driven to it. I was only trying, in the few ways left to me, to preserve what little privacy AIDS had not yet taken away from us.

So it was by stark contrast that on the day I went to get tested (at the government's Board of Health) for the first time in four years because my uncle had put the fear back in me, and the nurse asked me the first question on her intake form—"What is the reason you want to be tested?"—I could hardly wait to tell her the plain truth, more shocking than any lie I ever made up: "Because my husband died of AIDS and it never goes away, that's why." She must have seen it in my face when I blurted it out almost with a dare, as if it was her fault, because she did not ask me anything after that.

Two weeks of waiting followed, and the night before I had to go back to her to get the verdict, I could not sleep. I had not eaten, and I shivered alone in my bed. I remembered, again, what I had finally been able to put away and forget years before. I had had a virulent cold and flu that started in me when I first fell in love with Art—I later learned it was a common reaction to an infection, the way a healthy body tries to fight it off—and I kept hearing my uncle's voice warning that "it can lay dormant for seven years." I tried to distract myself by reading but could not, could only keep adding up my years as I had done so many times before.

I tried talking myself calm but my rage got the best of me. *I'm a perfectly logical person. Why can't I put this fear away once and for all? Why can't I resist the lure of pulling it up again even once more because someone who doesn't know thinks his need to make small talk about his curiosity is more important than my peace of mind?*

I very nearly decided I would not show up for the test result. My head was cramming full of *what if* questions, the questions without answers, and I was so afraid. *What if tomorrow it all ends? What will I do then, if, finally, I have AIDS?*

I decided to distract myself by making a list of the things I still wanted to do before I died—when all else fails, make a list that justifies why you should be judged worthy to live. I would find out what my reasons were *now*, and I laughed bitterly at myself for thinking, yet again, that I could bargain with the fates by going through this old exercise routine.

As soon as I started to write, I realized this wasn't going to be the same exercise as the last time. The words I was writing were no list at all—they weren't even mine. I couldn't find myself in these words, and I was certain they could not have come from me. I didn't know it yet, but my voice—which had only spoken to me once by that time—had entered the conversation:

> I want to see me enjoying myself. I even want to be loved and in love again. Mostly, I want to be happy, want not to be buried under my oppression, the constant sadness and fear.

> These words stunned me. I felt no relationship to them. Nor could I find any feelings to match their sentiment anywhere inside me.

Then there were more words coming:

> I hate the feeling that I shouldn't get happy, shouldn't want happy things, as if somehow that wouldn't be right, as if I can justify feeling anything as long as I am not happy,

and, finally,

> I want to feel alive again and not just wake up every damned day to the same sadness and longing.

I stared in disbelief at what I had written. Where had they come from? What was I supposed to do with such words as these? *I* wanted to be happy? How could *I*—so sure that happiness would never again be a feeling I could expect to wake up to—why would I have written such a thing as that? I thought I had been doing pretty well *mining* my feelings in the Caregiver's Group, but *this*? I was not prepared to initiate, nor contemplate, any new relationship with *happy*.

Sarcastically, I remembered all the others, who used to talk about how the night before you get the test result is when you reaffirm your commitment to your life. You try to make that deal with the higher powers, that if they let you live this time you will show them you are worthy of their confidence. Was that what I was doing here, bargaining by showing the fates I had good intentions for the future of my life so they should let me live? Only a few days ago, I had been so sure I hated the life I had been left with that I had no intention of even challenging what had become of happiness and love. I just expected I would never feel them again.

Yet, these words I had written spoke of a person's hopefulness and positive feelings. They expressed wishes, allegedly my wishes, for something so different from anything I believed were my true feelings. I was angry and maybe even desperate with carrying around so many heavy feelings, yet here I was writing words affirming that I wanted a life I could love. The words mocked me. I couldn't even feel happy just to know I wanted to be happy.

Ruefully, I remembered how it felt to know, even before Art died, that I would have the rest of my life to think about myself, and that I would, in time, feel better in spite of myself. Logically, I told anyone who asked that, of course I knew someday I would be happy again, because that's just what happens to people as they live. "It will happen automatically, with time," I always answered, and everyone eagerly agreed with me. Time, they always told me, was the great healer of all wounds.

But how could I want to be happy *now*, all of a sudden, just like that? Art had only died four years ago, and I was up to my waist in *mining* my feelings. I was suspicious. I was sure I could only have said those things about knowing I would get happy to placate whoever asked. I never really wanted or expected *that* to happen.

I wondered if the words had somehow forced themselves out of me. I did not even wonder if they might have something to do with that voice I heard, from that other time. I didn't ask if the voice had come again to show me I might have some other feelings I was afraid to acknowledge. I only wondered how the words I had written could be my own. Was I daring me, egging me on, trying to force myself to adopt some other way of thinking, all of a sudden?

It was obvious I had all the right words, but I couldn't let myself feel them. I could only ask, frantically, what would I do when I would *have to be* happy? Would there no longer be any more buried, hurtful feelings left to hide behind? I had no way of knowing I had started using my feelings as a barrier to keep happiness out. It had only seemed logical to me that I couldn't expect to be happy because Art had died and I had not.

What I didn't know was that I was convinced I did not *deserve* to be happy. I certainly wouldn't know what to do with thoughts of *not deserving*, so if I was aware of having them, I must have disallowed them. I was years away from learning about *Survivor's Guilt* and even more years away from understanding that thinking I did not deserve to be happy was a normal part of my experience. Some other day, which hadn't happened yet, the voice would come back and tell me I could continue to think about Art for as long as I wanted to and not have to abandon him at all. On that day, I would become able, finally, to acknowledge I felt guilty for having lived when he died. Only then would I begin to understand that, for so long as I could not give myself permission to be happy, no pile of words that might come out of me could ever make me feel any better. For now, all I could feel was blindsided by those words I had written.

In the morning, when I returned for the test results, the nurse greeted my sullen face with an unnatural surprise. "Go out there and have a good life," she said enthusiastically, waving me off with a wide, embracing sweep of her arms. She was so happy to be giving me the happy news that I was not infected. "Unless you change your behavior," she predicted, "I don't think you'll ever have to be tested again."

I didn't have to be tested this time, I thought resentfully after my night without sleep. And if it hadn't been for fear, I would not have had to take another test even when I knew—as Henriette had known—that I couldn't be infected.

Neither would I have had to confront the startling revelation I might really want to be happy. Nor would I have had to confront the new words I now didn't know what to do with: I might actually not deserve to be happy.

As I left the nurse's office, all I could do was feel sorry for myself, and angry. I supposed I should be grateful to know I was, still, not infected, yet it was an unseemly victory. The whole incident, from my uncle's call to the nurse's arms outstretched as if she were already celebrating my happy life, only made me sad to think I had become a sad person. That was when I remembered I had, long ago, declared myself to be a sad person. I had passed that exact judgment on myself. Was I still trying to live down that legacy?

Had I condemned myself to sadness?

When I was barely out of my teens, a wise professor asked me if I would describe myself as a basically happy or sad person. Secretly, I was aware I didn't know how to answer him, but with the bravado of a young woman, I knew I had to accept his challenge. "Sad," I pronounced, almost defiantly, trying not to sound as tentative as I felt. I liked the sound of that; it seemed like the *right* answer in a romantic, worldly way. Many of my old movie heroines were sad and melancholy, and as a young person, I had taken pride in placing myself in their exalted company.

Now, I was having a terrible thought I couldn't shake off. Looking back at my edict from the distance of time, I knew I had been naïve, at best. My old movie heroines, after all, had all been creations of authors and playwrights, and most of them had triumphed into fabulous happy endings. I hadn't believed what I told the professor, and now I was starting to worry if it was possible that I could have been so powerful as to make myself sad just by declaring it so.

I couldn't answer my own question. I didn't, at that time, have any way of knowing that we do have the power to make ourselves happy or sad. I only learned that later, when I conducted an unscientific experiment of my own. Now, I can tell you we can do this by using our unique ability to think: I envisioned myself changing my default posture from a basically sad to a basically happy one.

I know what you're thinking. I can imagine you sighing and maybe even rolling your eyes. Pie in the sky. New Age psycho-babble. If all we had to do to be happy was think ourselves happy, how come we're not all happy people by now?

About happiness: some thoughts revealed

There are some interesting answers to that last question up there. Some of the answers are more obvious than others.

For one thing, happiness is fluid. Over the course of a lifetime, we might all change our definition of happiness many times as we experience it in many different ways. For another, even though we might be inclined to *pin* our happiness on a particular person or object, that's not where happiness comes from. Even when we know this, we can get caught up in spending a lot of energy looking for what will make us happy where we can be reasonably assured of not finding it. We can convince ourselves it's *out there* and all we have to do is catch up with the right thing or person, which, or who, will bring us happiness. We can even decide to believe that if we're not happy it's because happiness itself has managed to elude us, as if happiness would somehow prevent us from finding it.

These misperceptions say nothing about happiness and everything about our own tendencies to keep ourselves in a negative frame of mind. That actually limits our chances for being happy, and we do that all by ourselves. Looking in all the wrong places and missing the points are two extraordinary ways we distract ourselves from seeing the simple truth of happiness.

Happiness is a feeling. We create it within ourselves, as we do all our other feelings. Only you know your feelings of being happy in just the way you do. It is not a gift you receive from out there in reality, even if you choose to believe your happiest moments were delivered by some things, or persons, who brought it into your world. It is a great gift you produce in the privacy of your own mind, and you do it by thinking it.

Reality, by comparison, is what we share with each other. It is the arena in which our actions, even our happiest ones, are operationalized. While my feelings may seem very real to me because I feel them strongly, they are only real to *me* and could never be held up for independent verification, measurement or evaluation outside my mind.

A wise friend once told me that all the feelings of love I have for another person exist only inside me; what I feel is *my* love. Perhaps you're thinking that's a simple statement and is obvious on the face of it, but you may want to look a little closer at what my friend meant by the possession of love. Because we all feel our feelings powerfully, we can sometimes forget they are only occurring inside each of us. We created them, and they belong only to us. Even if we choose to share them, the recipients of our love will only feel their own version of it. It is more than likely nobody has ever felt my love the same way I thought I was giving it, and the same is true for you and every other human on earth.

So my friend's words are worth repeating. Your feelings are yours, and only you can know what love feels like to you. If you show and describe your feelings of love to me, using actions and words that are very familiar to both of us, I may be able to see and hear your expression of love, but I cannot feel your feelings of love as you speak them. I can only interpret your words and actions in the privacy of my mind and create my own variation of the love you expressed. This is simply true because no two of us have had the exact life experiences that formed us into the people we have become. Thus, we can only decide to take each other *at our word*. Or, perhaps not.

This distinction can be useful as you are deciding which choices you will make about acting on your feelings. Once you accept that your feelings of happiness are yours alone, you can soon appreciate you are free to enjoy them as much as you wish, and then you can decide whether you want to act on them and how, or not.

Of course, you can also choose to be unhappy, not to be happy at all, even unwittingly. You can reinforce unhappiness in yourself by simply holding it in your thoughts without letting it go. No one will stop you from doing that if that's what you have in mind. Your brain is not an independent organ that can second-guess you. It cannot decide independently of you that you couldn't really mean you want to be unhappy, and it cannot decide to ignore your message of unhappiness by making you happy in spite of yourself. When you are imagining yourself unhappy, your brain is generating the negative neurons of unhappiness, and it is reinforcing them by multiplying them. It is only trying to give you what you *want*.

That's a good reason to be honest with yourself about what you feel and what you want for yourself. Imagine your brain as the central station for the processing of everything that pertains to you. It won't be making any demands of you, except, perhaps, that you be who you are so it can keep everything operating as you want it to. It is *you* who needs to be clear for your own sake, and it is to *you* that you need to tell the best true version of how you feel—in fact or in your imagination. Do you truly want to be unhappy?

For the record, it matters that actual happiness and the happiness you imagine for yourself are the same thing to your brain. Think of the times you believed you were the happiest you have ever been. Your brain accepts those feelings as happiness, and you will feel it. So, while the journey to an imagined happiness might not be as much fun as one you experience out in the world, if you really want to be happy, regardless of your circumstances, start adding some imagined happiness to your actual life. You may just find that the happier you imagine you are, the happier you will, in fact, feel.

You can think of this as an exercise regimen you might choose to follow and, while you're at it, imagine the kind of benefits you can gain from it. When you exercise your body you are first building muscles that change the way your body looks and feels, and then the way you feel and think about yourself follows suit. It's just the same with neurons—the nerve centers—in your brain. You can think of your neurons as muscles if you like, and you can imagine them getting stronger and increasing in numbers with your exercise called thinking-about-being-happy. It's an exercise your brain will love, because your brain is very malleable: it will change with your thoughts, experiences and the choices you make. Every time the possibility of feeling happy arises—in reality and in your imagination—you can reinforce it by reminding yourself that what you want is to feel happy. When you do that regularly, you can help happiness become your basic state of mind—and while we're at it, keep in mind that, even if this is hard to believe, brains all over the world have been proving it to be so, in neuroscience laboratories as well as out in the streets of the world.

Imagination is funny

While we're clarifying a few things, let's dispel some misconceptions about imagining. Imagining is not the same thing as lying, nor is it covering up a truth you may not want to know. Imagining is more honest than trying to convince yourself you are feeling happy when you know too well you are not.

Imagination is more like a decision you make to create a vision of what will make you happy, and the feeling of being happy that derives from your vision is as real to your brain as the happiness of actually changing your circumstances. This is also true of all your feelings—the positive and negative. You might say imagining is another creative way your brain helps you help it get its job done: maintaining your wellbeing. You might also think it is awfully nice of your brain to accept *pseudo-happiness* imaginings from you. At the risk of sounding ironic, this is way more than pseudo-happiness, and although it is merely obvious, it seems worth stating again: Your brain is *you*—and that's the point. Imagination is another tool in your non-physical sensory system.

A cautionary note

Of course, before you can be creating any kind of happiness for yourself, either in your mind or in actuality, you will likely have to resolve a prerequisite that may be standing between you and happiness: you have to *allow* yourself to be happy. Although this may seem peculiar— you're probably thinking: doesn't everyone want to be happy?—take a moment to consider this.

If you want to feel happy and you know all you have to do to feel happy is imagine yourself being happy, but you don't imagine it, there is probably an obstacle in your path. You may not be aware of it; it may be a story you tell yourself, about some way you are that keeps you from being happy. Maybe you think you don't *deserve* to be happy; would you be surprised to know many of us grow up feeling just that same way, for all sorts of reasons that are no good reasons at all? Since happiness doesn't have any existence without humans' brains, how can happiness decide by itself you aren't good enough to deserve it? It cannot. So what might be keeping you from living as a basically happy person if that's who you say you want to be?

Again, you have to allow yourself to be happy. Once you have your own permission, you can affirm happiness whenever you have an opportunity to do so. Your extraordinary ability to do this is right there in your thinking brain—the very same place where you keep all those thoughts, like *not deserving* or *not good enough*, and all the other stories you have made up about yourself.

I am not suggesting some mystical course in positive thinking, nor would I urge you to start pretending to be happy, just as I would not want you to deny that you sometimes have negative feelings or thoughts. There will always be things in real life that will suddenly appear, as if out of nowhere, to alter the course of your best intentions for yourself. Pretending and denying ignores how complex you are. You may know by now that I would certainly not suggest you ever feel anything other than the way you do. That never worked for me, and it took me a long time to undo the unhappy effects of denying my feelings.

Happy: an unscientific experiment

What would it take for you to allow yourself to be happy? What are those other things you might secretly suspect about yourself that you would have to put aside to make room for happiness?

In an attempt to make peace with what I had written the night before I got my fourth-year test results, I decided to conduct an unscientific experiment on the state of my own happiness. I also wanted to know if I could free myself from the way I once defined myself, as a basically sad person. Could I become a basically happy person? What would it take to make that happen?

For starters, I decided I would need a good working definition of happiness. This is the one I came up with:

> A happy person knows happiness is a feeling and it belongs to her. She is free to allow herself to feel as she does at any given moment, without having to attach any meaning to her happiness that it might not have. She does not think happiness is fleeting, and she is not concerned that sadness, when it comes in its turn, will overwhelm and replace her basic happiness. She acknowledges life is filled with all sorts of feelings that must be felt and, trusting her feelings, she is simply content to have them. All her feelings are welcome.

When I was sure I had a definition of happiness I would be able to recognize if and when I attained it, the next question was: How can I ensure I will remember to reinforce the positive neurons in my brain often enough to make happiness my basic way of feeling? I searched for something I do on a regular and frequent basis that I could connect my message to, in a way that would remind me to think about feeding my neurons as often as possible.

What I created, finally, was a link between my breathing and my reinforcing happiness message. I noticed that when I take a long, slow breath in, there is an empty space—barely noticeable—in which my breath is suspended for an instant before I am forced to exhale. I decided to fill that imaginary space with a message for my brain that I want to be happy.

I was sure that, with practice, I could become conscious of my breaths and use them to remind myself I want to be happy. In addition, even if I wasn't feeling positive enough to send the message along with every breath, or if I forgot to do so, I would still have many opportunities to send my message throughout each day. I was ready to start my training.

It was challenging at first, just as you might imagine any new exercise regimen would be. Sometimes I was grumpy and unwilling to choose happiness. At those times, I bargained with myself and chose to send no message at all rather than send a negative one. This was interesting in its own way, because I became aware of how often I contributed to my own feelings of unhappiness. If I felt downright hostile, I could forget the whole thing, but only if I acknowledged I was going to give myself permission to do so on that breath alone.

At other times, I felt happy just to be able to think I wanted to be happy. Each time I did so, I was rewarded by a flood of happy feelings that could have come from nothing other than my decision to take a stand in my own behalf. Disclaimer: All through this experiment, nothing actually changed in the physical reality of my life.

As I got used to playing this game, I increasingly found myself wanting to choose happiness whenever I asked myself about it. I started to feel as if I was doing something important for my life, and soon I *upped the ante* for my experiment. I wanted to see how many times a day I would be able to choose to be happy. Every time I managed to get all the way there, I watched in awe as my attitude changed and my spirits lifted.

I checked in with myself periodically to see how I was doing. It took a while, but gradually, over a period of months, I started to feel like someone I could describe as mostly happy—and even getting that far made me *really* happy. Eventually, I knew that, if asked, I would have to answer that I saw myself as a basically happy person.

From the vantage point of years since I undertook this unscientific experiment, I am happy to tell you that something did indeed change my default posture. The more I think of myself as a happy person, using my same definition, the more I want to think that; and the more I want to think that, the more I am, in fact, able to think it. Perhaps it is merely a self-fulfilling prophecy, but if it is, it certainly is one that has been worth making. I have reached a turning point at which it is no longer acceptable for me to tell myself I want to be sad. I do not.

At the same time, unexpectedly, my relationship with feeling sad has also changed. If I feel sad, I simply allow myself to feel it until it passes. I know it will pass if I allow it to run its course. Who knows? Maybe I'll develop the same kind of relationship with my other feelings, like frustration, anger, disappointment and even fear.

This was an unscientific experiment to be sure, but it was one guided by a lot of imagination. First, I imagined how my world might look to my brain, and then, to keep my brain healthy, I had to be willing to stop pretending I believed there was romance in melancholy (as I did when I was a young teenager). By now, I'm happy to tell you, I can't even remember why I ever thought so. Of course, I also benefited from more than a little help from my inner voice. When I'm feeling happy, *she* likes to send me images of me doing cartwheels of joy via my internal mailbox: my mind's eye.

This is so simple, really, and it's fun. Thinking I want to be a basically happy person makes me feel good, and feeling good makes me feel powerful—which, I believe, is a crucial ingredient for actually changing my life, if that's what I have a mind to do. Feeling good also makes it harder for me ever to want to choose to have negative feelings. Are you willing to undertake the challenge in behalf of your own brain?

The best part is you can feel it happening to you, no matter where you think you are in relation to happiness in the reality of your life. I would describe the feeling as something like running, taking a jump and then soaring. The simplest way I can explain it is to say it's just a feeling I have. It comes down to you, and me, as it always does. Your happiness comes down to you, as mine is dependent on me.

So, what is there to be afraid of?

4

Fear Weekend: Thinking Fear to Death

In my thirties and just out of law school, I used to love the laugh I got when I joked that I was afraid of everything. The good thing, I would explain when I had them waiting for the punch line, was I was afraid of everything equally. "All I have to do is fold my fears up and fit them into the back pocket of my jeans," I'd say—as I was making a neat little package with my hands, tucking it away in and patting my pocket. Then I'd conclude with, "this way, fear will never stop me from living my life."

Glib and sophisticated as I fancied myself then, I still look back at that joke with a grimace. Could I have truly meant to say I lived in fear? Did I think it was funny I carried fear around with me all the time, or that I had found a way to accommodate it in my life? How could I have ever enjoyed getting a laugh like that at my own expense, bragging I was afraid of everything?

Now that I'm older, I could roll my eyes in an *ah youth* kind of way and leave it at that, but as with many things I once joked about, I now see this laugh was overlaying a fundamental truth about me. It still makes me uneasy to think about it. Thank goodness my voice finally settled the matter of fear for me once and for all. Over the course of what I think of as my *Fear Weekend, she*—my voice—showed me just what kind of relationship I had with my fear, and then *she* told me the kind of relationship I could have. By the end of three days, I saw myself being transformed into a fearless person powerful enough to vanquish fear anytime I have a good mind to do so.

For clarity's sake, I'll need to distinguish what I call *my* fear, the fear that once held me in its thrall, from my oldest and most basic emotion of fear. Emotional fear is as old as we humans are. As you may recall, it is the fear that warns us we may be in danger and then forces us, immediately, to act—to run away, freeze on the spot or to prepare to fight—before we can even think about it. We can still trust this basic fear to be there when we need it; the earliest humans on earth came with this feature, and every human model since then has, too. We can pretty much presume, without having to think about it, that it will continue to operate automatically within us, preparing and then prompting us to act against threats to our physical wellbeing.

My fear, on the other hand—the fear I pretended to fold into my pocket so I could carry it along with me—would prove not to be a response to life that I have to abide. That fear has evolved in each of us as our lives have become more complex, but unlike the fear we do not have to think about, this fear seems to be woven into our thoughts in ways that can challenge us to our own detriment. It's the kind of fear that cannot make us feel confident we are living our lives deliberately, the way we want to; instead, this fear can keep us from acting in our own best interests. We would do well to figure out how to shrug it off, to act in spite of it or to get free of its grip in any way we can if we are going to live our lives as we want to.

In his book, *Synaptic Self*, neuroscientist Joseph Le Doux calls this *"defense conditioning"*, and as he describes it,

> *In modern life, we sometimes suffer from the exquisite operation of this system since it is difficult to get rid of this kind of conditioning*

once it is no longer applicable to our lives, and we sometimes become conditioned to fear things that are in fact harmless.[7]

These *fear things* Dr. LeDoux identified might be the most insidious of all the fears we humans confront. They are the fears that hang around us like a cloud, disabling us from seeing or thinking clearly about what we want and can do to get it for ourselves. They are the fears we embody in the words *can't, not good enough* and *do not deserve,* fears and even suspicions we are *too much of this* and *not enough of that.* They are the fears that can cripple our hopes and dreams for ourselves, impacting us with an intensity that won't allow us even to imagine reaching for our hearts' desires.

Left to our own devices to deal with this fear, some of us may have even gotten really good at using it as a weapon against ourselves. We have a fear of making a big change in our lives so we don't, even though we say we long to make a change and believe we are fully committed to doing so. Or we fear calling too much attention to ourselves so we try not to, settling instead to remain on the sidelines as if we were invisible in our own lives. These fears can make us afraid of risking, well, almost anything on our own behalf. What we do, instead of taking those great chances to make our personal dreams come true, is put together the very best words we can to try and convince ourselves that our actions, or inactions, are justified. Then, all that's left to us is to try and make *the best of it.*

By holding and thinking about our fears, we may actually be reinforcing them—remember that you can reinforce happiness by thinking yourself happy. Without intending to, we might be issuing our fears invitations to run rampant over the surface of our lives, to be the obstacles that will stop us from getting what we want. Were it not for these fears, we might all be fearless people. We would, of course, continue to have our regular, emotional fear and it would continue to safeguard our wellbeing. But these other fears cannot enhance our ability to thrive. Nor, in fact, can our brains use them to keep us safe from danger that may actually threaten us.

---

[7] Joseph LeDoux, *synaptic Self: How Our Brains Become Who We Are, p. 124*

If these fears underlie our important decisions, they can also undermine us by interfering with choices we want to make. Although these choices may have little or nothing to do with our actual survival, they are certainly connected to our quality of life, our sense of wellbeing and even our happiness. I fear we may have gotten hooked on these intellectual fears—the fears we give life to by thinking about them—and we use our thinking brains to fine-tune them until they are as wily and sophisticated as we ourselves are. Even unwittingly, we may be elevating them higher in our hierarchy of feelings until they have become big enough for us to hide behind, or under, providing us good excuses any time we need them, to avoid meeting the challenges our creative imaginations are dreaming up for us all the time.

We elevate these fears in a variety of ways. We personalize them. We refer to them as *my fear*—as in *My worst fear is that…*, as if we were putting our virtual arm around their shoulders and welcoming them into our family. Without realizing it, when we do that, we can also be reinforcing in our brains the messages these new fears are important to us and we fully expect they are here to stay. We give them the owner's seal of approval, the exact opposite of what we would want to do with such insidious fears.

We also personify *our* fears. We think of them as having physical characteristics, like *my eyes,* or non-physical ones, like *my sense of humor.* We nurture them by flattering them. Or we try to make peace with them as I did, perhaps by sending them the message we know we shall have to learn how to deal with this fear somehow, sometime.

Do we have to send fear such messages? Some of us talk about our fears as if they were entities that have invaded our bodies and demanded we negotiate terms with them before we can ever hope they will stop overpowering our other feelings.

At the other extreme, there is also another relationship with our fear that we must consider. There are those of us who deny they are afraid of anything. Instead of acknowledging they feel fear—remember, you don't decide to have a feeling; a feeling comes upon you—they might act as if they think fear will go away if they ignore it. They talk around it, as if they don't want to get fear's attention by calling it by name to its fearsome face. I have even heard people say they're afraid that, if they do admit to their fears, they will be held in a terrible grip of fear, perhaps forever.

Some people who want to deny they feel fear might also try to mask their fear by calling it more socially acceptable names. If you ask such a person if he is afraid, he might say, "No, I'm not afraid. I am simply thinking rationally." To assist him, you might compliment him for his courage or for exercising such *good, solid judgment* and mature thinking as he approaches his important decisions.

A plan like that can keep us from recognizing we feel fear, but it will not change what the fear itself is. It is still fear. We are fearful, and even with the support of one another, we'll still only be denying that.

Before too long, we'll have to deal with the denial of our fears in addition to the fears themselves. There's no getting around it, and for all our pretending we shall continue to feel fears nagging at us as we try to deny them and call them something else. So please, if you hear me insisting I am *simply taking a logical approach* to some issue at hand, feel free to look at me askance and wonder aloud why I cannot simply admit I am afraid. You would actually be doing me a great favor.

Not that it would be wrong to reflect on pros and cons as we deliberate the many choices and decisions of our lives. There is nothing wrong with being thoughtful, and active consideration for your own wellbeing can only be a good thing. Wouldn't you want to feel, always, you care about yourself and only want what is best for you? *Do* we care about ourselves enough to want only what is best for us, all the time?

I once knew a young woman who began every day with a fear exercise. Standing out in front of her apartment building, she could not decide which of several directions to walk in to get to her office. She said she was afraid to choose because she was sure that, if she chose the *wrong* direction, she would miss her one chance to meet the man of her dreams. While we want to be thoughtful and deliberate when we have important decisions to make, as long as it is our fears calling the shots it will be from fear we are operating, and fear can keep us powerless in our own lives.

When I have looked, I have found my fears behind every doubt I have about myself, every decision I try to avoid making. I have found them under every risk I have dared even to think I might take to reach as far as I could and take hold of what would make me happiest.

Confronting my fears, I have become convinced I do not always use my thinking brain well. I confess I have even relied on fear to nurture and empower other fears in me.

Yet, there is also this: what I learned about my relationship with fear from my inner voice during my Fear Weekend. In the end, my fear is no more than the air I breathe into it, and it is a lot less than all the words I use to define or deny it. My fear is a feeling and, as with all my feelings, I get to think about it as much as I want to before I decide how I shall deal with it.

It feels good to know I can vanquish my fear with my natural, human ability to think, the same ability I use to nurture fear. It's a relief to know that, if I find it in me, I can think about it, and when I do, I can dissolve that fear away.

What the voice knew

My voice has taught me that, if I ask questions of it, *my* fear cannot come up with any answers. If I try to chase it down by talking or writing about it, fear will just break up until I can blow it away like so much toxic dust. I may think it feels bigger than I am at first, but if I look again, I will find it is empty, not like me at all. By standing up to my fear I can reduce it to nothing. Of course, as with all victories of my mind, each time I force a fear to dissipate I gain the confidence that my brain has strengthened its resolve to do it again, and again.

On the basis of what I have discovered, I want to propose a new way of dealing with *our* fears: let's ask them questions to rout them out when we find them on our minds. The more we expose them, the more readily we shall be able to see they have no legs to stand on. When you find a fear in you, try starting with these simple questions. Answer them as fully and honestly as you can and then add your own questions as you go along:

What am I afraid of?
Why did I invite fear in?
Is this fear something real, and why do I have to be afraid of it?

Answering these questions can be enough to get you started on the path to confidence you can manage your fear. Your own answers can give you back the power you need to cancel those invitations you may be issuing to fear without realizing you are doing so.

If you think you are not yet ready to question fear when it arises, I urge you to start by calling it by its proper name: fear. Name all your fears out loud. Whenever you get a whiff of one, call its bluff. I am confident that, when you do, your fears will begin to crumble even as you're trying to chase after them.

How can I be so sure of this? It was my fear itself that taught me the truth about it, with my voice acting as the interpreter.

The fantasy woman

Finally, I was done with *mining* all my old feelings. The hard stuff was behind me and I was ready, and eager, to welcome joy back into my life.

I had learned a great deal about myself during the years that began when I joined the Caregiver's Group. Things that had not been as precious to me before I now valued greatly, and most of the things I had always relied on as signposts to identify my life had been dismantled. Where I had once been grateful to have my own law office to go to, to hide in each day, I knew for certain I would close the office—Art's last gift to me—because that work was much less important than what called to me now. I was embarking on an unknown path of work, and all I was certain of was I wanted to travel it for as long as I could.

For a number of years that began soon after I joined the Group, I was frequently invited to talk about my experience of AIDS in the context of hiv prevention education. I had learned much about how we keep ourselves safe—and also choose not to do so—and many teachers were eager to have me address their students. I started meeting with young people in their high school health classes, and soon after I was asked to speak with parents, caregivers and single adults—many of whom were divorced women who had raised their children alone and were ready to *"take on"* the challenge of falling in love again. Most women I met were finding relationships difficult to trust in what had become a dramatically different and harsh environment from the ones in which they had grown up.

Talking about what I learned from my own experiences helped me grow strong. Once I started talking, I did not want to stop. Luckily for me, many people encouraged me to keep talking. They said I brought them important things to know for their own lives as well as things to think about, and my words made them feel better. Wherever I went, people responded eagerly by talking about themselves, too, and I treasured those conversations. I began to realize we learn best when we can learn from each other. I saw the great power that is present when people are sharing their experiences in earnest conversation. At the same time, I had started to read and learn about the science of our brains.

One night, as I sat in the darkness of my bedroom with a head filled with thoughts about what I should do and how I should go about it, I saw an image in the dark. It was of a woman, a fabulous woman who felt related to me even though I was certain she could not be anyone I knew. After a while, I realized I was wrong; I did know her, intimately. I once called her my fantasy woman; the beautiful one I had imagined night after night in the dark privacy of my 13-year old bedroom.

I was a pretty ordinary teenager. I was so shy it hurt—shy: that's the polite word we give to a teenage girl's desperate longing to be invisible. If I was called on by a teacher and no less by classmates in the schoolyard, I flushed crimson, humiliated by my inability to speak. I felt betrayed by all the great words I secretly knew I carried around in my head, the ones I could not say when I needed them most. Over and over again I was reduced to mumbling, whispering and painfully exposing that self, the one I would gladly have traded for any other girl around.

As neither a beauty nor a scholar, I was sure my future, like the painful present, was going to be stocked with an awful abundance of ordinary.

But as miserable as I was during the terrible days of ordinary, the fantasy woman allowed me to celebrate a different life every night. Then, alone in the privacy of my imagination, I travelled to a magical refuge where she lived. She appeared every night on cue, and she stayed for as long as I needed her to help me fall asleep. She made it possible for me to balance the awful feelings of a 13-year old who was sure she would never make her mark on the world she would inherit, and to survive being her one day at a time. She was the image of a possibility for a kind of life I could only long for, and even though it seemed impossible, I knew I was somewhere inside her.

She had been the perfect antidote, the cure for a shy girl who couldn't speak for herself. She had all the right words at just the right times. She was smart and articulate, and people were happy to be around her. They were eager to hear what she had to say. They trusted her to speak simple truths, and she had a great reputation for saying exactly what she meant without wasting words. Of course, it didn't hurt my 13-year old feelings that she was vivacious and not at all shy. She was glorious to look at—I made sure of that—and she was happy. She made my heart sing with happiness just to see her.

Although I had no idea why I was seeing her again after all these years, I felt her appearance on this night was no coincidence. It was just a thought, but I asked if she was somehow related to what I had been thinking about the future I was moving into, and then, suddenly, I *got it: Of course.* She was a message sent to me by my inner voice. Then I realized, *it must have been my voice that sent her that first time, too, all those years ago.*

As I continued to look at and remember her, so familiar now, I gradually understood I wanted to *be* her. I wanted her life—the one I had created for her was the very life I wanted for myself.

Had I always been striving to become her? Might she have been more than a fantasy? I remembered how I had endowed her, so carefully, with all the details of characteristics I had most wanted for my grown-up self. They were the very same things I secretly cherished about myself as an adult, the ways I look at and live in the world, my values and now, the great decision I had made to start my life over with a bold, new kind of work. How happy I had been, loving the life I had given that fantasy woman, the life she had lived in my mind's eye night after night. I felt encouraged just to see her again, as if she had the power to connect me to my new life just by showing up.

I wanted to earn the reputation I had given her, to be the woman who could be trusted to be true to her word. As a child, I had taken great care to ensure she used words well and did not waste them. Now, I wanted to be the one who could be counted on to say exactly what I meant, what was simply true for me.

Excited to understand what our reunion might be offering, I promised myself as her image started to fade that I *would* make her life mine. I was moved to thank my voice for sending her again, for bringing me such an important truth about myself that I had forgotten.

The wind-up to my Fear Weekend

During the days that followed, though, as I set about to turn my dream into reality, I got frustrated by feelings of helplessness. I might have known who I wanted to be, but I couldn't figure out what to do to get there. Sometimes I couldn't even imagine anything bold enough I thought I was capable of doing, even though I said I was determined to do whatever it took. I had to admit I was having a hard time figuring out any action to take at all.

I can tell you, now, I was afraid, but I didn't know it; I was too busy pretending I had no idea what the cause of my inertia was. Without knowing, I was allowing fear to sabotage my plan. As if it was actually standing between me and what I wanted, fear rendered me unable to take any action or make any decision to make my dream come true. It had a way of making me feel frenetic even as I perceived myself slogging, slowly, or perhaps unable to move at all. Every time I tried to think of one thing to do, anything to get myself started, to break the deadlock of my immobility, my head felt flooded with *can't*. It echoed in the chamber of my mind until I had no room at all for good ideas about what to do first.

You might think that, if you are not feeling fearful, you cannot, by definition, be afraid. That isn't quite correct. We can generate fear from almost anything, and, of course, we can also convince ourselves we do not feel precisely the way our feelings are trying to tell us we do.

We can be fearful of things we don't want to confront, or things we don't want to do because we're afraid we will fail at them. We can be afraid of outcomes we only imagine. We can have these fears without calling them fear—they can be called hesitation, or procrastination, just two of the coats fear wears as a disguise. Regardless of what we do with it, this fear we choose not to acknowledge can be powerful enough to stop us from ever taking any action on our own behalf.

This fear can also become so familiar to us we think of it as a comfort, rather than an obstacle or the barrier it truly is. My fear comforted me because, as long as I didn't have to acknowledge it, I could talk indefinitely about how I was *so sure* I was willing to do *everything* I could think of to create my fabulous new life without ever taking any risk of action at all.

Deep in the part of me that knew very well I was afraid, I also knew I could rely on my fear to lull me into staying right where I was stuck. After all, I had created my fear with my imagination, perhaps the single most powerful tool for life in my body. I had already allowed the fear to convince me there was nothing I could do to realize my dream, so the rest was easy: I tried to do some basic business planning. To get organized, I made a list, asked myself *what are the components of the work I want to do, and what do I need to do to address each one?* I followed that with another list, of priorities, and even another list, creating specific goals and deadlines. Wasn't that what all the self-help experts said about how to start a business?

I told myself my problem was simple; I just couldn't pick a place to get started. I ruled out some things for lack of funds, others for lack of contacts. Not surprisingly, then, before long, whenever I started to think about what I wanted to do I felt panicked and frantic, as if I were racing around and around right where I stood, stiff and frozen. How easily I was beginning to convince myself I would fail to reach my goal because I could no longer even imagine how to get started.

It wasn't long before I started to suspect my dream itself might just be too big for me to manage: fear's victory, keeping me safe against my own Self. I settled into a pattern of concentrating on my failures more than anything else, and I went back and forth with that for a while. When I felt strong, I was able to build my confidence up: I could envision myself standing before a large audience and talking with them as I loved to do, then meeting with small groups to share our experiences of the ways we live in the world. It was a great fantasy, but it was one I could only stay in long enough to have it collapse again at the sign of nothing happening, still.

Anxiety grew the helplessness the fear seeded in me. I went on that way for months, until, frustrated that I had nowhere else to go, I finally asked no one in particular, *is there something I am afraid of?* Defensively, I answered immediately in my own behalf: *I don't feel afraid, so how can I be afraid? Besides, what is there to be afraid of?* Except for my imaginings and my dream of the kind of life I wanted for myself, very little had changed in reality. I had taken a part-time job after I closed the law office, and I still had my house. I was secure to near complete immobility.

Inside me, though, I could feel the chaos. We spend so much of our lives inside our heads, and no one can ever have as much information about us as we ourselves do. I was the expert on me, and I couldn't seem to figure out what was going on with me because I was invested in only one thing: my fear.

Finally, I decided that, no matter what it was holding me back, I was going to have to force it out into the open. I had to eliminate all my obstacles. It was time for another unscientific experiment.

This time, an Honesty Zone

I started by creating a virtual space in which I would do this work of confronting whatever it was that was stopping me from taking any action. I called it my Honesty Zone, an imaginary place I could get to by writing in my journal. Happy to be doing something—anything—I thoughtfully established some rules and made some agreements with myself about how I would operate in the Zone:

1. I would be free to question myself closely in order to be sure I was not keeping any secrets from myself;
2. I would be honest, even painfully so, as I answered my own questions;
3. I would stick with it as long as it took to reveal what was hidden; and

4. I would be grateful to discover the truth, whatever it was and whether I appreciated it or not once I found it.

Along the way, I gave myself permission to feel free to suspect my motives, to cheer at the uncovering of my truths and to cross-examine myself mercilessly about my intentions. For good measure, I added this: I would only allow myself to be hard on me as long as I also agreed to treat myself with unconditional love and trust. Isn't it peculiar how we sometimes have to remind ourselves to be kind to ourselves?

I have been writing in journals since I was 12 years old, when I got my first *Dear Diary*, complete with a little brass lock and key. Writing gives me freedom to express whatever I'm thinking, especially things I might be reluctant to say out loud. Now I keep a journal on a computer because it helps me keep pace with thoughts pouring out of me. When I'm done writing, I can save all my words to ponder, or I can delete them, tossing them away like so much crumpled paper. I can also save them to a flash drive, for privacy's sake.

More than once my journal has surprised me. Having to think in words on a page or screen is the best way I know to pull out through my fingers whatever is going on in my mind. It's like a deeply personal fishing expedition, being the fish and the fisher all at once. Many times, I have been caught off-guard by seeing the now-familiar words of my inner voice, telling me what I might be trying to keep myself from knowing I know, or feel. I imagine writing gives my voice a chance to speak *on the record*, and I get the added benefit of being able to keep what *she* says for later reference.

For all these reasons, my journal was a natural choice for the tool I would use in my newly created Honesty Zone. My voice would be there, too, and I already looked forward to her helping me *think through* to understanding what was undermining me. I knew *she* would; what I was unprepared for were the surprises *she* would also bring. *She* would show me what my relationship with fear was all about, and how easily I could change it, how I could manage it in a way that would free me from ever having to be held in its fearsome grip again. That would be an important thing for me to know, and, over time, I would get pretty good at it.

That wouldn't be the only surprise I would find as I wrote through my unscientific experiment. There would be surprising information revealed all along the way, words that I could not have expected was also waiting to be uncovered.

Fear: The Experiment, Day 1

Friday night. The first surprise was already cued to reveal itself as soon as I sat down at my computer to write late on Friday night. I could not have anticipated I would be there much of the night—I was—nor that whatever I wrote would turn out to be merely the preamble for what was to come over the next two days. It was.

As soon as I started writing, the truth started tumbling out as if it had been waiting for me to open the door for it. The first thing I wrote was *I can feel fear mocking me.* That set a tone, and this quickly sharpened it:

> *It's whispering in my ear, telling me I have done a thorough job of creating a dream as big as I can imagine, but I've done nothing at all about making it come true.*

The words made me feel defensive, as if fear itself had written them to boast about its power over me. Duly noting I had been denying fear, I immediately began to reason with it in my old familiar way: trying to get around it. I reminded myself of all the steps I had tried to take and explained, to no one except my fearful self, why I hadn't been able to get it done. Even as I wrote my excuses, I had to admit I hadn't actually tried to do any of those things on my lists. I had simply thought about doing them and talked myself out of each one.

How could I have acted otherwise? I was frozen in place, trapped by a fear whose name I had refused even to ask. Before long, I began to suspect *this* wasn't about my dream of talking with people. I suspected I was about to uncover something else, something much more fundamental about myself. *What was I so afraid of?*

I resisted the temptation to feel defensive and told myself to think, instead. These first words I had typed were a signal of something beginning, as if the territory to be examined was becoming defined. *This is exactly what I need,* I told myself, and I promised I would try to be patient and let it unfold. I decided to keep my Honesty Zone open so I could write whenever something bubbled up inside me. It was one of the things I had learned while I was mining my feelings: Buried feelings rarely just pop, fully formed, from my mouth or through my fingers. They come out in little scraps over periods of time, and I had learned it is precisely when a scrap of a feeling appears that I most want to be available to coax the rest of it out by writing about it. This would prove to be particularly true about my feelings of fear, although I didn't yet know what it had in store for me.

All I knew was I was writing furiously on and off through the night, the kind of writing that is like a warm-up exercise. It consisted of mostly random thoughts I hoped would lead me to something substantive, as if I were trawling in murky waters.

This came out, a clue perhaps:

My fear is familiar. That's why I'm holding onto it. It isn't comforting me but certainly comfort can come in some very uncomfortable packaging. There is comfort in the familiarity of my fear.

That made sense in a very disturbing way, because I didn't quite understand why I wrote it. I pondered it awhile. Then this came:

In the past, whenever I have gotten myself into something I thought was too big and scary for me to handle, fear always made it possible for me to make an excuse to get myself out of it. I have always counted on my fear when I've gotten stuck.

What kind of a message was I trying to send myself? Was this my 30-something bravado coming back to haunt me forever joking about how I folded my fears up and wore them in the back pocket of my jeans? Did I really think fear was my friend? Had I truly counted on it to help me get out of things I have been afraid I cannot do? I certainly wouldn't think much of myself if I trusted *fear* to get me out of things, I said I wanted.

And why would I have to do that? I alone created this dream of mine. Surely, I could walk away from it if I thought it wasn't viable for me. I could very easily get out of it. Who would care enough to try and stop me? Who would even be interested enough to judge me?

I wanted to keep arguing about that in my own defense, and as I started to wander away from my computer to do that, I made myself stop and go back. Even if the words were true, they didn't tell me what I was afraid of. That was what I was looking for.

Then these words appeared in my head even before I got back to the keyboard to write them. The voice came quickly, gently and precisely, in *her* usual way:

> *I—would be disappointed to know I never even tried to do something big for myself, like make a dream come true, just because I was afraid of my own dream.*

Yes! That was true. I knew I could just walk away, but I also knew if I did abandon my dream—and especially if I didn't even try to make it real because I was *afraid* of it—I would spend the rest of my life wondering *what if* and feeling very disappointed in myself.

But why was I afraid of it? Although I was still walking around it, I was starting to accept I did, indeed, have some kind of powerful relationship with my fear. So far, it was a relationship in which I didn't like myself very much.

Even so, what had been feeling so heavy inside me was already starting to break up, as my thoughts began to separate out from one another and define themselves. That's a kind of clarity writing in a journal has always brought to me. I could feel excitement that, soon, I would be able to consider each of my separate thoughts individually. I thought—incorrectly, as it would turn out—I might already be very close to having my answers. I wrote:

> *Is that the best I can do with the great opportunity I have before me to transform my life—run away from it in fear?*

Now I was getting angry with myself. Anger is a great emotion, because it always moves us into action of some kind. I kept on writing, whatever came into my head, anything I could think of to keep the thoughts and feelings stirred up. I was hot on the trail of answers, and I wanted them.

After some time passed, I finally found the courage to challenge myself:

If my dream is too big, then isn't it too big for me simply to walk away from it?

Yes, again. And:

Even more importantly, if I do not want to use my fear as a hiding place anymore, doesn't that mean I will have to walk right through my fear?

It does. I remembered my voice told me—years before, when *she* first spoke—that I must walk through the feelings that hurt me and not around them anymore. I knew if I didn't do that now with my fear, regardless of what I named it, I would be responsible to myself for allowing fear to stand as an obstacle in my way, perhaps for the rest of my life.

I was on the line. I had already done all the thinking I could for one night.

Day 2

Saturday. I woke early, immediately feeling a bit of a letdown. I felt I had been working at it all night as I slept and still didn't know what I was afraid of. Although I have had the experience of going to sleep with a question and waking up with an answer, I had not asked a question this time, and no answer had been forthcoming. It was clear I was just going to have to let whatever was inside me come out in its own time.

In the meantime, neither I nor my voice seemed to have anything to say. I decided to take a break from the intensity that was crowding my mind; I called a friend and arranged to spend the warm, sunny spring afternoon with her. She listened sympathetically as I continued to argue with myself.

Several hours later, when I had not gotten any closer to exposing my fear, my friend urged me to make a collage. She thought it might help me clarify my thinking. She even sent me home with a batch of old magazines she no longer wanted. Later that evening, I started the project she suggested, more as a way to relax during what had become an emotional weekend than out of any enthusiasm for the project itself.

There was that old skeptic in me again, looking for a way around something I didn't want to do. The handful of old magazines my friend had given me, with strict instructions to choose photographs randomly from all of them for the collage, were not the kind I had any interest in reading, so I decided ahead of time that it was unlikely I would find any photos resembling what I was dealing with. However, I had nothing to lose, so dutifully, if skeptically, I half-heartedly flipped through them while I watched an old movie on television. When I was done, I put the magazines and the little pile of photos I had cut out on my table and called it a night.

I went to bed wondering how this weekend would end. There was a lot more brewing inside me that would have to make itself known before I could find out what was on my mind, and I wasn't feeling at all confident I could get it out. Maybe my fear would come out on its own, but I was going to have to wait at least one more day for any answers.

Day 3

Sunday. It started quietly with its routines of coffee and driving into town to buy the newspapers. It gave me no indication that, by the time it was over, this day was going to take me all the way to surprising and even startling revelations—including a new relationship with my fear.

I have always believed life-altering advice can come from the strangest sources, and I felt completely ready for whatever this day might have in store for me. As it went on, though, the day seemed to offer nothing at all. There wasn't much to write about in my journal and, although I kept the computer ready, I had done no writing since

Friday night. Whatever it was that had been moving me through the weekend seemed to have suddenly become decidedly still.

That is, until I settled down to read *The New York Times Magazine* late in the afternoon. There was a featured article about a woman whose work I had admired when I came across her book: *A Framework for Understanding Poverty*. I was eager to read the article in the Magazine, because Dr. Ruby Payne had intrigued me into curiosity about the woman behind it.

The article was about Payne's journey from an educator and high school administrator in Houston, Texas, to a premier teacher of teachers. In her work in an inner-city school system, she had been confronted by the singular challenges of students who lived in often extreme poverty. She had created a plan for meeting those challenges in her classrooms with what sounded like great results, and she was now travelling widely to give her colleagues the benefit of her experiences, as well as her extraordinary interpretation of them.

As I read it, Dr. Payne explained she had started with a dream. She had wanted to *"make a difference with children"*.[8]

A financial adviser to whom she had spoken about how she could make her dream come true had referred her to what she called an *"odd book."* It was *"ostensibly dictated to the authors by two 'spirit guides...,' called* Creating Money. *The advice it gave was to 'Make a list of what you want in your life and ask the universe to bring it to you.'"*

So she did. *"And it happened!"*

As I read her words, something started to happen in me, too. I felt excited, as if I had been a hidden fan in the bleachers all along. I jumped up from the couch and started pacing around my living room, talking out loud and waving my hands and arms in the air. I felt exhilarated, like Sherlock Holmes hot on the trail of I knew-not-what discovery.

Yes! I shouted, and *You see?* —without even knowing what it was I was seeing. In my enthusiasm, I asked what was different about her, and about the countless other people whose similar stories I had read or heard over the years. Every one of them had credited something for

---

[8] *The New York Times Magazine,* June 10, 2008.

their success. It had always struck me as curious that, many times more than once, the something had been invisible.

How were all these other dreamers different from me? I demanded. Whatever they had, I wanted it for myself.

My voice could not even wait for me to get up the stairs to my computer before *she* started answering that question. *She* was talking as I ran up, and her words nearly stopped me cold in the middle of the climb:

> *They all believed they were good enough to get what they wanted and were asking for. They had not wondered if their dreams were too big, or about how to make them come true. They just believed they were good enough.*

My head was spinning with these words that didn't seem to describe me at all. How could that be the answer? It felt like a condemnation. Didn't I believe I was good enough? Wasn't I trying to make a happy new life for myself? Why wasn't that enough to prove I'm committed to my dream? All I had were more questions, and there was no one who could answer them for me.

She wasn't finished. I no sooner got done typing what *she* said than my voice started *speaking* again:

> *My fear is that I don't deserve to have my dream come true.*

At that, I was stunned. There it was again, the suggestion I thought I did not deserve to have something I wanted for myself. It had first come up years before, when I had thought I was nearly ready to allow myself to be happy again after years of grief. I had forgotten all about it—*not deserving*—which had appeared so suddenly wearing a jacket of Survivor's Guilt and thrown me off my course when my uncle's call from California had scared me into thinking I might be infected with the virus when I had known that could not be possible. I had been afraid when I found those words there in me the night before I got my test results, the possibility I might be my own obstacle against becoming happy. Not knowing what to do with thoughts that I was undeserving of happiness, I had settled, then, on pushing them aside until later, until some other time when I might be ready to confront such an idea. *When had I thought that time might ever come?*

Now, as I stared at the words on the screen, I felt betrayed, but I couldn't figure out who to blame for it. Just as I had rejected any suggestion, I thought I did not *deserve* to be happy, I wanted to refuse to believe I could possibly think I did not *deserve* to have my dream come true. I hated knowing I could even think that about myself. It presupposed a terrible judgment against me—with me as the judge.

As I continued to stare at the words, I suspected that, no matter what I thought or wanted to be true, I could only have written them because Survivor's Guilt was still there behind my thinking: I didn't deserve to have anything good or happy because Art had died and I had not. Although I had forgotten about that after putting myself through the ordeal of being tested for the virus yet again, it was plain now I had not stopped thinking that about myself. Although it shocked and hurt me to see it, at least I could admit it was likely I still felt that way, even now.

What I could not acknowledge so readily, nor understand, was how fear had arisen out of thoughts of *not deserving.* Why was I using the fear to prevent myself from acting in any way that might make it possible for me to prove I could have what I wanted? Wouldn't that proof put to rest any further question of what I thought I deserved? Was the fear of my own guilty feelings more powerful than the guilt itself? The words I had just written seemed to be suggesting it was.

I had wanted to know the name of my fear, and I guessed I had found it, although I couldn't even begin to imagine what I could do about it. To tell you the truth, I was afraid of the thought that I didn't deserve to have a happy life. What could I ever do about a fear like that?

Returning to my journal, I started to write. I was writing that my fear felt familiar and I was holding on to it, but then I stopped mid-sentence. I remembered I had already written something like that only two nights before, at the start of the weekend. When I went back to what I had written Friday night, I found it there in my very first journal entry:

My fear is familiar. That's why I'm holding onto it. There is comfort in the familiarity of my fear. Fear has always made it possible for me to make an excuse to get myself out of anything. I have always counted on my fear when I've gotten stuck.

How complex was the relationship with fear I had invented out of being afraid of it. Even though I had not understood how those same words applied to me only two days before, their meaning was suddenly painfully clear to me: I used my fear to keep me from doing anything I feared was too big. At the same time, when I gave in to my fear, I made it impossible to believe in myself, and that prevented me from trying anything at all. For good measure, I allowed the fear to harden into judgments against myself, and then I held those judgments as even more proof I could not bring my dream into reality. By the time I was done thinking about it, instead of simply acknowledging I felt fear, I had decided I had failed in every way to accomplish whatever I set out to do.

Now seemed a good time to admit that, in fact, I had actually done very little; mostly, I had been busy thinking negative thoughts about myself. By calling myself a failure, I had enabled fear to *comfort* me with words like *can't* and *too big*. Fear was indeed comfort that came in a very uncomfortable package. I had even stayed right there with it until I could finally let myself off the hook by thinking up my fallback excuse: maybe it was a good thing, after all, that I realized—before I got too much more involved—I might not be able to make so big a dream come true.

All of this could only make sense because I had allowed my fear to get so powerful that it grew into the suspicion I did not deserve to succeed. To sustain a fear that big I would have had to reach as far as I could to undermine any belief in myself to the contrary. That was exactly what I was reading in my own writing now: me, counting the ways I used my fear to keep me from having what I wanted. It seemed as if I had created a perfect definition of a vicious circle and I could not break away from it. If I didn't believe in myself I could not make my dream into reality. If I couldn't realize my dream, how could I ever get to feeling good enough about myself to believe I deserved good things?

But, was it, really, a vicious circle? Might it just be a circle I could break apart if I could find another way to look at the same information? If I thought of *deserving* as I think of happiness—that is, as a feeling that can only come from within me—could I change the verdict against me to a new opinion, that I deserve to have everything I want? Surely I could change anything about my feelings; I had changed happiness to my default posture. When I changed the way I thought about my fear, wouldn't I be able to take myself all the way back to believing, again, I deserve good things? Couldn't I change the old script by retraining my brain to accept a new truth?

That seemed an enormous task for the moment, and I still had not resolved my relationship with fear. It was fear preventing me from moving forward, and this time I was sure there would no longer be any comfort in its familiarity. There could be no excuses because, this time, I wasn't working toward *some goal.* This was about the dream I had invested with my fantasy woman all those years ago when I was little girl. She had held it for me until I had grown up and could come back to claim it, and I would not so easily walk away from it. It was made of my work, which I loved and which nurtured me; it had grown out of my experience of loving and losing Art. This time, if I could not move the fear out of my way, there would only be my disappointment in myself, no matter how carefully I crafted words that would try and explain away my inability to get past it. If I could change my relationship with my fear, I might win back my belief in myself, and that might be powerful enough to take me all the way to where I wanted my life to be.

I was determined to stand down the fear. I started writing to it. I told it I would never again allow it to grow roots inside me. As of right now, if I started a thought or a sentence with *my fear,* or if I even suspected fear might be anywhere around me as I was trying to make my dream real, I would refuse it. Growing angrier as I wrote, I warned fear to be ready. *I'm going to demand answers from now on, demand to know why I am afraid, and whether I truly have to be afraid of anything I think might try to stop me. I'll never give in to my fear again.*

As I continued to tell fear how I felt—typing furiously in my journal as I went along—I became aware the weight of the fear was getting lighter inside me. I felt as if it was breaking up, and I imagined helping it with my fingers, crumbling it like stale bread until it was smaller and smaller still. Until it was so small it turned to dust, I could blow away.

Then it was gone. It was no longer a weight on my chest. It was out of my mind. For the moment, I sat perfectly still with my hands in my lap in the extreme calm it left behind. To be sure it was gone, I took long, deep breaths to find out if I could feel any remnants of it anywhere inside me. I tested myself by thinking of what I would do first to make my dream real. I was sure I did not feel any fear at all.

In the stillness that followed, I promised fear I would do the same thing just that way the next time it appeared, and I would continue to do so every time after that. I would challenge fear by *thinking it through*, as I had just now—I would think it to death—and I would drive it away.

Fear Weekend: the aftermath

The day after my Fear Weekend, I noticed, when I came home from work, the magazine photographs I had left on the table. I placed them on the large sheet of cardboard I had bought for the purpose of creating a collage. On the back of it, I had written the question I had thought of Saturday, as my friend instructed: *What is the next right thing?*

As I took a phone call from someone at just that moment, I absentmindedly moved the photos around on the board. When I stopped talking and took a look at them, they told the entire story of my weekend. It was an amazing story.

Without realizing I was doing so, I had pulled out mostly photographs of women of all ages, from children to elders, doing things that seemed very brave to me. They were all engaged in what looked like joyful celebrations of life.

I had found those photographs Saturday evening, when I had been feeling not at all celebratory, nor even much encouraged. Yet, in some of the pictures, women and girls were waving their arms in victory after sporting events. Others were holding up globes of the world, or barbells or their arms, joyfully showing off their strength and courage. There were women talking together in groups both large and small from cultures all over the world, and there were couples in intimate romantic settings as well.

The collage told a thrilling story of me, in a variety of fearless celebrations of my life—happy and fulfilled—just as I was feeling now as I stared at it. It spoke of the next steps I had asked for, and it held out to me the certainty of my success and the joy of it all. As I glued the photos down to hang the collage as a reminder, I marveled at what I had produced completely unaware. For weeks and months after that, I kept smiling at it staring down at me from the wall, reminding me of the possibilities I was creating for a fearless future, and showing me the promise that I could have it all.*

Now, many years after my Fear Weekend, I still find *"fear things that are in fact harmless"* showing up inside me—maybe they're just facts of life in a complex and challenging world. They are masterful in their creativity—like I said, my fear is wily and sophisticated, exactly as I am. It may still take me a bit of time to realize it is fear I am feeling, but *I* am the change in my relationship with my fear. Even if it does arise with the intention of protecting me, I respond as I promised I would, every time. I ask it questions. I challenge it with an intention of my own: think about what it means to have that kind of fear. Is it really bringing me a message I should heed, or am I merely having a knee-jerk reaction to a challenge I might be uncomfortable or uncertain I can meet? These are important answers for me either way, and I must have them before I can decide what I want to do for my life, deliberately.

Soon after my "Fear Weekend," I was trying to explain to my friend, Frayda, that I was having trouble making a decision to do something in relation to a particular aspect of my work. She asked me what it was I couldn't decide about and, as I started to answer her, I suddenly

---

* There is a step-by-step description of making this collage in appendix A.

envisioned the words as I was speaking them: "I'm afraid I—," I said and, immediately, I saw my fingers chasing after the words, trying to grab them. I could not catch them. They were breaking up too quickly and turning to dust just beyond my fingers' reach.

My fear always shows up prepared with its own list of perfectly reasonable excuses for why I cannot do what I intend to do. While Frayda waited for me to answer her, I was watching the first item on fear's list as it dissipated before my fingers could grab the words. Then the second good reason crumbled to dust, as the first one had. When it happened just that way to a third set of fear-words on the list, I stopped trying. I took a deep breath, imagined myself blowing away all the dust and sat quietly for a moment to collect my thoughts. I was smiling at what I had just seen. Turning to my friend, I laughed and said, "I guess I'm not afraid of anything. I'm just going to do it."

Frayda, a therapist, offered that I had made a new friend of my fear. She explained I use it to help me think my way through to making decisions. She said I invite it in and watch it build, and I wait until it reaches its climax, then I blow fear up, exploding it. In the aftermath, as the dust settles around me and life returns to normal, I make my decision by stepping over the dust of my fear and continuing on my way. She said she thinks that's very brave of me.

It doesn't feel brave to me, although it does remind me of one of the journal entries I made at the end of my Fear Weekend. I wrote, "I have used fear as an excuse *not* to do something I wanted to do for myself." Now, it pleases me to think I might be using fear as a way to affirm and strengthen my resolve to have exactly the things I do want for myself.

My new truth is that I am no longer afraid of finding fear in me. I am confident it is just a matter of time before the fear I think about will reveal itself again—it's connected to my ego it seems, and ego always wants to win—and I will make it disappear, again and again. I have engaged my fear in a great game we play together, and because I can think it to death, it no longer has any power over me. With "my fear" *harmless*, I have only the fear mechanisms nature intended, still operating where they were intended to be—keeping me safe from actual harm without my having to think about it.

Dina L. Wilcox

Living with, but not in, fear

Long after the weekend was settled in my memory, I continued to think about what might be going on in my brain. I wanted to know if it does what it does with any intention, and what that might mean for a brain. Could the thing I've been calling *my fear* have started as one of nature's evolutionary experiments? Was our fear once, perhaps, evolution's latest great new idea for supporting my life in the complex and confusing world we humans live in now?

What I had learned so far was that it is possible for me to make happiness my default posture. That's great, because being happy feels good, and it's even better than that. When I'm happy I am more likely to make good choices and decisions in my own best interests—which keep me feeling happy. When I'm feeling happy, I'm also feeling positive and strong, and that encourages me to live my life deliberately.

Now, the Fear Weekend had something equally important to add to my growing fund of information about myself. Maybe we all have to learn we are capable of managing what Dr. Ledoux calls our "harmless" fears. They, like happiness and all our other feelings, are responses whose jobs seem to be to get us thinking about ourselves. That makes it very important that we know whether, and how, we can consciously participate and impact what our brains do.

Indeed, it is our capacity to think about things that seems to be central to who we are as humans. We think automatically—that is, we don't have to decide to think in order to be able to do so—and yet we do have to think deliberately, with our consciousness, about whatever feeling-messages our brains are transmitting. The more I learned about my brain, the more I saw myself as a whole with amazing parts that, when they work best, are all working together, in a perfect balance. I wanted to participate actively—consciously—in that process, to make my own, deliberate contributions to the tiny dominion I was starting to think of as *me*.

If there is any challenge to being fearless, it must surely be in the decision we have to make first. As with happiness, we must decide to allow ourselves to live without our "harmless" fears. It is not a matter of whether we can or deserve to be free of fear, nor does it have any relationship to judgments we may pass against ourselves, like *we are not good enough*. We can simply know our brains have us thinking about fear in order to protect our wellbeing. If fear is part of our biology, then it seems only logical we should be able to choose to grow fearlessness in ourselves.

We do that by thinking about fear consciously. The more we strive to be fearless, the more often we will find ourselves feeling just that way, and every time we make another move in that direction will be a trip worth taking. We will be reinforcing the messages in our brains. That, it seems to me, is the perfect way to build confidence in ourselves, consciously.

We can do that whether we are scientists or not. Using our consciousness, we can know when we're feeling fear, and then we can use our conscious thoughts to meet our fears face to face.

You may want to take that thought with you the next time you go out to conquer the world. If you choose to do so, you will be giving yourself a great gift—and you *deserve* it.

Either way, you get to decide.

5

Of Adventures, Detours and Distractions: "I Just Want Someone to Love"

Has this ever happened to you? You decide you need a change. Maybe you're longing for a different job or a new career, or perhaps you've decided you need a whole new outlook on life. You're thinking you'll change your style, the way you live, bring some new people into your world; maybe you'll move to another town or a city and *start over*. You talk about it with friends or your family, explore your options. A Plan begins to take shape and you're thinking it will be perfect: *just what I need*. You're excited, and you're ready.

Then, just when you are about to take those first critical steps that will signal the start of your new life, your eye catches the sparkle of something newer still that you've never seen before, just up ahead of you, within your reach—could *that* be the new possibility sent right to your doorstep? It touches you, perhaps as your favorite comfort food would, or maybe it carries the scent of excitement, a thrill you can't resist. It's alluring, that's for sure, a some*one* or a some*thing*, the sound of music to your ears, the essence of a perfect fit. It's just the thing you've always dreamed about that you didn't even know you were dreaming about.

Why Do I Feel This Way?

Whatever it is, it's unexpected, certainly not part of your Plan, and it has distracted you. You've got to check it out. You can't let it get away. Maybe you won't get a second chance.

When something unexpected shows up in our lives it can make us wonder if fate is knocking on our door, even if we never believed in fate before. We're excited to think it could change everything in the most wonderful ways. Perhaps it's the serendipity that will make life worthwhile, the kind of opportunity that will challenge us to rise to levels we have never reached. Romantically, we might imagine it may demand we be brave or, at least, it will give us an opportunity to realize we have been brave all along. We might discover we love being who we are, we're proud of ourselves and we can, at last, allow ourselves to feel that pride. How could anyone resist such an invitation? Don't we owe it to ourselves to go after it—even if we have to put our Plan aside?

For some of us, the lure of an adventure can be so powerful we shall spend all our time going from one adventure to another, making these distractions the *fix* we cannot live without. Others may never quite manage to walk down the path to following an adventure, and still others will always be grateful they resisted all invitations. For them, it will be enough to savor the sheer pleasure of wondering, forever after, *what if I had?*

Some detours from the paths we've made for ourselves can take us all the way to realizing what will make us truly happy. Others, in retrospect, can leave us angry, not happy at all, even bitter. The some*one* wasn't true, and when the glitter of the some*thing* wore off, we couldn't help but notice it hadn't been as wonderful as we had imagined. Maybe we'll feel regret for the time we wasted. Or worse, maybe we'll be left wondering how we could have been so wrong to think we ever needed it. We might suspect we somehow summoned it, brought it on ourselves by thinking we wanted a change—are the fates trying to punish us for such hubris?—and, if we did, how or why could we have done such a thing to ourselves?

The adventures we choose for ourselves may or may not deliver on their promises, and it may simply be that we're all bound to follow one every so often. Whether we do or not, one thing is certain: they have things to reveal about us. After they're over, you may discover your unhappy adventure took you down the fast-track to true happiness, right there in its wake you found something you are certain you wouldn't have been able to know about yourself, some new truth that only *that* kind of adventure could have brought you. It might turn out to be a *blessing in disguise*. Once the dust settles, you might even pick up your old Plan again, elated to find it still there, and isn't it wonderful that the wisdom you gleaned from your adventure was perfect, big enough to help you, at long last, transform your Plan into your new reality?

The truth about these glittering adventures is that they call to us when we least expect them, and they can turn out to be much more than the life-changing distractions we hoped they would be. They can show us things about ourselves that inspire or force us to change the way we know ourselves for the rest of our lives.

Memories can be so inconvenient

One evening, I was sitting on a couch in a friend's living room where a few of us had gathered to enjoy a Friday night end-of-the-week glass of wine. A woman who I was just getting to know was talking about her marriage, which she had recently ended. As I watched and listened to her, I felt myself drawn into a powerful bond of empathy and understanding with her.

She explained she had been quite young when she married a man more than a few years older than she and, although she had been in love with him, she had quickly come to realize he was an angry and manipulative husband. In retrospect, she said, she may have chosen him because he had made her feel secure in a way her unavailable father had failed to. As she grew stronger, she knew she was going to have to leave him, because he would never allow her to manage her own life. She was a lovely young woman who was a talented singer and, at the time I met her, she was on the verge of realizing her dream of a musical career.

As she was describing her relationship with her former husband, my mind wandered in the direction of a memory of my own that matched hers. Almost five years had passed since I had ended a brief marriage that could still get me shaking my head in wonder, even from the safe distance I had finally managed to put between it and me. I had ended that marriage when it forced me to realize I could not live with it any longer, and after I did end it, I spent a long time thinking about why I had chosen it in the first place. In the years since, I had gotten all my answers, and I had learned much about myself in the process.

So, I was surprised when, having barely reached the tip of my memory, I suddenly heard my voice shout—loudly—knocking my attention right off its train of thought. So loud was the sound of the voice I had to look around the room, furtively, from one friend to another, to reassure myself no one else had heard it. While I did so, I tried hard to get my face—which I could feel had flushed to red—and my expression—which I knew looked startled—to return to normal before anyone would ask if I was okay. It seemed impossible, but they just continued talking as if they had not heard any sound at all.

Nonplussed, I tried to slow my breathing back down to normal, even as the words my voice spoke were reverberating in my head:

Because you *didn't think you deserved any better. That was why you married him.*

I didn't disagree with what the voice said, and I knew *her* well enough by this time to know that *she* must have intended to stop me from thinking about those memories. But why? As *her* words kept pulsing in my body, I couldn't help but wonder if there was more I needed to know, and what it could be. This was no time to be thinking about it, so I made a mental note to write later and returned to my friends, more than slightly surprised to find they were only just beginning to move on to another topic of conversation. I tried not to look as I felt, as if I had returned to the room after an absence.

When I got home, I ran straight to my computer. I typed in what the voice said, and then what the woman had been talking about that had triggered my memory in the first place. After that, I sat back to ponder.

It was easy to remember how much that experience changed me. I had gotten distracted just when I was most certain I knew exactly what I wanted to do with the rest of my life.

I had made my Plan. I was going to create the life I had once imagined for my fantasy woman, whom I had loved since I was 13 years old. I had even started to carry the Plan out. After I closed my law office, I began to travel around the country, speaking at conferences about how we can keep ourselves safe in the age of AIDS. As the epidemic evolved, my work in HIV prevention changed, too. I considered myself lucky, so lucky to be able to meet and talk with people of all ages and different backgrounds about how we make choices and decisions as we go out into the world to look for love. I loved doing this work, and that meant so much to me. I was content to think I had found a way to make something I could live with come out of Art's death. More than that, I believed it was the work I was *meant* to do.

My relationship with my feelings had also changed by that time. I knew I needed to trust the way I feel and not fall back into my old practice of denying feelings that made me uncomfortable. That had been my old pattern, and I believed it started when Art first got sick. After he died, I made a commitment to acknowledge all my feelings, whether I wanted to or not. Secretly, I was pleased to think I was learning to trust what they had to tell me about myself. I thought I had finally gotten everything I needed for my life, and I was happy.

None of that stopped me from being tempted by the glittering lights of an unexpected adventure that suddenly started to call to me from the road just up ahead. Even if I could forget what happened during that adventure, I would not soon forget how ready and willing I had been to abandon my own intentions for myself. Without thinking too much about it, I had taken a sharp detour from the path that led to my perfect Plan, and headed straight out, right into the arms of an adventure that would change forever the way I see myself. I fell in love.

Happily ever after

Falling in love. Just saying it makes you want to smile, doesn't it? The feeling comes over you quickly, and it's so delicious you cannot resist it. And why should you? Everybody wants someone to love. For me it was like a soft, spring wind after the raging storms of loneliness that followed Art's death. Didn't I deserve to be happy? *I* thought I did.

I met a man at a friend's house and in a matter of days—mere weeks it seemed—we accumulated all the right words for starting to think about *happily-ever-after*. We hungrily got right to it: the long, romantic dinners, holding hands in the movies, talking together late into starry nights that looked like nothing so much as the stars in our eyes.

More than anything, I marveled at how much we had in common, our backgrounds and childhoods, even the places where we grew up and lived as children. We loved to dance to the same music; we had one sense of humor. It seemed uncanny, as if we were custom-made for each other. I wondered if it was fate, and as if to reaffirm the truth of it all, he lovingly spoke my own thoughts even before I did. In months, he sold his house and moved into mine; we brought our families together and celebrated Thanksgiving, then a new year; we talked about getting married in the spring. I was breathless, swept away with the romance, the finding of a new soul-mate—how lucky was I? We were so much alike, how could it ever be any different between us?

Just before the end of our first year we married, in a small and lovely garden ceremony at my, now our, house. If I wondered by then, just a little, whether I was doing the right thing, I reminded myself we loved each other, and we had all the reasons we needed to be sure we would be happy. *After all*, I reasoned, we were adults. We had life experience, and we could trust ourselves to know what we were looking at.

Still, it hadn't been as easy settling into real-time as I had expected. There had been arguments, and some of them had been frightful in their intensity. I reassured myself everyone has things they have to get used to and compromise about. Of course, I had been surprised when he asked me not to invite my friends to our wedding because he had only a few people in his life and it would make him uncomfortable to celebrate his marriage with strangers. That hadn't felt good, but I had acquiesced. *There is love beneath it all* I told myself, and my friends would understand when they got to know him. We were going to be good and solid, as the earth. I loved his family, and my family loved him. I told myself these things as I reached for proof from anywhere other than inside myself that we would be happy together. I never even thought to ask if *I* would be happy with *him*.

I knew I was deeply embedded, and I was convinced it was right for me to be there. On the day we were married, I told myself I had made promises and commitments and these mattered more than anything. Then, as if to put a cap on it, as I walked out of the house to join him in marriage, I smiled a know-it-all smile to think I would not be able to get out of it now, even if I wanted to.

Six months after our wedding, I told him I would agree to pretend we were still married if he would agree to counseling, and one interminable year after that failed, my surprisingly bitter divorce was completed. It would take me longer to figure out what had happened than it had taken me to get into and out of the experience.

So what happened?

It was an adventure I simply could not refuse.

A few words about loving

When I was in my twenties, I had a theory that every new romance was going to introduce me to another kind of man, and every new man would make it easier for me to know what I wanted from *the* man with whom I would eventually choose to spend my life. I believed all I would have to do was add up all the things I had learned and I would know exactly what kind of man would make me happy. I would never have to settle for anything less than that.

Now I know that loving has always offered to teach me many more things about myself than I could even have imagined there were to learn. Often, the most important things have had nothing to do with what I want and do not want from someone else. Mostly, my romances have taught me nothing about falling in love—except, of course, with myself. Always, the most important lessons have been those that have taught me how to love myself.

What I had not known about myself until the day I discovered my adventure was over was that, even though I had promised myself I was never going to ignore my feelings again, I had been doing just that since the adventure began. *That*, and there was one old feeling buried deeply within me I had never come to terms with: I was still living with a fear I did not *deserve* to be happy. If you had asked me, I would have vigorously declared that any doubts I still may have about what I deserve had long since been put to rest.

Only with the distance of hindsight would I come to believe this falling-in-love was custom-made for one purpose only: to bring me face-to-face with that fearsome judgment I was still holding against myself. As it did, my adventure would, once and for all, transform me into a person who trusts what her feelings are trying to tell her.

Now, back to the story

Truth be told, I very quickly found myself up to my neck in adventure. Love stopped feeling good right after I finished falling—maybe it even broke my fall—and the dust started to settle in thick around us as things piled up and got away from me. He made promises in the innocent, early weeks, pronouncements, really, about ways he wanted to be for me and things he wanted to do to honor our love, things that later—when promises proved lies—he would accuse me of having tried to trick him into making.

In a short time, a pattern developed between us that someone would later tell me was *toxic*. He would start out sounding as if he wanted to have an intellectual conversation, because, after all, we were educated, professional people who paid attention to life around us. It could have been some fine philosophical point, or something we had read in the news. But as talk turned to argument about it, whatever it was, he made it deeply personal. He got angrier and meaner, baring his teeth and spitting-shouting as he leaned into my face. He seemed determined, not to make some point, but to beat whatever might still be good and loving between us into the ground, so he could march across the top of its grave and off and away into some place I could never go to with him. I tried to fight back, even just to hold my own, but I was no match for him. I would try to keep track of what he was saying so I could answer, but I'd be trembling so hard on the inside I finally had to stop talking altogether and wait for it just to be over so he would let me go. Soon, there was no ground on which we could ever stand together again.

I thought for a while I was still me, but I wasn't sure at all about who he was, and it wasn't much later before I had to admit I wasn't even so sure about me, after all. I developed allergies, which I had never had before; a homeopathic doctor would tell me later they were a symptom of grieving. Then I lost my voice. For months, I would start out speaking only to fall into laryngitis that diminished me to a whisper.

Worse than all the arguments, he seemed to think he was the expert on me, and he made it plain he had his work cut out for him if he was ever going to get me into shape to meet some standard he had in mind for a wife. Somehow, trying to look at me through his eyes, I could see that nothing about me seemed right, as if I had changed in the middle of the night, while we were asleep, and neither of us could figure out what to do about me in the morning. In no time, it seemed, I couldn't even keep track of what I was trying to stave off. I thought I was thinking about trying to find the answer to *wasn't what we had a good thing at the heart of it, well worth fighting for?* The harder we fought, the more elusive the thing itself got.

And then there was my Plan for my work—the one I had so lovingly developed and begun to breathe life into—to travel and talk with people about the things that matter to us as humans, the things we have most in common. He had been so excited about that when we met. He had called my work *organic,* and I had been flattered at how proud he was to think that.

After we got married, I stopped traveling so we could be together. Soon after that, I got to be too busy trying to brush away one thing after another that kept blowing up in my face to be telling anybody else about what matters in life, and even much less to think I had anything to offer anyone else. I could barely seem to help myself. I couldn't even count on my voice to be there when I opened my mouth to speak.

I still don't know how I did this, but early on I made one good decision: to protect the Plan for my life's work. I told him I was simply changing my mind, changing my course. I said it would be too much for me to do after all, and why didn't we just focus on being in love instead?

I told him that, but the truth was I wanted to protect my precious dream, to keep it from getting lost to me altogether. He was making his own plans to expand my work to fit himself into the center of it. It was mine, and even if I was helpless, I knew for certain I would never allow him to take that away from me. I may have forsaken my friends for his sake, but, even unconsciously, I would protect my dream. I would hold it in reserve, in case, so it would still be there for me if I ever got ready, again, to pick it up. That seemed unlikely, but at least I could be sure I wouldn't lose it altogether.

So the questions were begged all right, and they remained that way for a full nine months after we got married. Then, one sunny Sunday morning as the winter was beginning to let go, I was raking old leaves to clear ground for planting around the house when my mind wandered into an argument with itself.

My voice to the rescue

Suddenly, there *she* was—at first, I noticed with some curiosity that *she* had been very quiet while I was busy falling in love—and *she* spoke up for the first time in years. *She* asked me, ever so gently, in her way implying nothing: *Why are you feeling so unhappy in your happy relationship?*

My voice: *she* always touches me in just the right way. When *she* speaks to me, no matter what *she* has to say, I always feel loved, foremost and unconditionally.

Tentatively then, and carefully, I took a deep breath of what felt like the freshest air I had had in ages. Feeling as if *she* was holding a mirror up to my face, I looked into it, and my heart sank. I saw myself as a woman I was never meant nor ever wanted to be, someone he needed me to be for his sake, even against my own best interests. As I looked behind that woman, I could also see the woman I was never going to be if I did not stop this from happening to me.

As I stared from one version of myself to the other, I had the sinking feeling my adventure was over. I knew the answer to the question the voice asked me: I wasn't happy because I was being terribly hurt, over and over again. I wasn't getting what I needed. Not from him, certainly, and as long as I remained helpless under the weight of him, not from myself either. It was time for me to return to my familiar life, and that meant I was going to have to end this marriage. *I* was somehow going to have to find enough courage left within me to stand up to him and take my life back.

In that moment I realized, once again, I had been stubbornly refusing to allow myself to know the simple truth about how I felt. I was afraid of him, and getting more so all the time. I had become afraid of him as far back as the first day of the first argument, which had scared me with its vehemence months before we had ever talked about getting married. Yet, instead of protecting myself at that time, I had smiled ironically on my wedding day to think I could not back out, that I would not ever again be able to reject what he was offering and run as far away as I could—as if I had strapped myself in for the whole adventure, ensuring, perhaps, I would be here to know the feeling of this, precisely this, now: feeling my fear, I knew I was going to have to confront it—and him—to rescue myself.

The smile on my face was full of regret, and there was a bitter taste in my mouth. What had I done to myself? How could I have allowed such a mean-spirited relationship come into my life to take it over? How could I have willed it to be called love? I was disgusted with myself. *Strap myself in to keep me in it?* What was I going to have to do to get myself out of it?

Standing there in the dirt with a giant rake in my hands, I suddenly felt so small. I had let myself down, and in the worst way: by denying my feelings.

This time, I hadn't done it because I had been afraid of how I felt; that reason had belonged to Art's illness, and I could see this wasn't the same at all. This was about how, from the outset—in the first easy, happy, falling-in-love days—there had been a reality I had liked so much more than the one I had been living in alone. I had wanted that—someone to love—and I had thought that would be worth risking everything for. Isn't that what everyone thinks about falling in love? I could never have imagined the cost of having love would ever include risking or even losing myself.

No amount of white-washing around the simple truth so I could pretend loving was there was going to make it so. The truth was quite something else. I could see that clearly now. If there had been a loving relationship at the beginning, it was long gone. There was no happiness in my house. Nor was he the person with whom I would be willing or able to spend the rest of my life.

I started asking myself some hard questions, like was it possible I had wanted it so much I had willed myself not to see he was nothing like me, that we really had nothing in common at all? It had always been a point of pride for me to think of myself as a perceptive person, a woman who is determined to see through to the truth about everything. I had always trusted that about myself, and people often said it as a compliment to me. But I had missed my mark by a wide swath this time, and I couldn't understand how. How had that happened? What signals had I missed? Had there been any clues along the way? Had I forced myself not to notice all we had between us were the words we had spoken in the first few weeks of our meeting? All of a sudden, my head was filling with questions I was dreading, and I had no answers.

Not now, I thought abruptly, still standing with my big rake in my arms. My voice could help me, later, as I searched for all the answers I needed, but it was too soon to be putting any energy into that, now. I knew I was afraid, and I could not stay where I was. I needed to do something. Whatever it was, it was going to demand all my attention.

I decided to move slowly. I talked with my friends, the few people who had somehow managed to fight against me and stay in my life, who loved me and knew me well. Why hadn't I ever noticed they also seemed to know about relationships with angry, manipulative people who would rage at you? I had a surprising number of friends who knew about people like that, and they all responded in the same way. "Abuse," they told me, although I never used the word. "You're being abused," and every time I heard it the word clanged in my head the way the metal doors of the high-security prisons used to when I went to visit clients. They cautioned I might be in for some danger if I provoked an end to what had started as merely a joyful adventure, and they helped me make a new plan. Then they lined up together in front of and around me, to hold me and shield me as I carried it out.

I thought they were being melodramatic, and I might have even laughed at them as I nervously defended what had been my falling-in-love. I was certainly not comparing myself to a woman who has been abused. "That is so much worse than this," I told them. They just smiled at me.

It would take me a long time to appreciate that the fear I felt was proof enough of what they said. He and I never spoke to each other again. I stayed away from my house as often as I could until he moved out, and I tried not to feel bad that it had become a victim of my mistake. I left it unprotected and unloved, a hostage to someone who could not care. My house had always been filled with love.

I kept an emergency bag in my car, packed with clothes and things I would need in a hurry if I had to leave home. Carefully, I picked a lawyer from among my former colleagues, a woman bigger and stronger than I who made me feel safe in her presence. I felt very small indeed. A friend traveled with me to and from court. When he finally moved out, I put locks on doors and windows I had never seen the need for in the almost 15 years I had lived alone in my house on an old country road.

My divorce decree would say cruel and inhuman treatment, further proof, for me, of the truth my friends had spoken. I had not been physically battered, but I had been struck into realizing I had been abused.

How had that happened to me? I had always thought, working with so many women who needed to divorce men who abused them, that I could never be one of them. I had thought I would see it coming and I would be able to prevent it from ever getting that far. It had seemed only logical I would be able to recognize it, since I had learned so much about abuse. I had believed I had all the answers I needed. If it wasn't apparent at first, abuse would show its hand at some point—it always did—and then I would end what had started and move myself to safety.

Surely, I thought, I would do that, and I had believed I would. I had, for so long, thought I would have time to act quickly because I would recognize it as soon as it started, and now I saw I could only think that because I had never experienced abusive behavior before. Abuse doesn't wait to start until you become comfortable enough to see it for what it is, and it doesn't wait, politely, to begin only after you've finished falling in love. It is there at the beginning, right there even in the early, happy-to-be-happy stars-in-your-eyes days. It had been right there as we planned our wedding, happening already when he asked me to keep my friends away and I had consented, thinking I was being respectful of his feelings when all I was being was afraid to start an argument. I had hurt my friends on his behalf, and I had felt helpless against losing them for the truth of it. My adventure was unlike anything I had ever known before, but not in the way I had ever anticipated. By the time I saw it for what it was, it was already too late to do anything about it. *That* is the way abuse works.

I had been wrong, simply wrong on all counts. There were no differences between me and any other woman who had ever been abused, certainly no differences that would have enabled one of us—me—to prevent abuse. I had been kidding myself to think *this* one can learn from *that* one's experience, no matter how many marriages I had objectively seen up close as the lawyer on the case. Abuse doesn't begin because of the way any woman is, nor anything she does. Abuse begins because of the way abusers are, and they carry that with them as they would any other disease you can't readily see. If you are not an abuser, or if you have never tried to love one, you cannot even imagine a person acting in such a way. Nor could you ever anticipate that someone you love could ever put you at the receiving end of it.

I had been wrong to think this relationship would make me happy, but not for any reasons I could ever have thought up. We always want the person we're falling in love with to be like us, to like the things we do and to want the things we do. Love that brings serendipity makes us happiest, the more uncanny the better, and the faster we fall in response to it. There had been no way I could have known in advance that, even from the very start of it, my adventure was threatening to change me into someone I never meant nor wanted to be. We are never taught how to fall in love. How would we know how to distinguish between falling in love with someone with whom we honestly have things in common and with an abusive person who falls in love with us by filling him—or her—self up with *us*, with *our* things, and then reflects them back to us for us to fall in love with in return?

Bigger lessons still

Over time, I would learn to accept these things. I could accept, gratefully, that I had gotten out of there when I was sure there was nothing else I could do, when I could see it was just no good. I could accept that. But for a long while afterward, I had a hard time understanding why it had taken me so long to acknowledge it was no good.

That's when my friends told me abuse contains a feature that seems designed to keep a person locked into it. They said abuse knows better than I that it can count on me to make excuses for it, and that I will use my good and loving heart to keep my brain from figuring it out for as long as possible. If abuse gets lucky, by the time I do figure it out I might even be convinced I am too far gone to be able to break away.

I heard what they said, but I was not satisfied. I was haunted by the memory of my own smile on the day I got married, as I thought I couldn't undo what I had done. How could I have gotten so deeply entrenched, until I almost disappeared altogether, and then kept myself there, unwittingly? Blocking out everything else was the picture in my mind's eye, me looking satisfied, as if I had gotten what I deserved on that day I realized I had *strapped myself in* just to keep myself in such a relationship? How, and why?

"Don't worry," they told me, and "don't blame yourself. Abuse comes with its own straps," and they had been slipped onto me long before I ever got to my wedding day. Over time, I would come to understand that by the time I got married my fear might have anesthetized me. That kind of fear made it much more likely I would over-emphasize whatever happiness passed between us, as I would over-minimize our unhappiness.

I never could figure out what to make of the arguments, though. They had felt so violent to me, like nothing I had ever experienced. Early on, I had tried applying my old argument-rules to them—examining my own behavior to see how I might have contributed, and trying to get him to talk with me—but once I understood these had been the rages of abuse, all I could do was allow they didn't have anything to do with me at all.

Perhaps this will sound peculiar, but knowing I had not provoked or contributed to the rages brought me no comfort. It embarrassed me. I felt humiliated. Who was I, this woman I never thought I would ever become?

"You were out of your league," one friend explained. "All you wanted to do was love someone, and you gave the best loving you were capable of." She told me I could be proud of myself for being able to love with a whole and open heart, and she explained I didn't provoke rage, just as I didn't deserve the fear that rage caused. Although I didn't feel it at the time, she said, "You can be proud you got yourself out of there as quickly as you did, and you weren't hurt any worse than you have been. You took good care of yourself, and that's all that matters."

I was gratified to hear what she said, and so glad to have gotten away, but even that wasn't enough when she said it. No matter what anyone told me then, I was obsessed by that *smile* on my wedding day. It had come from inside *me*, and I needed to know why.

I took my question to Anne, the woman who had facilitated the Caregiver's Group years before. Although I had not seen her in some time, I knew she would make herself available when I called to say I needed her help.

"Survivor's guilt," she said. She had talked about it years before, and I had learned about it from her. While I was busy caring for Art, I had thought *we* were living with AIDS, and I had been confounded that I had not died with him, even though I was never infected with the virus. As I had talked about my feelings with the Group, I understood, intellectually, that I had done everything I could to keep him alive, but my feelings were saying something different, and I had not been able to comprehend that. I felt I hadn't been good enough to keep him alive, hadn't worked hard enough or known the right things to do. Somehow *I* had lost him; *I* was to blame for letting him slip through my fingers. I had survived.

Had I brought that guilt with me into this marriage, and could it in some way have caused me to stay there, perhaps even to deny how unhappy I was? I remembered I had told myself, at the outset, that I deserved to be loved—even loved magically—but had I truly been driven by an older fear that said I didn't really believe I deserved happiness at all?

Talking with Anne, I saw that the kind of love I had chosen was only what I believed I deserved. I believed it was the best love I could ever hope to find again—who else would love me, a damaged woman who had not been good enough to keep her husband from dying? I believed *that* on the day we met, and I still believed it as I stood in the yard raking old winter leaves away for the sun to warm the ground on which I stood. It was only my voice asking *her* question on that day that forced me to ask if I deserved more than I accepted. It was only because *she* challenged me by holding up a mirror in which I could see what was truly happening to me, that I finally became able to say I had enough, on my own behalf. It was only because I had been threatened that I could finally say I did not deserve what I had settled for.

You may recall my telling you that, on that morning of raking leaves, before the voice asked *her* question, my mind had wandered into an argument with itself. I had been angry about another argument that had happened earlier that morning. As if I had been found guilty of something, I had been forced to listen to a description of myself that had hurt me; it had been all wrong. He didn't know me at all, didn't even have any idea who I was. When he looked at me, if he thought of me, he saw someone else, and I had no idea who she was. Instead of letting it go and holding my silence as I usually did to keep a lecture from growing into a rage, I had corrected him, argued against him for my own sake. I remembered I had done so after I had this thought that I had nothing to lose anymore so why shouldn't I say whatever I wanted to?

That had pleased me in a vicious way, although I had not understood the feeling in me at the time. It had felt significant, as if there had been a turning of the wheel.

After that argument, I had gone for the rake so I could be alone with my thoughts in the sun's warmth. Without my realizing it was happening, the truth of how I felt was beginning to push out of me. I had, even without knowing, put myself out there in the sunshine to collect my truth.

As I raked, I was finishing the argument with him. "No," I said, "that's not who I am." I was not an angry woman, nor a woman who wanted to alienate herself from other people. I rejected that completely. "That's who you are," I had said, "and that's who you are trying to make me into." I was not like him, not at all. Nor could I ever be. I didn't want to be.

I loved being with people. That simple truth made me ache all over from the pain I had caused the dearest people I had sent away in his behalf. I had abandoned everything that was true for me. I loved meeting people and talking with them, learning from them. I loved most what people have to bring to one another, their experiences brought with good intentions to be shared like nourishing dishes at a potluck supper. I have always believed that is the best way we learn about being human, by being with other, earnest humans, asking questions we need answers to and having a good time doing it. Hadn't that been what my work was all about?

My work. Suddenly, the ache spread to missing my work, and myself, so far away from where I had gotten to. It had been just at that moment that my voice had spoken and held *her* mirror up to my face. *She* had thrown me a lifeline, and I had grabbed it.

Putting it all together, again

As I sat at my computer pondering these memories after enjoying Friday wine with my friends five years later, I thought I had learned every lesson that adventure had held for me. But, if that was so, why did my voice shout to stop me from recalling my own memories?

In some time still ahead of me, I would learn all memories are not created equal—in fact, no memory I could recall would ever be precisely the same as it was at the moment I created it.* In their own

---

* You'll read about this in chapter 6

way, our old memories eventually become the stories we tell about our lives. When I learned that, I would understand what my voice intended: *she* shouted precisely to break my train of thought. *She* wanted—needed—me to stop thinking about that "adventure" and re-telling this particular story, and I would eventually understand it was also time to stop reinforcing it in my brain by thinking about those unhappy memories. *She* had been right to stop me. As far as I was concerned, *she* was simply completing the job *she* had started with *her* question on the day of the rake.

Of course, there are all kinds of adventures out there for the having, and some of these have nothing at all to do with romantic love. Some are more powerful than others, and not all adventures are cloaked in what we might later call wish-it-hadn't-happened clothing. You might, at a business meeting, find yourself deep in conversation with a captivating new friend, one whose marvelous influence inspires you to take that bold step and change your life. Or you might find a book in a library that unexpectedly becomes just the thing that shifts your perspective about, well, everything. You might even find a little dog, abandoned and walking the streets of your town, and discover you must take him home with you so you can experience loving and being loved by him, unconditionally. There are countless adventures waiting to be had, and each of them may have only this one thing in common with all the others: each will surely bring you opportunities to learn something important about yourself, something you may not even have thought was there for you to discover.

Romantic love may be the grandest of all adventures, and it can also be the most distracting. Yet, it may be just this intensity about romance that makes it the perfect setting for unlocking valuable information about yourself. This shouldn't be surprising, because loving means allowing yourself to be vulnerable, and that makes you more likely to act on your feelings without censoring them. Feelings, as you know, always have things to tell you about yourself, even things that are unexpected.

Maybe we have adventures deliberately, to summon up feelings we might not ever have otherwise. Maybe, since we can be so good at dressing up our feelings in any clothing we may want them to wear, we need to have powerful adventures to reveal the truth of what our feelings are telling us. Even as I was certain *I just wanted someone to love,* after my adventure I could appreciate that loving can be complicated by fantasies, needs, fears, longings, likes, personal experiences and dislikes, not to mention confidence, self-esteem, memories both remembered and long-forgotten—and, of course, the ever-present influences of all those novels, songs and movie adventures that ended in happily-ever-after. Every one of these things can be as a smokescreen against learning what I might have preferred never to discover. Maybe we should think of our grandest adventures as, finally, clearing away the smoke that gets in our eyes.

I had thought my adventure was going to be about falling in love, and I guess you could say it was in one important way. It was all about falling in love with myself. How could I have ever known *that* kind of falling-in-love would offer me the perfect environment for resolving the one question I had not been able to settle on my own, the lingering question of what I thought I deserved? Out of the answer to that question came a realization of something wondrous, even miraculous: I discovered how much I matter to me. I care about me. I like myself, and I love thinking that about me. I have felt my own worth, and feeling it threatened, I rose to my own defense.

The voice, revisited

This time, I learned my voice was not merely the sound of my own thinking, *she* could also tell me things I was certain I was not consciously aware of knowing. After my adventure, I wanted to know more about *her*, where such a voice had come from. Had anybody else also discovered their own *her*?

I was interested to read that, as far back as the 1920s, a metaphysical teacher named Florence Scovel Shinn was teaching her students we all have a *"still small voice"* within us.[9] Shinn said it's *"not an actual voice, though sometimes actual words are registered on the inner ear."* She

---

[9] Florence Scovel Shinn, *"The Collected Wisdom of Florence Scovel Shinn,"* p. 178.

likened it to *"intuition,"* which she called hunches.[10] She also reported the voice is frequently referred to in the Bible.

This made me curious, but I was not surprised. What Shinn described sounds a lot like my inner voice, and the private conversations that I recognize as the sound of my own thinking.

My own experience argues for Shinn's *"still small voice"* being the source of internal wisdom. Much of what we know about ourselves comes to us through our feelings, which are our responses to all the things we experience. Can it be that our feelings use our voices to communicate with us, to help us think about how we feel so we can decide how we want to act on them?

When my adventure was over, it was important for me to know my voice did not force me to act, but only gently challenged me to do so. It was always my choice. We always have free will. By asking me *her* question, *she* did not tell me what I knew but gave me the opportunity to think it through for myself. This was especially important because I am more likely to value something I learn for myself.

It also mattered that the voice did not try to prevent me from embarking on my adventure at the outset. *She* did not try to warn me off a potentially dangerous liaison. I have no doubt that, if *she* had, I would have ignored such outrageous advice, even if it *was* coming from the best intentions. I was under the spell of an adventure at the time, and I would not have wanted to be reminded I was at risk of abandoning a plan I had made for my life.

I am the only creator of my life on earth, as you are the creator of your life. Without our awareness, we are vastly creative, and even when we are not consciously aware of doing so, we are always challenging ourselves to learn more, and still more, about the truths of who we are.* This is what I mean by "adventures".

I appreciate that my voice helps me access my own wisdom. It simply tells me what it knows, what *I* know is true for me, and, after that, it will grow silent again. It can seem as if it doesn't even exist, but I know better. *She's* there in my hardware, and I'm sure you have your

---

10   *Ibid.*, p. 152.
*   Shinn, see Bibiography for evidence of these statements.

very own voice "in there," too. It's been there for as long as you have been able to think, and it will continue to be there for you for as long as you live.

If you think you have not yet heard your voice speak, it might take you a little while to separate its sound from those others you keep in your head. At first, its messages might be so soft you can barely hear them, but you needn't be concerned. Your voice will become stronger as you get better at listening for it. It has not disappeared for lack of use. I am convinced that, no matter what we call them, our voices have been built right into us by evolution, and they are always ready and waiting for us to summon them. All you have to do is listen for it and question your own thoughts and feelings. Some people call their inner voices their *"Higher Selves."*

Know that words are filling your head all the time. In Appendix A, there is fun exercise you can try for clearing those words out every so often. Once you have gotten that under control, here are some of the ways you can recognize your inner voice:

- **When your mind is wandering, or when you see an image in your mind's eye, get curious.** Ask some questions. *What is this about? How am I feeling?* Look for the details. Can you relate it in any way to other things you have been thinking—or worrying—about lately? It might help to write the details about these thoughts or images so you can put them aside for a time and then recall them when you are ready to give them your full attention. Whether you are aware of doing so or not, you have attracted those words and images, and you and your voice have already begun to think about how to make their meanings clear.

- **Your voice will never be forcing opinions of its own upon you.** In the process of working through to knowing what is simply true for you, you may form opinions, which will likely harden into beliefs. As you know, opinions and beliefs are nothing more than conclusions you arrive at in the normal course of thinking. You deliberate—that is, you think—and when you decide, an opinion is born. Then, if your voice tells you you're feeling something other than what you decided you feel, you may want to consider you might have invented a story to support an opinion you like better than your feelings. Your voice might be suggesting you do not truly feel as you have declared your opinion to be, but it will never be trying to force you to accept an opinion of its own. By definition, your voice cannot have any opinion other than yours.

- *Fear is not your inner voice.* Your voice is the anti-fear. If your voice suggests you are afraid of something, it does so in order to help you, not to challenge you. Perhaps it is trying to enable you to realize you can think away your fear. This can sound difficult, but I know it's possible. During the Fear Weekend, my voice actually helped me think my way through to understanding what my fear was made of, and when I got there, the fear was gone. *She* showed me I had all the power I needed to change my relationship with fear: I could think it to death. That power resides in you, whether it is your opinion that you can be powerful against your fear, or not.

- *Your voice is not your conscience.* Although popular culture enjoys depicting people with an angel on one shoulder and a devil on the other, arguing into each ear about whether they *should* be good or bad, your voice will never be *shoulding* all over you. It has no reason to use guilt as a strategy for reaching you, and it is quite content to leave you to your other devices to figure out how to live with your conscience.

- *Your voice will not judge you, nor humiliate or embarrass you.* Your voice has no investment in bringing you down by proving itself right or smarter than you. It *is* you, and it knows its job is to tell you what is simply true for you. You might think of it as the objective constant in your mind, that part of you that gives you what you need so you can decide how to use what you know in your own behalf.

Why Do I Feel This Way?

Sometimes, I have to write at my computer with my eyes closed to listen to the sound of my inner critic. The critic is just one of those other voices we carry in our heads that can be less than helpful. By comparison, my feelings and my voice aren't concerned in the least with where I put commas in my journal, or whether all the words are properly spelled and in good grammatical order. These things preoccupy my inner critic and, frankly, they can get in the way of my listening. Try to silence yours so you can write in peace if you're keeping a journal.

Your voice knows you are the best expert there can be on the subject of you. Think about this: You are the one who knows you best because you are the only one who can know everything that goes on in your head all the time. Think about the many things that pass through your mind that you choose not to share with anyone: the things you think are trite or trivial or too dumb to mention. We all have doubts or suspicions and fears about ourselves, things that embarrass and upset us that we may have long ago been led to believe we cannot change. Remember, your beliefs are only opinions; they are not facts. They are there like secrets in your head, right alongside the joys you never tell anyone about, what you love about yourself and the amazing confidence you are sure you have, that you could, if you have a mind to, imagine yourself into any future you want for yourself.

If that isn't enough, think you are also the only one who is always with you, wherever you go, the only one who sees things exactly the way you do and who experiences your life just the way you do. You are the one who has the greatest investment in your own health and happiness. You are the only one living inside this thing you call your life.

You can trust yourself to have the answers you need because they are there inside you, even—or especially—the ones you might try to hide from yourself. You are the greatest source of information about you there can be on this earth. All those experiences, everything you know and all your adventures teaching you more all the time. These things make you the definitive library and museum of yourself. Perhaps your inner voice is the curator and the internal spokesperson for your vast collection. Whatever metaphor you use, it is simply logical that this wealth of information you are so busy collecting all the time would have the greatest value for helping you manage your life.

As the person in charge of my life, I can tell you that, thinking about my voice being there in my brain, experiencing my life right along with me, comforts me even without my ability to know how it got there. It makes me think I am wiser than I know and I am always looking out for myself, and that helps me avoid the feeling I am the victim of what life seems to throw at me. I am way too important to be a victim; I am the reason for everything I do. It is for my benefit that I extract whatever comes from each and every adventure I may have, for that becomes my wisdom.

In the meantime, I can think of my voice as the part of me that knows me best, loves me unconditionally and only ever wants what is best for me. *She is* me, and her presence means *I* am always there, watching, vigilant, all the while, ensuring I get from my adventures whatever I might have come for. Even if I do not know at the outset what it is. Even if, sometimes, I forget to give it a conscious thought.

6

In Search of the Elusive Memory

I have a confession to make. There was one memory that was left over from my adventure of falling-in-love that I could not put down with all the others, no matter how hard I tried. During one particularly mean-spirited argument, I had been told what *my problem* was: I didn't know how to tell the difference between when I was feeling and when I was thinking. It had been intended as an insult, a way to debase my ability to think, and I had known that at the time. Ironically, though, I hadn't received it as an insult at all.

I can still see myself getting up from the chair to leave the room. The words zoomed straight into me like little darts that started pulsating as soon as they hit. No one had ever said anything like that to me before. My first impulse was to defend myself, to refute the charge, toss it off, but I chose to say nothing instead. I simply walked away, silent. Somehow, the words attached themselves to me, immediately, and for good.

They stayed attached for years, until long after I had learned everything I needed to get from my adventure. Every so often I revisited them, wondering whether or not they might hold some important truth for me. I asked myself if I ever felt differently when I was thinking, from the way I did when I was feeling, and I tried to imagine myself thinking first and then, quickly, feeling, to see if it was different. All I could feel—or think—was unsure of the answer.

One of the times I thought about it I remembered that, when I was nearing the end of my twenties, a psychic told me I think too much. I thought she was implying that was a bad habit of mine, and I shrugged it off with a laugh of recognition. Now, as I matched her words to the accusation that I couldn't distinguish thinking from feeling, I started to wonder if I might have been missing something important as far back as *that* conversation.

I had been pretty sure the first time I ever thought about the subject of my feelings was when I was overwhelmed by the fear and sadness of losing Art. I was single-minded about being a good caregiver, so it had been easy, then, to decide to push all those feelings down deep inside me, where I imagined I couldn't feel them and could keep them from getting in my way. I had even made a deal with them, that I would take them out and do something with them some other day—anything to help me think I was being practical and logical, and I was still in control of my life. I had needed time to think, not to feel.

Years later, after I told the Caregiver's Group all about those old feelings as I *mined* them, I promised myself I would trust whatever my feelings had to tell me and never deny them again. Of course, then I confounded myself by doing exactly that when I wanted my adventure to bring me a happily-ever-after ending it could never have produced.

Even worse, something important was different by then. At the time of my adventure, I had read enough about the science of feelings to know they are our early warning signals. They tell us a very simple truth of how we feel so we can make good choices and decisions in our best interests. I had disappointed myself by putting aside everything I knew and treating my feelings as if they might undermine my happiness, and now, even though it was long after my adventure, I was still debating why I might have done this. I knew too much to accept my own stories without questioning them.

In reality, my feelings had often been contrary to my thoughts. I could have simply allowed I might have conflicted feelings, but I had willed myself not to and, after my adventure, what I had growing in my mind was a new dilemma. When it really mattered, would I ever be able to use my feelings in the way I believe they were intended to be used? The very suggestion seemed the proof I might not be able to use my feelings at all, because I didn't know what they were.

The thought that I couldn't tell the difference between thinking and feeling, added to the psychic telling me I think too much and my own experience of not trusting my feelings over and over again, seemed to add up to one conclusion only. I had a problem with my feelings, and it was more likely than not that my problem had started long before Art got sick—no matter what I thought.

What if I was unable to tell the difference between thoughts and feelings, and what if choosing to trust my thoughts instead of my feelings was actually harming my ability to make good choices for myself? What if it had been doing just that for a very long time? What I had learned about my feelings from the science I was reading told me they are much more important than I appreciated, and way too important for me to ignore. What could I do to right such a serious wrong?

I started to think about thinking—which I have always loved to do—and feeling, which suddenly seemed much more complex and even painful to me. Were these supposed to be equal things inside me?

The more I held the two alongside each other, the more confused I was. I knew I had never tried to compare thinking and feeling before, and I was pretty sure I had never learned any particular strategies for dealing with either of them. If feelings were supposed to be helping me, then why did I have to have feelings I didn't want? There were so many of them, and they seemed so often to get in the way of what I was sure I did want. And what about the ones that just plain hurt too much to bear?

Did all people think about their feelings, and did anyone else think the way I did? Is it just a part of human nature to wonder about them? Or did something happen to confuse me about my feelings? I suspected the accusation that I didn't know the difference between them had stuck in my mind because it held a ring of truth, and that meant I would have to find out what the truth was. Might I have even grown up not knowing there was a difference between thinking and feeling? I wondered if my whole family might not know the difference—what if we were all defective in just that way? Did anybody ever get to learn about their feelings? If so, what had other people learned that I obviously did not know?

These were peculiar questions, but they made good points. They showed me it would be worth my while to try and answer them if I could. They had certainly gotten me stirred up, and thinking. If I did find the answers, would I be able to use them to make a new relationship with my feelings, once and for all? Was this some grand new adventure, an opportunity I shouldn't refuse?

Those last two questions were easy to answer immediately. If I could, I decided, I would most want to make a new relationship in which I could have better control of my feelings. I remembered that, when I was a young woman, my father had often referred to my mother as *too emotional,* and I had been uncomfortable with that. How much *emotional* was too much? He had often expressed frustration about having to choose his words carefully when he spoke to her. I hadn't really understood that—my mother always seemed a solid and practical woman to me—but I had never forgotten *too emotional* must be a very bad thing to be. I had wanted to preclude the possibility that anyone would ever accuse me of such a thing.

For the moment, it seemed, I had all these questions piled up and no way of answering any of them. I decided to pay attention for a while and see what developed. Whenever I thought I was having a feeling, I tried to examine it as quickly as I could, before I would even think or speak about it further. Then I would quiz myself: Quick—was that a feeling or a thought? I wanted to be sure I had the right one, at least to prove to myself I knew the difference. To my consternation, I had to admit I wasn't always sure.

In fact, the more I thought about it, what had started as a curiosity had turned into something else, and it was making me very uncomfortable and more than a little defensive. Although I couldn't yet say exactly what it was, I was convinced it was very important for me to figure it out.

As I continued to watch myself thinking and feeling, I slowed my process down so I could be very deliberate about it. Each time I was having a feeling, I noticed I became aware of it because I had started to think about it. The line between feeling and thinking seemed very thin—had it always been so? Was it supposed to be so?

I did think it was odd that, as soon as I noticed I was having a feeling, I also thought I was having an *aha* moment—as if I had somehow caught myself *red-handed* having a feeling. Regardless of what the feeling was, I noticed I was thinking about how I could deal with it in some way. I was scrutinizing my feelings as if I had some general plan in mind to think them away or to diminish them until I just couldn't feel them anymore. Either way, I seemed compelled to get right to work as soon as I uncovered a feeling inside me.

Realizing that, I became suspicious of my motives. Whatever it was I was intending to do to my feelings, I was uncomfortably sure my actions were not exactly what nature must have intended I do with them.

For instance, if I noticed I was feeling anxious, instead of asking myself why I felt anxious, I would first notice I was feeling anxious because I was already thinking *"no; I'm not anxious"*—obviously denying I knew very well I was anxious. Once I secured myself in *not-anxious*, I would start to look around for something else to call the feeling, something that would neutralize it or intellectualize it—anything that would prevent me from having to give in to the feeling of being anxious. I might toss it off with an *"Oh, I'm not anxious; I've just got this deadline coming up at work and I want to make sure I meet it"*. *Just* became my favorite *go-to* word, the one I used every time I had a need to reduce a feeling to its lowest common denominator: simple, logical, nothing emotional about it at all. As soon as I had something else to call the feeling, I held onto it as the proof that, indeed, I was not anxious. I was *just* being responsible. That seemed much more rational and a good thing. It would enable me to move away from the feeling, and I could start to breathe normally again.

With some feelings, though, I noticed I also set out to conduct a little *damage control*. I started to prepare an explanation I could use to describe a sanitized version of the feeling, as if I thought I needed to have it ready in case I was ever called upon to justify having a feeling. I would hear myself suddenly explaining to imaginary people who were not in the room with me that I wasn't anxious. I *just* wanted to be certain I got the work done in a timely manner. What I really wanted, though, was to be sure I could *convince them* I wasn't feeling anxious. I wanted them to believe my version of my story. I would try out all sorts of explanations until I found the perfect one, and then, after rehearsing it a bit so I would remember it, I might finally be able to put the whole thing out of my mind.

Except, of course, that, for all my rationalizing, I still felt anxious. I never did put any of my feelings out of my mind. I could see that now. The feeling of being anxious hadn't gone away, and while I was noticing, I reminded myself none of my other feelings had ever gone away just because I had tried to dress them up in new, rational coats. I had simply moved them over into the cage I kept in my mind called *denial,* from where—I had already learned the hard way—old feelings do not go away by themselves. They just keep waiting to be acknowledged.

Why was I thinking so hard about this? Why couldn't I *just* let myself feel anxious, or anything else? Why did I think I had to have an endless supply of reasonable explanations to justify myself to no-one-there *just* because I found a feeling in me? Who else would care what I was or wasn't feeling? Who was there to judge me?

Those were questions I forced myself to answer, and the answers proved as simple as they were unsettling. Of course, no one else cared, and that made it even worse. I needed to be satisfied I had all my feelings under control. I could not have said why that seemed to say something pretty bad about me, but I knew it was something I did not want to hear. Maybe I didn't need to make a new relationship with my feelings in which I could have more control over them, after all. Maybe the thought that I needed to control my feelings was the source of my dilemma in the first place.

Curiously, I had never before been compelled to ask myself why I thought I ought to control my feelings. I had never even noticed. If someone had asked me, I was certain I would answer, *"feelings are just feelings and the only thing you can do with them is feel them"*—wouldn't I? Wasn't it? So why was I acting as if I believed my feelings were nothing more than theories that pointed up ways in which I was defective? What made me think my feelings had to be dealt with swiftly, as if I would have to be ready to prove to the invisible people in the room that I was not defective?

Cautiously, I took my case both for and against my feelings to my friends, hoping someone could offer me a valuable insight. Maybe someone wiser than I would tell me they felt the same way and validate my relationship to my feelings. Then, perhaps, I might not have to be so concerned I was acting unreasonably. I heard myself asking them, *"Do you think I have a right to feel this way on the basis of these facts?"* Each time, after they stopped laughing at how much I sounded like a lawyer, they would tell me, *"They're only feelings. They don't have any right or wrong. You just feel them, that's all."*

"Of course," I would say, defensively, pulling back as if I had touched a hot stove. I knew that. I would have said just that to someone else. You can't control your feelings. They're just your feelings. Yet, each time I caught myself having a feeling, there I would be, at the beginning of the same process of analyzing, rationalizing and trying to turn a feeling out of being a feeling and into facts, so I could pretend I was able to live with it without having to get *too emotional* about it.

Soon, I had no doubt about it anymore. I had a problem with my feelings. The more I thought about it, the bigger it was growing, and it seemed full-blown.

But what was it, exactly? Could I find out why I acted toward my feelings as I did? Could I ever get all the way to allowing myself to feel as I do, boldly and without any embarrassment? Might I ever truly believe my feelings are things I can trust? How would I know if I didn't try?

Memory: the unscientific experiment

That was the moment I started using the information neuroscientists have been learning about our brains. I have always been curious to know how I operate. How do my hands and fingers, for instance, know what to do when I'm not at all aware of what I want them to do? How does it happen that I am attracted to the things I am, the particular music, activities and places I think are fun, even beautiful? Why does blue make me feel a certain way and red another? How might I be a different me altogether if I chose to do one thing instead of another, and why is it often impossible to go back to the beginning—after you've done something—to try and do it over again, differently? I've often been suspicious of my own motives, and I have even been curious to know if I might find, if I knew how to look for it, someone inside me who was entirely other than the self I know so well.

It was this passion to know about myself that motivated me to start reading science books, where I discovered just how many other people were asking and coming up with new theories for the same kinds of questions I had, about how humans' work. I was intrigued. Once I started reading, I couldn't stop, even when much of what I read seemed more than I could interpret. I have no background in science—that's a polite way of saying it. In the fifth grade, I was supposed to make an engine from a teeny-little kit whose pieces would *worry* in a happy-engine sound when I put them together correctly, and I couldn't. I put it together all right, but it refused to do anything. I still have a memory of my science teacher—a big, burly, red-faced kind of guy with white hair who scared me mute—holding my engine up as I stood next to his desk trembling while he told the whole class it was hopeless—*I* was hopeless—and after that I never had any interest in learning about scientific things again.

That is, until my curiosity drove me to find answers to my own questions. I always have questions, so I was excited to read about what was being discovered about my brain, and the more I read the more I found what I thought were the really important things to know about being a human. Determined, I kept reading, searching for something that had been written specifically by scientists who had asked questions about feelings. If I was lucky, they would tell me what I needed to know.

One book told me it was likely I had learned about my feelings from my parents, not only from what they told me, but, from the ways I had observed them treating their own and each other's feelings.[11] That made sense, but I didn't know what to do with it. It was then I realized I was starting to collect facts I could use to construct another unscientific experiment of my own. Immediately, I started to make

---

[11] Daniel Goleman, *"Emotional Intelligence: Why it can matter more than IQ,"* pp. 189-90

notes and collect information that encouraged and tantalized me, anything I thought I might be able to use as the foundation for an exploration of my own relationship with my feelings.

It was pretty clear to me that I knew exactly what I was doing with my feelings, but I could not find myself in all the scientific language. I determined that the moment called for bold steps, and inspired, I created my own category: denial. I was simply in denial about my feelings. This is the definition I gave to *my* category, denial:

> *The person in denial is aware of her feelings as she is having them. Where her style differs from others is in the way she chooses to manage her feelings. She does not feel swamped by them, but neither is she accepting of them. She may judge them to be defective, objectionable, even inconvenient. Doing so, she chooses to deny them. She may also choose to suppress, refuse to acknowledge, and even obfuscate her feelings altogether. Such a person might actually transmute her feelings, that is, she might think about them until she convinces herself they are something else, thoughts, perhaps, and not feelings at all.*

I took a long time to create it, and, once I was satisfied with my own definition, I studied it. Finally, I was clear and ready to begin my unscientific experiment. It occurred to me that my *style* might not be unique to me. As an unscientific person, I believe it is unlikely I am the only human who ever lived, who might do or think *this* or *that*, whatever these may be. Perhaps with a bit of grandiosity then, I easily projected my contribution to the science of feelings onto others who could fit themselves in this category right along with me.

Ready, I opened the door to my imaginary laboratory. I placed my newly defined category alongside the other pieces of information I had collected so far on my imaginary lab table, and I continued on with my reading.

As I read, it fast became clear that before I could have any hope of improving my relationship with my feelings, much less understanding it, I would have to know as much as I could about what my brain had to say about a few select things I had stored in it. All avenues were leading me to memory.

Step 1. The research

As I suspect many people do, I used to think of my memory as a kind of file cabinet I kept in my head. When I wanted to recall something, all I had to do was think about it. Instantly, the picture of it would appear, revealing all its colorful details to me just as I remembered them. When I was finished with the memory, it would somehow find its way back into the right file, where I could trust it would be safely stored until I might summon it again. All my memories did just that, I thought, every time I wanted or needed them. I never had to think about how it happened. If I had thought about it, I would have said I take for granted my memories will stay just where I put them for the rest of my life.

Now, the scientists who study our brains tell me I may continue to think that, but I would be wrong. Our brains have actually revealed they have no *Savings Bank* called *Memory*. And it isn't likely any of us will be spending a lot of time taking nostalgic walks down *Memory Lane* with all our fondest experiences just the way they happened, either.

We will remember many things, of course. Occasionally, especially as we get older, some things will seem to have disappeared altogether—what *was* the name of that girl in high school, the sorority sister in the red and white sweater who I can still see flashing across my mind's eye, with her perfect blond hair, who always made me feel—?

You may be surprised to know this, but even the things that do not disappear altogether are never really quite themselves once they get settled into our brains. Every time we recall a memory we change it slightly, adding some new colors and deleting some old facts. We will keep changing our memories again and again every *next-time* we recall them, so what we see each time is only the most recent version we recreated of that memory.[12]

We won't know we're doing this, of course. Instead, we remain blissfully unaware we are looking at a changing reality in our minds. We continue to feel just as comforted by seeing our same old memories

---

[12] *Ibid.*, pp. 47-48.

back again every time we recall them. As you might imagine, though, toward the end of their lives our fondest memories might look a lot more like things we have completely dreamed up than anything we actually experienced. We'll just never know that. Every time we sit back to relive our good old days, they will always look just as good as we remember them.

Our brains do not seem to be at all troubled by this high-tech *bait and switch*. In fact, this kind of activity fits into a major part of our brains' vast scheme for memories. While we may think our precious memories are all about preserving our past, memories are, in fact, all about how we live into the future.

Memory is a unique kind of critical thinking helper. It holds and updates information from the past in case we might find it useful in the present—that's why our brains discard the old versions in favor of what we're telling them is the new version of our fondest memories. Memories make it possible for us to recall things we know, so we can draw from and use that information to make new decisions the next time we find ourselves in a similar situation.

For instance, if you ignored the needle on your car's gas tank being near-empty when you started out on your last Sunday drive, and you were forced to walk back four miles with a gas can just so you could get home again, your memory of that walk might return every time you slide into the front seat of your car after that: a gentle reminder to check your gas tank.

This is a grand idea, and it sounds so simple. However, while the goal may be simple, memory itself is anything but.

For starters, we don't have single memories we summon at will, even though we think we're doing just that. Our brains process every new memory by breaking it up into individual pieces and stashing the pieces all around itself. When you *call up a memory*, you are actually sending a signal to all the places in your brain where it has stored that memory and instructed each individual *piece* to travel to a central site so you can *recollect* it, forthwith.[13]

---

[13] Daniel Levitin, *This Is Your Brain On Music: The Science of a Human Obsession*, p. 165

Let's look at this from another angle. Without your awareness, your brain somehow:

1. manages to send the right signal, which
2. manages to get to all the right places, so that
3. all the right *pieces* it has stashed away can travel and arrive at a single place together, instantly, just to
4. enable you to recall the particular memory you wanted.

With so many tiny *pieces* having to move instantaneously, you might already be starting to suspect it is miraculous you can ever remember anything at all. While you're at it, keep in mind this memory reconstruction is happening at the same time all your other bodily systems—like breathing, hearing, seeing and whatever it is that enables you to remember how to make and drink your morning coffee while you get yourself out of the house on time for work, and maybe even concentrate on what you're reading in the morning paper before you do, so you can talk about it later, with your colleagues at work. Your bodily systems are continuing to do their jobs as if they had nothing else to do. You might not be wrong to think remembering seems like a miracle.

Disturbing the peaceful picture you have of your memories even more, when you're thinking they are safely tucked back into their file cabinets, your memories are still pretty active. They get pushed around, overrode, and blended together; and each time new information emerges, it blurs the outlines of what we knew before. In the process, some memories will be intensely edited this way, while others will be erased altogether.

If this doesn't sound chaotic enough, here's something else to remember. When you act under stress, your jostling memories cause *static*, which can make it impossible for your brain to pull up any memories on demand. So, the next time you're grabbing your head and shouting, *I can't even think straight*, try to remember that's because your brain isn't listening. When you got to that point of distress, your brain has already turned off its thinking machinery altogether. That is, it activated its automatic shut-down mechanisms for dealing with the neural static of stress. Try to relax and let your brain do its job. If you like, while you're waiting for the power to come back up, you can consider this: one of the things your brain just did was instruct your emotions to take over until you could settle down and start thinking clearly again. Emotions, unlike feelings, operate automatically: you hear a loud bang and you automatically stop and look around for the danger. Somehow, your brain knows what your priorities are, and it will always opt for keeping you alive over enabling you to recall a memory. How it manages to do that, you may never know.

This news was food for thought to me. Perhaps this information could help me, and everybody else who needs to get over a prejudice that people who we think are *too emotional* must be weak and unreliable. The next time your rational brain cannot think straight and it has to call upon your emotions to help you manage the situation, you—and I—might use the extra down-time to marvel at how efficiently our emotional brains step in to help us survive in their own, unique way....

But I digress. Please consider this: When you walk past a flower garden in full bloom on a warm and sunny spring afternoon, and you take a deep breath of everything it has to offer, you may revel in the feeling that the very scent of it is relaxing you. But your brain isn't relaxing. It's hard at work. It has to pull up all the information you have stored about those scents and flowers, and maybe even spring days and sunshine, and all the other times you have ever experienced them. It does this instantaneously. Before you know it, you're reminiscing about some other spring day when you were eight years old and wearing that brand new lavender outfit you used to love so much, walking with your favorite uncle past that garden kept by those two elderly sisters who lived together, and one of them scared you once because she popped up—*remember?*—from the flower bed, just as you were bicycling by, that other time. And whatever happened to that bicycle, anyway, the one you swore was the very best and you would keep it forever to give to your children when you grew up and they were old enough to ride?

Ahem; I got a little off the path with those memories that I love so much. In the meantime, my brain was using its *working memory* here. As the name implies, working memory is beyond merely a temporary storage system; it serves as an active processing mechanism vital for thought and reasoning. It's been said that working memories can hold as many as seven different *pieces* of information at a time, for as long as two minutes. This system enables you to do things like remember how to brush your teeth without referring to the manual, and to recall and hold in your mind long enough to dial correctly the seven digits of the phone number of your dentist. It can also scan the whole landscape of everything you've ever seen, heard, done or imagined, all the facts of your life. Working memory makes it possible for you to remember who you are so you can *just* be yourself.

While I'm being myself, if memories are made of this, I'll have to think twice before I declare my certainty that any experience I ever had just had to have happened exactly as I recall it. It's my brain doing all the hard work, and if it has a plan that demands a willingness to let a few things go by, I can certainly cut it some slack.

Step 1.5. *Two memory systems working in there*

Okay. So I was willing to acknowledge my memories seem to live a pretty flimsy existence. I even agreed to accept I have transformed what I once thought were the *simple* facts of my life into the greatly embellished stories I love to tell. At least, I decided, I can feel confident I shall be able to remember *something* about my past, and that might help me understand what happened to my relationship with my feelings.

Not so fast. We actually have not one but two memory systems: one for the facts and another for our emotions, including the emotions that are attached to some of those facts. Before you run back to collect up all your fragile memories in self-defense, you'll need to know it's already way too late to retrieve the memories in one of these systems. It prefers to keep its memories to itself. Well, sort of. Our two memory systems have been called *explicit* and *implicit*.*

Our e*xplicit* memories hold the facts we've been discussing so far—yes, the very facts we're changing every time we recall them. Our *implicit* system stores all our emotional memories. The more we know about our *implicit* system, the more we might appreciate we have any versions of our memories left to us at all. The *implicit* system acts as if those are *"its"* memories and it has a right to block us from having access to them. Yet, even from their seemingly secured bunker, these memories can continue to impact us throughout our lives. Since they can, you can rest assured they do impact us, all the time, in the most important of ways.

Let's take the two systems one at a time. *"Explicit"* memories begin to gather in us when we're around the age of two; it is not at all a coincidence that this is just about the same time we start to use language. *"Explicit"* memories are based on the facts as we know them. In order to know them, we need our language skills, so we can name and describe such events as that walk past the garden with our favorite uncle.

As anyone over 30 can tell you, when we reach this age, our factual memories begin to lose some of their glow. When you think you are *"losing it"*, especially after 30, perhaps you can take heart in knowing it may not be your mind that is at risk, but only your memories.

In fact, the next time you can't remember where you put your keys or have forgotten your own telephone number, think: only human. Hmmn…maybe I can finally excuse myself for once carefully placing my eyeglasses on a shelf in the refrigerator and then forgetting all about them as I tore my house apart looking for them. Given how much our *"explicit"* memories go through over the course of our lifetimes—stress, jostling and vivid imaginations re-creating just about everything—it

---

* To be precise, there are also specific memory systems for how to do things, like driving, and for semantics, the words you *pull up* when you're speaking and writing. Explicit memories are also divided according to the senses that use them (seeing and hearing, for instance). Implicit memories distinguish how a given moment felt, from these other, *how-to* matters. *Ibid.*, p.113

shouldn't surprise anyone our *"explicit"* systems might get a little weary around the edges as they get older.

By interesting contrast, our *implicit* memory systems never seem to get too old to remember what they have learned. They appear to be downright covetous of that information and, perhaps, even a little more independent than we might prefer. They are likely to decline any invitations we might issue for permission to access our own emotional memories.

This *implicit* system begins its work even, apparently, before we're born, when it enables us to become familiar with the sound of our mother's voice and the language she speaks—which, in turn, makes it possible for us to recognize her as early as 36 hours after we meet her face to face. This system is fully operational from the outset, and it remains active and vital throughout our lives. Were we able to access these memories, we would truly have a valuable tool for understanding ourselves in all our glorious humanity. They are the record of every emotional experience we have ever had.

Nobody can recall their emotional memories, nor is anybody aware of having any such memories.

Although we may be able to describe, even in great detail, what happened that led us to feel a certain way, once the memory of that feeling is stored in our brains, we cannot re-have the feeling itself. We can only wonder about, and imagine, how that experience made us feel. Recalling the facts can ignite strong feelings in us—we might even be brought to tears—but our responses to what we recall will be made of who we are today; we can never know the feeling of how we felt at the time. This may be curious, given how much we are editing old factual memories, but because we cannot recall our emotional memories, we cannot change or delete them.

If it makes you feel better, your brain doesn't withhold these memories with any malicious intent to make your life more challenging. Remember, your brain is *you*, not some renegade freelance organ you brought in to do its job. Your emotional memories started to be formed before you had any language skills. Even as an infant, you were very busy watching and listening, feeling and reacting. You simply had no way to articulate what your senses picked up from all that was going on around you. Nor would you have had sufficient language skills built up to be able to understand any wordy explanations that might have been offered to you by some compassionate adult at the time.

Silently, wordlessly, you processed the impact of what you observed and heard around you, and you stored that impact as emotional memories. This is important to know: regardless of the shape they're in, your feelings about these things have remained the same as they were on the day you first had them. Knowing this can help explain why you may have misunderstood more than a few of the things you experienced at the time you were beginning your life. It's equally important to know that those things may have had a dramatic, or even traumatic, impact on you and could easily be impacting your choices and decisions today, whenever they are triggered by what your brain now perceives as similar events.

It is likely you continued to misunderstand your old feelings even long after you became an adult, because they remained untouched, locked up inside you. You have no access to update them with new information you learn as you grow older; you just keep collecting new emotional experiences. Indeed, it seems the only thing you may be able to do with your old emotional memories is act on them for the rest of your life without ever knowing why.

Acting on what you seem to know without ever knowing you are doing that, and even without asking why or how you came to know it, also describes something we call intuition. To our detriment, intuition has had to endure a reputation as one of our least valued social characteristics—until now, when science has begun turning a revealing light on it.

Maybe intuition started as an afterthought. Maybe, when nature began to realize we had no direct access to our emotional memories, perhaps it searched around for something it could substitute as the next best thing.

> *Intuition is that sudden thought or image that flows into your present life, right out of your knowledge of the past, the perfect memory of just the thing you need to apply to your present and future situation.*[14]

---

[14] Thomas Lewis et al., *A General Theory of Love* (New York: Vintage Books, 2001)

Can you—the expert on you—think of a better way to problem-solve than by being able to use a tool as unique as this? It comes directly from your own experience; you come by it naturally. Does knowing this make you suspect you're a powerful person who may, after all, be one who trusts her or his intuition to tell the truth about him or herself?

Before we leave it, here are two final pieces of information you may want to have about your implicit, emotional memory system. It is the home of your ability to feel. It has also been called your guide to falling in love.

Step 2. Creating a hypothesis for my feelings

As I read about emotional memories, I imagined somewhere in my brain there was hiding whatever it was that caused me to stop trusting my feelings. What bothered me was this: If something that happened long ago was still actively influencing the way I think of my feelings today, and if I have no way of knowing what that might be, could I ever expect to create a new relationship with my feelings? I knew I needed to do exactly that for my own sake, because, otherwise, my unremembered past would always determine my present and future way of thinking about my feelings. Maybe it was already the reason for my not trusting my feelings even after I promised myself I would.

By now, I was pretty sure treating my feelings as if they were my enemies was interfering with my life. It made me think I couldn't trust myself and I was undermining my own intentions. If I was doing that because some very particular something happened once, long ago, that caused me not to trust feelings, wouldn't I need to know what that was? I hadn't, after all, been able simply to change my behavior when I became aware of how I was acting, so, yes, I decided, I needed to know. The question I had to answer was this:

Can we ever expect to change any of our behaviors, even if we dearly want to, without knowing what caused them?

I wanted to do whatever I could to help myself stop thinking my feelings were unreliable. Since I couldn't access my emotional memories directly, I wondered if imagining old feelings I could connect to factual, actual events I could recall—in effect, applying my adult thoughts to what I imagined were my childhood feelings. Might that be powerful enough to help me change my behavior? If I recalled as many relevant facts about my life as possible, and if I applied them to what I know about my feelings now, could I construct an explanation for how I might have come to think my feelings were suspect? What, if anything, would happen if I came up with a conclusion that contradicted the actual truth hiding in my emotional memories?

If I could find—or establish—or even create—something that could help me manage my feelings better, would it have to matter that I made up some or all of the feelings I was remembering? Did the truth according to my *implicit* memory system have to be the only, once-and-forever truth about me? After all, those were all my memories in my brain, my version of my own feelings I had attached to what I saw and heard. I had already learned I could change my default feelings from negative to positive if I had a mind to, so couldn't I sort-of do the same thing with old emotional memories by presuming some things about them if I couldn't have the emotions themselves? They would never be proven independently if they didn't come out of hiding, so how would I ever know they would be invalidated by any conclusions I might draw?

A bigger question was starting to emerge from these, and it intrigued me. Does the meaning of an experience come from the experience itself? Or, do I independently create the meaning I give to the experience by feeling a certain way in response to my own, personal perceptions of it?

To ask this another way, if I had put no meaning on any particular experience in my childhood, would it have any meaning? Might I be the sole creator of all the meanings of things I have witnessed and, perhaps, misinterpreted as a very young child?

The other people, who might have been actively involved in those same events I witnessed, would certainly have come away with each of their own versions of what happened—people do that all the time.

Since that is so, why couldn't I look at some old events of my childhood and *re-see* them, give them new meanings, using what I know now as an adult? Might I be able to create another way of feeling about some things that happened to me a long time ago, and then use my new information to change my relationship with my feelings? That seemed as good a hypothesis as I could hope to work toward.

Walking rapidly back to my imaginary laboratory for another unscientific experiment, I decided the end would justify the means. At least, it seemed the effort was worthy of my consideration. It was time get into action.

Step 3. Working with my memories

It was immediately clear from all these questions that, if I was going to have any chance to change the way I managed my feelings, I would first have to manage to put together some actual facts. Even though not much of anything else seemed clear at all, that much, at least, I was sure of.

I began rummaging through my memory of facts in search of any times in the distant past when I might have tried to control or deny my feelings. My intention was to find myself acting in the same way as many times and as far back as I could recall. Those memories, I thought, might enable me to develop a theory, identify the pattern and, if I got lucky, even find a common cause for my behaviors. If there were answers to my emotional questions, those old facts about my life would be the only things that would hold them, and release them.

There was one, lonely memory. It suggested my relationship with my feelings had been confused as far back as when I was 17. I remembered I had made a very deliberate decision, then, to rely on my ability to think rather than on my ability to feel. I had no memory at all about what might have caused me to make such a decision, but I did remember deciding that would be a better way to navigate the world. This memory was saying that, at the age of 17, I already trusted my thoughts more than I trusted my feelings.

I could imagine it must have seemed sensible to do it that at the time, because the world beyond the safety of my parents' home had been increasingly unfamiliar and more than a little scary. I had joined the workforce early, just out of high school, and I had taken an unsophisticated me into the world of adults before I was quite mature enough to be there. I had no memory of how I might have made that decision to override my feelings with my thoughts, but I easily remembered enough of my experiences during that part of my life to be able to see *why* I would have reached for any strategy that could make me feel more secure. Small wonder it wasn't long after that the psychic told me that I think too much.

I also remembered I had represented myself to the world of my early twenties as glib and sophisticated and, with pride, just a touch cynical. I wondered if that persona might have come about from emotional experiences I had when I was around that age, too. A little chagrined, I also recalled I had actually modeled myself after the professional women I had grown up adoring in the fabulous romantic comedies of the 1940s Hollywood cinema. How I had loved, secretly, the quick wits and bright minds of my favorite movie heroines. They always seemed to be more alive and to have more fun than the women who were soft and vulnerable—like me, I thought—as they competed in the cold, hard world. In my youthful naiveté, I might have decided that, if it worked for them, it would work for me. After all, in all the old movies everyone always lived happily ever after, and they all got just what they wanted all along. While I hadn't been, even then, so naïve as to believe there was truth in all those stories, I could envision myself being sufficiently naïve to reason some of those happy endings might, at least, have carried a grain or two of truth.

Now, as I gazed across the years and looked back at my younger self, I could see clearly how truly permeable my protection was during that time. I could still see me (*ouch!*) being knocked over easily and repeatedly by the longings and confusion that raged in me, not to mention by the many opportunities youth itself presents for being *swept away* into adventures. I could not remember how I might have acted toward my feelings, but I was impressed to discover I was, even as early as my late teens, uncertain about trusting them—uncertain enough to try and bypass them altogether. From the distance at which I now stood, it wouldn't do me any good, but I couldn't resist reminding myself that, whatever I did, the remedy I chose to steer my life with, probably did not improve much in the way of outcomes for me.

After that, there seemed to be no more I could glean from those facts. They represented an interesting recollection about me, but they didn't arouse or seem to lead me to any particular triggering events. They were more like the pattern I continued to act out as an adult, only in a younger format. It seemed unlikely, therefore, they would help me figure out what I needed to know at this moment.

That is, until my voice weighed in, with the gentlest of reminders, a single word barely spoken, more like a thought placed quietly into my mind. *Protection:* keeping myself safe any time I was feeling insecure. Could this be the common thread that caused me to negate the very feelings I was looking for? Had I been trying to protect myself in the only way I knew how?

It had been *protection* from my feelings of loss and fear which I had acted on as I tried, frantically, to keep Art alive. I had also been trying to *protect* myself from knowing the painful truth, that my adventure would not bring me happily-ever-after. Clearly, I had just identified my 17-year old self's decision, unilaterally, not to trust my feelings in favor of thinking as a way to keep myself safe. These were all connected. They all represented important times in my life when I had tried (and failed) to control my feelings by relying on my ability to think them away. Each time I had done so with the same good intention of safeguarding myself as best I could.

I was on to something—but what exactly was it? More importantly, when did it happen for the first time? What I needed was to find out if there had been an event even earlier than 17 that caused that same intention to arise in me. I suspected that, if I could find a few older facts, I might well find a powerful trigger that had set me off in the direction of protecting myself from whatever feelings arose in me in response to facts.

I can say with confidence I was never taught to distrust my feelings. I am quite sure I was never taught anything about feelings at all, in the way I was never taught how to breathe properly or how to watch with my eyes and listen with my ears. Those things were taken for granted as part of being human when I was growing up.

Thinking back, I remembered myself as a young teenager, when my feelings routinely ran the gamut from hurt and disappointment to—albeit less often—soaring with joy, and I saw myself bumping along the ground making stops at every feeling between the two extremes. I recalled times when my parents tried to offer the best advice and guidance they could from their own, comparatively limited life experiences. The world they had grown up into had all but disappeared in the brave, new energy of my '60's world. I had figured out pretty quickly that I was on my own in my world, and I would have to learn how to take care of myself.

Try as I might, though, I could not remember anything about acting a certain way toward or about my feelings having ever come up during my early teens. Nor could I find any other facts in my memories of those years that could help me attach a specific event to a decision I might have made about my feelings. It seemed my experiment might have come to a complete halt.

Luckily, then, I remembered what I had read about the influence of parents on young children. I was pretty sure my parents never told me I couldn't trust my feelings, but what about the ways I had seen them act in relation to their own and each other's feelings? What would my *implicit* emotional memories, if they could speak, have to say about things I might have seen or heard when I was too young to understand them?

I can already hear you scoffing about how, as a very young child, maybe even under the age of two, I could not possibly have decided my feelings were not trustworthy. Of course, you would be correct to think so; I could not have thought my way through to such an intellectual conclusion without words.

Even so, I was, as you were, creating emotional memories all the time. They were simply the responses I had to events I observed and conversations I overheard, other people's events and conversations, and their feelings, which I may have felt empathically but could not have named. They would have taken hold of me, right at the start, the powerful feelings, perhaps of fear, of being threatened or realizing my instinctive drive to protect myself. My emotions were born right along with me, as much a part of my biology as my digestive system and my eyes. They would have led me to the feelings that were now—still—buried in my emotional memories, the feelings I was not able to re-feel.

Those memories were, however, attached to the facts that generated them, and it was these facts I hoped I could still find in my *explicit* memory system. So, taking a deep breath as I prepared to dig through my oldest facts, I asked one more question, almost its own hypothesis:

Could I find something in my very young childhood that caused me to grow up believing I could not trust my feelings?

Like an archaeologist newly arrived at the site of my dig, I carefully searched for anything that might be related to feelings in any way, without disturbing too many other things. Since I didn't really know what I was looking for, I decided I would be willing to examine any facts that even suggested the possibility they could be attached to an emotional event I might have experienced.

To my surprise, my first stop was at the sight of a very old and long-familiar memory of an event that happened when I was about five. It was something I never could have forgotten; it stood alone among my childhood experiences. I have always thought of it as a singular event in my life, unrelated to anything else. I was aware that, much of what I knew now, came not from the event itself but, rather, from what I had remembered previously, over the many times I had thought, heard and talked about this event over the course of my life. What I didn't know was that this time, although it was old and familiar, this memory was going to impact me in a very new way. I would also discover it was not at all unrelated but was, rather, a seminal experience from which many others followed.

A favorite cousin of mine, who had been born with heart disease and had been an invalid all her life, was 17 when she and her family boarded a plane from New York to Florida on a doctor's urgent recommendation the trip was necessary to save her life. Many of my extended family of aunts, uncles and cousins were present on the airport observation deck to watch as they walked to the plane, with my cousin in her wheelchair, directly below the balcony on which we stood. We later learned she had difficulty breathing during the flight and died in a hospital soon after they arrived.

Not surprisingly, almost all the details of this memory have disappeared from my brain by now. There are only two images that linger, and I think I may only remember them because I have seen them in my mind's eye so many times that they have been reinforced enough to stay. Even so, I was only able to pull them up and hold them for the length of a flash. I saw the family wheeling my cousin to the plane and looking up at us to wave goodbye. Then I saw this: me, small and searching for something around the railing, frantically, then holding my finger up to show it to my mother, who was bending over me. She was wearing a long, dark coat and a hat.

I remembered I often thought about this experience as I was growing up. I had started to cry, and I had stopped my tears to search for some way to hurt myself, so I would have had a *reason* to cry. I had searched the railing we were leaning against, single-minded in my purpose. It had been very round and smooth, like polished steel, and I had tried to find a sharp place where I could cut my finger and make it bleed. I had also known, as I had held my finger up to my mother, finally allowing my tears to flow, that I had been feeling a little guilty. I had been thinking, *"it isn't really very much, only a little blood,"* but it had been the best I could find. I had hoped it would be good enough.

As I had so many times before when I recalled this experience, I was provoked again by my having believed, at five, that I could not cry unless I had a *good* reason to do so. This time, I also wondered, for the first time, why I would have believed my fear for my cousin would not have been considered a sufficiently good reason to cry. Now, I wondered how long I had known, at five, that I might be called upon to justify my feelings. Regardless of the answers to these questions, I was now starting to feel confident that what had happened in my past was going to answer the questions about my present reality.

I had grown up with a large extended family around me, one that seemed to love spending hours sharing endless stories about who we were and how we had gotten to be that way. Most of these stories were told as loving reminiscences, typical ways families like to sustain themselves. I had often been reminded I had been especially dear to my cousin who died. They told me she had loved me and I had been her special pet while she was ill; I had visited with her often at her home. Even as a little girl, I readily saw that my mother and aunts were greatly comforted by retelling these stories about our friendship, and I was always flattered to hear them.

Maybe that was why I was already an adult before I ever started asking questions about the details surrounding that period of my life. My mother had often told me, with pride, I had once gone to live with my aunt, the mother of my cousin and my mother's favorite sister, and her family. Although I only have the faintest memories of myself at my youngest ages, one image used to appear often in my dreams: me, as a very young child, getting up during the night and walking down a dark hallway in my nightgown toward the bathroom as everyone in my aunt's house slept. I had never questioned this image, although I had always wondered about when it happened.

Now, it seemed suddenly significant that no one had ever told me anything about the events that led up to my having gone to live with my aunt, nor why or even for how long I had been away from my parents' home. I needed to know the details. I went to a cousin who I knew would have the answers: she had been 13 when I was five, and it was her older sister who had died. Perhaps she had been the one pushing her sister's wheelchair toward the plane as I had watched from above them on the observation deck.

My cousin explained that, two weeks after her sister died, our maternal grandfather also died, and his death thrust my mother into a deep depression that had greatly concerned and even frightened our extended family. She said it had been in response to their concerns for my mother's wellbeing that I had gone to live with my aunt, for what she thought might have been *only about two weeks*.

But, she said, it might have been longer; she didn't really remember how long the time had been.

I knew, because my mother had often told me, she had been *sad* for a period of time when I was a little girl. I have also been told stories about how, as a very young child, I had been afraid to leave my mother alone, although I had not been told, nor was I able to remember any details about this.

These adults who loved to tell me their stories while I was growing up could not have known that anything they said to or did with one another would have had any significance for me when I was so young. They would not have thought to worry I was observing things that went on between them, or that such things as I observed might have been disturbing to me. If they had thought about it at all, they would have said I was too young to understand what went on between adults and could not be impacted by any of it.

Indeed, even years after these events, they continued to recount their most memorable parts of my life growing up: how my cousin had loved me; how close my mother and I had been when I was a little girl; and how devoted to her I had been. They thought it sweet that I had been afraid to leave her side for any reason, and it showed how much I loved her. They had even seemed the smallest bit proud I had been the little girl in kindergarten who cried inconsolably when my mother left the room, until finally, the principal had to call and instructed her to come and get me one last time, suggesting she try and enroll me again the following year because it was obviously too soon for me to be separated from her.

I was certain I had collected enough facts for my experiment, and I was eager to apply my question to them:

Had something happened in my very young childhood that caused me to grow up believing I could not trust my feelings?

Writing the question again released a flood of new questions, and I scrambled to get them all out before I could even think about whether or not I had any answers. To my surprise, the questions themselves would serve as their own answers.

When I was around the age of five and, perhaps, starting with the time of my grandfather's death, had I eavesdropped on conversations between my parents, or between my mother and her sisters? Had I felt I must have done something bad that caused my parents to send me away to live with my aunt? What had I felt? Wouldn't I have mimicked the same fear and anxiety as the adults around me were feeling about my cousin and grandfather dying? Had I cried when my mother left me alone at kindergarten because I thought she would not come back for me since she had left me at my aunt's house?

It seemed likely I witnessed my parents talking. Perhaps I had been frightened if they seemed to be arguing about my mother's *sadness* as she tried to explain to my father how she was feeling. Had he expressed his own frustration or disappointment, and had it been these events that caused him forever after to think of my mother as *too emotional*? Had she felt defensive?

Were my feelings matching my mother's, and were my fears the very things that became emotional memories saying it is not good to tell people how you feel or to show your feelings? Had I, in fact, been trying to protect myself as I had so many times after that?

I thought about how I might have felt when I went home again after living with my aunt. Did I hide my feelings to show my parents I was *good enough* to keep? Was that when I taught myself how to justify my feelings, in case I ever got caught *red-handed* having a feeling again? I couldn't answer any questions about why I tried to hurt my finger at the airport, but it seemed to suggest I had already learned something about needing to have a good reason to cry—just like my mother told me to. I also thought, from remembering my frantic search at the railing, I seemed to have already decided my feelings would not be a good enough reason. I never did find out where that might have come from, but I did soon discover it would not be necessary to help me complete my experiment.

My intuition was telling me what I did know was a credible version of our truth. I could imagine my parents arguing, my mother feeling guilty as she tried to explain her inexplicable depression to her husband, and herself. I could visualize her sisters, all older than she, reminding her by way of warning, she had a family whose needs she must put before her own feelings of sadness and loss. How easily I could imagine my aunt, my mother's wisest sister, intervening, taking matters into her own hands and me into her home for a time so my parents could be alone with each other, to try and *work things out*. These would not have been unusual things for a family in crisis to have done. Who would have been able to explain such things as these to me? Who would have thought I needed an explanation?

With this mixture of thoughts, memories, questions and my own imagination flooding my adult mind, I could almost put my own words to what I would not have been able to verbalize then:

If that's what happens when you tell people how you feel, then I'm never going to tell anyone how I feel. They'll just get mad at me, yell at me, blame me, and send me away.

While I was at it, I had a message for my feelings:

Nobody really wants to know what you're feeling, anyway, even if they ask you. They just want you to feel the way they want you to feel, the way they feel. Feelings just get you into trouble.

That would be just like me. Wasn't it, in fact, just like me?

A surprising reaction

The next thing that happened in my imaginary laboratory was completely unexpected. When I had exhausted myself with questions and was done putting words to the feelings of the little girl I imagined caught up in events she could not possibly have comprehended, an eerie stillness overtook me. It was decidedly different from the tension and excitement that had taken over when I started to trace my steps backward over the facts of my life.

Looking at those facts from the distance I now had, the adult woman in me found nothing but ways I could have easily and obviously misinterpreted the actual events occurring around me for days, weeks and perhaps even years. Applying my rational, adult-mind's standards, the events themselves generated no independent evidence my feelings could not be trusted.

Indeed, my feelings had proven eminently trustworthy. I had recognized all too well that my family was in some kind of trouble and distress. There had been no wrongdoing intended to make me feel defensive in any way; I could see my aunt loved me and stepped in to take care of me, as she had done all my life. I could not invalidate in any way my child-self's great effort to protect herself, and I could easily see I had simply been a very little girl who could not have understood, nor been made to understand what she had seen and heard happening around her. Those things had upset and scared me, and I had interpreted them by applying them to myself, my only frame of reference.

I could accept as fact that those things I saw and heard did not have the meanings I gave them. I had, in fact, invented stories about them, presumably in order to help myself deal with how they made me feel, and to cope with feelings I did not understand. My stories created meanings for everything that happened, and the meanings were based solely on my feelings, the feelings I had in response to what I perceived. I had simply been too young to have sufficient skills to do anything else. In fact, the adult I was, had to admit that the child I had been, had certainly done the very best she could. Even so, I could see clearly, now, that the stories I had made up out of my fears did not tell the story of what had happened.

In the stillness that replaced the excitement of questions and speculations I had raised in my search, I was, suddenly, silent. I was not prompted to ask anything further, nor did I want to say, to anyone, what I had found or thought on my own behalf. The matter seemed to have closed itself, leaving me with no need for answers or explanations, from my parents or anyone else. I did not have any need to have my childhood experience validated in any way.

In the now smoothed-out places where the knots had been, I was cautious and confident that, the next time I had a choice to wander down my familiar path of mistrusting or denying my feelings, I would be able to remind myself I had once been a very little girl who had tried to protect herself in the only ways she could. I no longer needed to rely on her protection. I was sure I had found my *event,* and even if my questions had re-created some of the feelings and emotions that event triggered in me, they had also set my feelings free to come and go, unmanipulated by me, without apology and without justification for the future. I felt confident about that.

Cautiously, just to be sure, in the days and weeks that followed, I tried to test myself, to figure out if anything had, in fact, changed about my relationship with my feelings. I noticed and imagined feelings and watched myself to see if anything was different. Each time I did, I also sent a strengthening message to my brain, telling it what I wanted was simply to allow myself to feel as I did. I wanted never again to believe I needed to think my feelings away. I was surprised to find nothing but the same, total stillness inside me in return.

Any concern I had, about new thoughts and old feelings contradicting actual memories of feelings buried in my emotional memories, seemed to have been resolved as well. I was content to trust that, if there was a different truth within my *implicit* memory system, it was not necessary for me to know any more about it than I did now. It seemed not merely possible but a certainty that, when I looked at the child's events through my adult mind's eyes, I had re-formed my relationship with my feelings. I had gotten to a clarity I could never have had as a child, and through my new clarity I could see my feelings did indeed have important things to tell me about myself. They had always been trying to do just that—as they are meant to do—even when I had been unable to comprehend or accept their messages.

We bring our own meaning

I shall never know if my version of my family's experience would match anyone else's. I am certain everyone's version of *the truth* would be different from everyone else's in one way or another. Since it was apparent I had created the meaning of those events for myself, I could readily believe each of my family members who participated in those events must have done precisely the same thing in the privacy of their own minds.

Does that mean there was no single, actual meaning in reality, but only events themselves, devoid of meaning but for the meanings each of us created in our own minds? I suspect that is so. If I could so readily end my old relationship with my feelings and immediately begin a new one, it seemed more than likely that there is only meaning when we create it for ourselves.

That makes sense. Only we perceive what only we see and hear. When I, as an adult, reviewed those old events of my childhood, I had merely updated what I previously knew in a way only I could. I had done it to give the youngest part of me the benefit of an understanding she could not have reached herself: my adult wisdom about those events. At the same time, I had also released my adult self from the burden I had been holding onto all my life.

Even if my personal truth would not have met a scientific standard for proof, I could not dispute the very real feelings of peacefulness and resolution the stillness brought me. As I write this now, years later, I no longer have any moments when I am inclined to mistrust or ignore my feelings. I can, and do, simply *let them be*, without any of my old needs to change or think them away.* Even more importantly, I know every time I do that I am strengthening my ability to do it again, the next time I have a feeling. Something indeed shifted in my relationship with my feelings as a result of my unscientific experiment.

Now, I no longer worry when I find feelings showing up in my thinking brain. I simply know that feelings are there to be felt, as they should be, and I do not have to suspect myself, or feel ashamed or guilty that I have deliberately put them into my thinking brain so I can manipulate them away. I have it in my power to choose not to make excuses or apologies for how I feel, nor to figure out any strategy for dealing with my feelings.

While I was at it, it was time for me to dismantle that cage in my mind that I marked *denial*, that handy repository for what I had once thought would be a good place to stash my errant feelings. I would never again bargain with any false promises that I might eventually take those feelings out and examine them when I had more time or inclination to do so. Rather, finally understanding that I could never, as a matter of biological face, *re-feel* feelings once they had passed through my brain; I would choose to feel them as they show up for the first time. I would, with the help of my voice, understand what they had to tell me about myself.

---

* I can say the very same thing even in 2024. Since this unscientific experiment, I have never again questioned my feelings, nor suspected anything wrong with me for having them. Hence, this experiment was well worth creating, as it set me free to feel only as I do.

In the end, the matter of managing our feelings may be all about biology. We will always be aware we are having feelings; we'll notice we're thinking about them. That's not because there is something defective about us, but, rather, it is just the way it is with humans and their feelings. The halving of feelings is automatic, and it is fundamentally connected to the taking of action in our lives. The actions we take are informed by the particular feelings that motivate them. What we do with and about our feelings matters greatly to us, and *that* it does is itself a matter of great importance.

Even in the earliest years of our lives, before we can possibly have any understanding of ourselves as humans in the world, our bodies are protecting us and keeping us safe. Throughout our lives, whether we have been aware of it or not, we have participated, in any number of ways, in taking care of ourselves to the best of our ability. Much of what we do we do automatically, and that enables us to begin to act as soon as possible, in our earliest hours as infants, even when we are far short of having any recognizable capability to act deliberately.

For many years, my voice had been trying to help me understand that I could trust myself to take good care of me. As you may recall, the first time I ever heard her speak was when *she* told me I had to *"go through your feelings and not around them anymore"*. I had trusted *her* instinctively, without understanding *her* message, until the day when, finally, I understood the great significance of what *she* had said. My voice had been trying to show me that if I was to live *my* life deliberately, I must know what my feelings are trying to communicate about me, because only that way can I know how I want and need to act in my own best interests.

Maybe we should not be asking whether we can ever learn the truths that are hiding in our *implicit* emotional memory systems. What if, instead, we were willing to ask ourselves questions as adults that can help us replace the old truths with new ones, truths that are borne of our growing wisdom? What if we could think of asking such questions as merely one way to update our old information and put to rest any lingering impacts we might still be feeling from old experiences? We can choose to think of that as our own deliberate use of our memoirs, putting them to work to update our old stories and alleviate the meaningless meanings we have invented for them.

It only makes sense. When you ask *How can I ever expect to change any of my behaviors?* You are signaling a readiness to journey to that centermost place with you, to where your first perception, and misperceptions, reside. From there, you can seek to balance who you know yourself to be with whom you most want yourself to be. Then, you can steer yourself, gently, toward living the life you want for yourself.

Emotional memories and falling in love

You may want to consider one more thing about your emotional memories. You may recall I referred to your *implicit* emotional memory system as your guide to falling in love.

It is most likely that your fundamental feelings about love began to develop when you were very young, under the age of two. For years before you could understand or appreciate what you saw and heard, you eavesdropped on love as the significant adults in your life experienced it. Yet, you could not have asked them to explain it, any more than they could have explained it to you. You learned something, though, and you stored it in your brain.

This predicament—let's call it a rather large gap in our communications capability—may be why so many people think of love as complicated and confusing. You and I have learned most of what we know about love from an infant.

The ramifications of this are astounding. I can almost feel your mind starting to reach out, and back, toward your memories of the adults on whom you depended as a very young child. It would be their characteristics and interactions you would have memorized. It would be from them you learned to know the ways *you* exhibit *this:* your particular version of what love is all about today.

If you saw angry people, or people who denied their feelings, if your adults were afraid and insecure, sometimes, many times or all the time—and almost all of us have been at some time—you would have registered that even though you had no awareness of doing so, nor any context in which to have placed it. If you heard arguments and saw reconciliations, or if you saw other patterns and mood swings—in short, if you noticed all the things you think of as ways people normally behave when they are not trying to be on good behavior for your benefit—you would have felt your own responses to these things and interpreted them in the only way you could have. Even as the rest of you matured, those emotional memories remained just as you left them. Even right now, they are motivating and influencing the ways you act in love; only now, they're complicated even further: you have added your own experiences of love along the way.

As adults, we look for familiar things, the things we recognize as love. Our most familiar traits come from our first and most powerful experiences of what love is all about. It is that one powerful, first definition of love that we are bound to seek, over and over again. How else could we recognize love?

Along the way, you have learned many new things about love. Even as these conflict with the old ones, they never quite seem to override the old ones as you start out looking for love. Have you ever heard anyone say they always *seem to fall in love with the wrong people?* Have you ever despaired of finding a good, loving relationship, or thought that, maybe, you'd be better off if you just stopped looking?

Well, this might be a good time to remember you created your own emotional memories. Think about what you know of your adults, the ways you saw them interact with their own and each other's feelings. Even if you cannot get all the way back to the earliest times you observed them, you can look at your own recent memories and ask them the questions for which you might be longing to have answers. Is *this* what you might have learned there, or that? You might not even notice them for their familiarity, but they are likely to be the very same things you saw and heard passing between your adults when you were *eavesdropping* on their relationships.

What if you could edit these memories by updating your old information? It's your information, and you can always reserve for yourself the right to challenge your memories, to update and re-create them with new information that you reinforce in your brain.

As you know, your brain makes no distinction between an event that's happening and one you imagine is happening. You are not bound to be the victim of your grown-ups' pasts.

Let's add another complication and see how it impacts what we think of as our *ability* to love. Remember that little hook of *not deserving?* Is it possible you suspect you do not deserve to be loved because your experiences have confounded you? In the next three chapters, I offer a broader sense of what our lives might look like from our brains' perspectives: what our brains might tell us if they could describe themselves.

We have evolved to maximize our wellbeing in order to survive as a species. Barring biological discrepancies, we all have pretty much the same mechanisms for responding to life. You might be surprised to know how many of these mechanisms—which you will read about in chapter 8—seem to have evolved in us for no other purpose than to bring us together, in friendship and even love. Maybe watching as young children, we got confused into thinking love is hard to find, even harder to sustain—what would you think if we found out love is the most natural thing we humans can do, and the most powerful? What if we discovered all we have to do, truly, is utilize these mechanisms as they are intended and then allow ourselves to have love, and give it? In the face of powerful evidence such as your brain could provide, you might have a hard time holding onto any biases that suggest you are a person who is not deserving of love, regardless of attempts that did not end the way you had once hoped.

As always, you get to choose to use what you know to help yourself in ways you could not have in the past. You can decline an invitation to hold onto the possibility of such things as your old, emotional memories being judgments against you. You can decide, instead, to use what you know about being human to lessen the power of your familiar, your automatic motivators, your *triggers*. Maybe, with practice, you can eliminate them altogether—wouldn't that be worth trying to achieve? You might even be able to do that without ever knowing precisely what they are. Try making some up, imagining them on the basis of whatever facts you do know you learned about love. Your brain won't be concerned you are lying to it when you imagine a new truth for yourself. See if it fits, if it works for you, and then you reinforce it for your brain, which will simply treat it as your new truth.

You might choose to do your work as I did my unscientific experiment, alone. You might just as easily choose to invite others to work with you: try dancing, and laughing together; these are two powerful mechanisms nature has built into you for this purpose.

During the years I spent talking with the Caregiver's Group, it was so easy to learn how much can be gained by talking with other, earnest people about the things we have in common. That had been a surprise and a new experience for me, especially after my solitary years of caring for Art and then surviving my loss, alone. I had incorrectly thought no one could offer me the kind of help I needed, as if I was the *one lost cause* in the universe. Yet, within the Group I felt safe, and talking there always seemed to help me move closer to my center, my point of balance. It was while I worked with the Group that my voice started to speak to me, to help me figure out what was true in my life, and what was not true.

Over time, it has been my trusting of the voice and, through that, myself, that has made me fearless about facing down whatever I might find in my old memories. I know if I keep searching and probing, gently and steadily asking myself questions, I have nothing to fear from what I might find rummaging through those memories. More importantly, if I feel the least bit of anxiety or fear about what might be hiding in my mind, or even if I decide I do not want to do my work alone, I can easily bring together a group of friends, one or more, who I can invite into my imaginary laboratory. Certainly, I can also seek out a mental health professional as a guide if that is what I need.

For me, there is great courage in knowing one of the possibilities for our lives is we can make changes whenever we decide it is in our best interests to do so, and we can reinforce the importance of those changes in our brains. Knowing there are other possibilities you can choose, and you are not locked into choices you made when you were two or 12, or 40, you can climb out of anything you may have *fallen into* just because you have a mind to: it is power-making. It says you have within you the ability to figure out a way to bring about the changes your heart desires.

Change, as we are so often told, begins when a single step is taken and is then followed by another, and another. Steps can be asking yourself questions about who you are and who you want to be, and then making an honest effort to answer them in the context of what you want for your life. Steps are also the decisions you make about whether you want to *go it alone* or invite others to bear witness or help you in your journey. Giant steps are the ways you make the choices that act on your decisions.

Each of us is a one-of-a-kind human with our own, unique experience of the life that is ours alone. This, I believe, is one of the most important messages our brains, with the help of our voices and a little neuroscience, have to tell us. Even as the messengers teach us about our extraordinary individuality, they prove to us there are also countless ways we are just like each other. A great comfort can be found in our sameness. We might even be surprised to discover, in the process, how much we truly need one another to fulfill our individual missions of living well.

7

Telling

"I'm only one, but not alone."*

Telling: *verb – transitive.* *"To communicate by speech or writing; express with words…."* An easy definition for a familiar action word. Devoid of subtlety. Broad in its subjective inclusiveness. General…and deceptively simple.

This definition, as you can see, does not contain an advisory, although perhaps it should. Warning: *Telling* may impact the substance of your emotional life and seriously mess with your feelings. Yet, telling can prove to be vital to your health and wellbeing. Hence, telling may top both your lists of *do* and *don't do* at the same time.

As little kids, we might tell *on* someone who wrongs us to someone bigger, older than we are and can mete out justice in our behalf. As adults, we tell one another all manner of things, what the weather is, how to get to the movie theatre and the latest news. We tell things we think others want to hear and just as likely things that are only on *our* minds, maybe in our hearts. We tell one another off. We tell people we love them.

---

* With gratitude and permission from Albert Hammond for the quote from their fabulous song, *"One Moment In Time,"* by Albert Hammond and John Bettis.

We also have our own, personal relationships with telling. We tell ourselves the truth as we believe it to be, so we can act in our own best interests. We do not tell ourselves the truth so we can avoid having to act altogether. Or, vice versa. We tell ourselves stories, about everything, how we feel, what we want more than anything in the world and, even endlessly, what we *really* think about all those *others* who have transgressed against us. We tell ourselves it's the simple, obvious truth we're telling, but often, when push comes to shove, we'll tell ourselves afterward we knew there was another truth all along and then wonder why we didn't tell ourselves that before it got to be too late.

On the night Art was diagnosed with the HIVirus, he told me he didn't want to tell anyone he was infected. After he died, I told myself he forgot to tell me what to do with his secret. I had promised I would never tell. I assumed it was over, that the secret died with him just as the virus did, and I would no longer have to think about it. I didn't want to have to tell anyone, didn't want anyone to know, so now it was mine because I had promised to keep it and there was no one else to give it to. I wanted never to be challenged by it, and I planned to keep it forever.

Then I broke all my promises about it. It proved to be too hot a secret for me to hold onto, even as a legacy.

Before it was done with me, the secret would force me to identify precisely all the ways I had had my own, separate experience of Art's experience. I would see our two experiences had been completely different—and that didn't even include the one I had gotten caught in alone, the one that seemed never to end and didn't even begin until after he died. The secret that he died of AIDS would play a starring role in that experience. It would be the decisive moment of betrayal for me, without which I could not be set free.

In Art's experience, I was the keeper of the secret because I had been charged by him with ensuring no one ever learned it. It was my job to *head them off* if anyone seemed suspicious that something had become imperfect in our perfect life. That was a charge I took to heart, and my record of vigilance was unblemished for so long as he lived. Of course, there was that one important telling I could not have avoided, for both our sakes.

By striking comparison, in my experience, I was going to have to tell everything that happened to me before I could ever hope to re-fill the empty spaces his death had left inside me. In the process of coming to tell, I would learn about how we tell and why, why we choose not to tell—and what the great price was that I would have to pay for trying to keep myself from telling what must be told. Telling would force me to realize I was, after all, only human and I could not hold back the power of such a secret as I had inherited, not for all the best intentions in the world.

So maybe it was ironic that, in my telling, I would find the gold. There, in all the giving up and letting go telling demanded of me, I would find connection, and that would be as breadcrumbs for me to find my way back into my own life. I would learn I could bond again with people, people could care again about me, and I them, and I would begin to appreciate that even our brains were in on a great conspiracy to bring us together, to learn from and teach each other what matters to us all.

At first, when I became certain the secret was not going to go away by itself, I resented that it could force me to choose between my promise to Art and my own need to keep on living. There was no way I could do both, no way I could help myself without telling on Art. I never wanted to use what I knew against him, and for years after he died, I continued to protect him at a great cost to myself. I was completely unaware of it, and in those bitter years, it seemed only cruel and unfair that I might ever have to sacrifice his good name to save myself. Why would I have to do that, when it was his secret and not mine at all?

Before I could even hope to answer that question, I would first have to learn to be willing to remove the bindings I had kept the secret wrapped in, and I was fearful of doing that. I kept myself bound up in protecting Art without even noticing he had stopped needing my protection anymore. Instead, there was only me, and I desperately needed my own help.

I would have kept on going, but the secret wouldn't wait for me to get over my fear. It would come bursting up from inside me into the light of day, all by itself. For me, that would prove to be the final rending of all that had held us together. It would also signal the beginning of the rest of my life.

Telling, I would learn, is fundamental to a human. Telling would set me free.

The secret takes root

As I told you in chapter 1, on our first official night as *People Living with AIDS*, Art declared he didn't want anyone to know he was infected with the virus. He had interrupted my racing mind, which was busy making a list of the people I took for granted we would have to tell because we would need them to love and help us. I was trying to keep it short because I knew he would not want everyone to know, but it did not occur to me that the people on the list I had in mind would be included in his edict. I was ready for any kind of conversation he might want to have, except, as it turned out, the only one he, in fact, wanted to have. While I was waiting for him to say who we would tell and who we would not, he had gotten lost in his own thoughts. I hadn't noticed. I was nowhere in his sights.

While he had been in the hospital with pneumonia for the two weeks before that first night, I had watched him struggle to reach for anything he could find that would give him a feeling of control over the future he already saw ahead of him. Calmly, as though he had carefully thought through all the little details of a plan while I was at work one day, he had told me we could go to the Caribbean for a vacation and take a little snorkeling boat out into the Sea. With my deathly fear of drowning, I had been immediately uncomfortable before he got to his point, and I could hardly breathe by the time he had finished describing his plan of falling backwards off the boat into the water, the way you do when you're going to snorkel, only not coming up again.

When he had gotten all done telling, he had asked me what I thought about his idea. Sick to my stomach as if I were already drowning, I had answered slowly, making my answer up as I spoke, without even realizing what was on my mind. "I think...that...if...you're the only one who is infected...I will try and help you do whatever you want to do. But if I'm infected too...I can't really say what I will want to do."

What little color he had in his face drained completely out as he stared back at me, stunned, as if I had slapped him hard with my words. Was it possible he had not even told himself I might be infected too? It had been obvious I broke his reverie by making him think about what was on my mind, even though I had had no idea what that was until I heard myself speak. I had only been trying to answer his question honestly.

I had been vaguely aware the moment might have changed everything between us. It might have forced me to realize Art had stopped thinking about me because his need to control what was happening to him, alone, was consuming him. But because I would never have allowed a thought as dangerous as that, I had sat, perfectly still, waiting for what might come next. Gratefully, it had been nothing. We had held each other in our eyes and let the conversation end, not intentionally, but as if we had been rendered speechless to realize we had nothing more to say to each other on that subject; we had allowed the conversation to pass quietly by itself because we didn't know what else to do with it. After that, there would be no more conversations about what we would do if he got a positive diagnosis.

When we reported to the doctor's office at the start of what was to become our first official night in the AIDS epidemic, we went to talk about what was suddenly not Art's health but his *status*. I asked, innocently, what about me? *What should I do to find out if I am infected too?* I was so certain the doctor—who got a strange look of horror on his face when I asked—would bring it up himself, that, when he didn't answer he would test me too, maybe even right away, that night, before we left, I was jolted right back into that other moment in the hospital in which I seemed to be all alone, thrust out from Art and no longer thought of. I saw I must have decided too quickly that we three were a team. I could see I had only imagined, in my growing hysteria, we had made a pact, formed a little cottage industry called keeping Art alive, and now I was forced to see I was wrong. The doctor told me I had to call the health department. "Private physicians aren't allowed to test people who aren't already their patients," he told me. His look, however, told me something else, what he did not want to tell. He was relieved not to have to do anything about me. Even as I fought against it, I felt abandoned in spite of myself.

Afterward, when Art had the taxi drop me off at the drugstore to have his prescription filled while he went home, I sat a long time in the crowded pharmacy waiting for my package to be readied. I arm-wrestled with thoughts that wanted to wallow in the impossible feeling I had been forsaken. *I don't need that,* I told myself sharply; what I needed was to pull myself together in time to figure out what I might have to tell the pharmacist, who now knew exactly what had happened to us. I could see the word was spreading fast: four of us in less than two hours, five if we counted the doctor's nurse. Even worse, the pharmacist had been around for years of Art's kids' growing up and they had a warm and friendly relationship. When he walked around the counter with his hand outstretched toward me, I tightened every muscle in my body as I reached for the package and nodded my acceptance of his good wishes for Art's wellbeing. I was grateful he had chosen to say something that did not require any words back from me.

My head was already jam-packed with conflicting feelings by the time I got back to our apartment, and I tried to comfort myself; I felt ready for anything that might come up in our conversation. Yet, when I looked at Art I saw immediately I had come home completely unprepared. Whatever I might have thought our next steps were going to be were not even going to show up on the agenda in his thoughts. In our little bedroom, which held so much precious intimacy, we stood on opposite sides of the bed as he started to tell me what was on his mind.

I had known, because Art had told me when we met, his family taught him no one would want him if he got sick, and I knew he believed his family and, presumably, everyone else, would abandon him now if they knew. He was determined not to give anyone that opportunity. To drive the point home, he demanded a high price from me. He told me I would have to leave if I could not help him keep the secret. I saw in his eyes as he pleaded his case near tears, that he was ashamed and had already equated his illness with the end of loving. I was uncertain and, frankly, for the first time since I met him, I was afraid. He seemed hell-bent on forcing me to realize we were no longer who we had been only a couple of hours before, and I did not understand. In my mind we were in this together, and whatever it was going to be, *it* was going to happen to both of us.

How had we gotten all the way to leaving—*my* leaving—and so quickly, without my even having been a part of the conversation?

I promised him, on that night, I would keep his secret—"I'm not goin' anywhere," I mumbled defensively in response to his challenge—because I could see he was already convinced I was going to leave him anyway no matter what I said. I finished the thought in the privacy of my own mind, the only place left where I could still find myself: *You'll just have to wait and see.*

I could easily convince myself there might be no room in Art's mind right now for anything other than *his* disease, *his* death, and these had sucked up all the breath he had inside him until there was just no space left over for things that might have to do with me. Thankfully, I had come to know him well before this night, and I was confident he did not want me to leave. He was only afraid I was going to and he needed, as he had in the hospital, to seize control wherever he could find it. But between *leaving* and his doctor telling me he could not help me, that indeed there was no team, only me on the outside of the actual new relationships that had formed that night—Art and *his* disease, and Art and *his* new doctor and *his* disease—I was struggling hard against feeling I had somehow been thrown away in the frenzy of diagnosis.

Desperately needing to get away from the terrible feeling threatening to hurt me, and still seeing the look on the face of the pharmacist as he sadly acknowledged what had just become Art's secret, I was determined to get us past this night. I needed to begin to concentrate on what *I* thought I had to do. I would have to ignore everything that threatened to get in my way of beating my enemy, the virus responsible for what was happening to my happy life. Silently, I promised Art he would never have to tell anyone anything he didn't want to. I pledged I would prove to him I could do everything I had to, to protect him in every way I could. I would show him we were in this together. All he would have to think about was staying alive. I would do the rest, and I would be there regardless of what he thought, whatever it might cost me.

On that night, telling started to teach me things about itself I could not have figured out in the abstract rooms of my mind. I could not have anticipated telling would have to finish what had begun with that conversation about leaving, nor would it wait inside me as long as it had to for a chance to do that. I believed I had no choice but to act as I did because I rejected the only other choice outright, and I surely had no context, then, for suspecting *not telling* would prove so powerful a potion. How could I have known I was setting myself on a course that, years later, I would not be able to get off of with even my most stolid denials that keeping the secret had nothing to do with how I was feeling?

Instead of telling what was merely so, for years after that first night of the diagnosis, I lied to everyone who mattered to me. Recklessly, I made up stories and told myself they were only what was necessary to protect Art, *that* was all that mattered, until I convinced myself it was so and there was no other way. Yet, the more polite people there were to make it easy for me to lie, the more contemptuous were my thoughts about them. My innocents. I mocked them in near-derangement as I realized the full extent of what people do not want to be told, and I played a dangerous, desperate game in which I dared myself to come close, so close to telling them every hideous detail of what had happened to us, what was happening still, that I wondered how they could not know something was terribly wrong. Viciously, I told them in my head how lucky they were I was bound by my secret. If I could tell, I could blow up every pretense we had of decorum.

Yet, for all my bitter contempt, I could never understand, nor could I ever tell anyone, how it hurt not to see in their eyes the reflection of what I watched day and night after day and night: the vastness of pain and sorrow that was devouring Art as his relentless disease wore him down. On that first, terrible night, I was decades away from realizing what telling would, eventually, have to reveal, a seeming lifetime away from discovering it could have been a release valve all along, and if I had known, I might have been able to use it to keep me whole so I would still be myself, later. Would it have saved Art? I had no way of knowing any of that at the start of the upheaval.

Secrets and lies

By the time we left New York City for the northern mountains of the Hudson River Valley, where Art would live for another six weeks, I was grateful to get away from my home town. I knew I was being unreasonable, but I blamed the suddenly-ugly city for making him sick. I was tired of nearly three years of acting light-hearted and happy in my love, telling our families and our dearest friends the reason they were seeing less and less of Art was because he was working hard at his great job. The truth would have stunned them. Even seeing him would have taken their breath away by the time we started pretending we were moving to a wonderful new life in the mountains, to build our own law practice together. I told myself it would all be for the best. They would never see him, or me, again, so we could leave them content to remember our unmarked happiness.

Yet it seemed bitterly ironic to me. Art's whole life was about loving, the having and the giving of it without holding anything back and, always, the celebration of sharing our love. I learned so much about loving from him—he was the first person I ever met who loved openly, shamelessly, joyfully—and there was still so much more I needed to know. No one would have believed that he, of all people, would choose to hide away from the very ones he loved the most. He was too sick to go out much of the time. He couldn't eat and he lost weight he never regained. In no time, it seemed, he became frail and stooped. He walked slowly when he could move at all, and the pain of neuropathy* showed in his face even as he tried to hide it from me. I knew he didn't want anyone to see him the way he looked, but I knew him well enough to know that wasn't the reason he pulled himself out of the life he loved so much. He was trapped by the terrible secret of his own making, and he just never had enough time to figure out another way to live with it.

---

* Neuropathy is a condition that is called, in AIDS parlance, an *opportunistic infection*. It numbs and destroys the nerve endings in fingers and toes.

By then, what I knew made me angry until I hurt. I told myself I was disgusted with the charade that counted on our friends being too respectful to challenge me, and I was glad to be moving away from them. I never once allowed myself to ask what my life would be like when I could not see them or interact with them at all, even if I was approaching them from behind the fiction I had created. I felt as if I had split into two people under the weight of the secret, although I told myself it was the weight of the disease that was getting me down. I lied to myself to cover my lies to everyone else because I had made a promise that demanded I lie even as the costs mounted around my feet, and I never let myself think twice about anything that might have contradicted my lies. I told myself everyone was just someone outside the Art-and-me fortress we had built around ourselves and they, I knew, would survive my perfidy. As far as I was concerned, I told myself, those things that were only about me didn't matter. I, as everyone else, would have all the time I needed to do something about me, later.

Once we were out of the city, we spent most of our time working frantically to get our tiny law office ready to open. We had no time to dedicate to making new friends or getting to know the neighborhood. That didn't seem relevant anyway.

I wasn't able to tell myself Art was working furiously to make the office ready for *me*—I wouldn't know that until someone older and wiser with clearer vision than I had, would suggest it to me sometime later. I surely knew I was nearly hysterical about helping him in any way I could just so I would be able to watch him. By then, watching him had become my primary activity as well as my reason for living. Anyone watching me would have thought I believed I could keep him alive just as long as I held him in my sights.

For all my effort, when the silence finally came rushing in to take over his place in my life, I was caught unaware. I felt blind-sided and I looked around me, confused, as if the car we had been riding in had been hurtling toward a stone wall that would stop it, and it suddenly had. Weirdly, on the morning he died, I misunderstood why I had been left behind to sit in my chair looking at hands in my lap that no longer had anything at all to do. What was I supposed to do?

Everyone recognized me but me

I was supposed to get up from my chair the week after he died and return to work, whether I was ready to or not. We had new clients at our new law office in our new town. They had started coming as soon as we hung our signs with the cartoon of the dog. Everybody, it seemed, had been saving up some legal matter for our arrival from New York City, and then there were all the people who wanted to find out for themselves if the dog—our English bull terrier puppy Art had turned into our logo and whose face was appearing everywhere around our hamlet—really worked in the law office and if she looked like her caricature in our signs. They were thrilled to discover she did, on both counts, and she soon became a celebrity in our little community, just as Art had predicted she would.

As for me, as I dressed for work that first week, I was surprised to see I had dissolved down to bone-thinness. My clothes hung off me even as my body felt heavy and sluggish and I had to drag it around everywhere I went. Immediately, my calendar was filled with meeting people who reached out to me for help and advice. Sloughing off the irony that I might be able to advise anyone about anything having to do with life, I gratefully kept myself secreted within a threshold tenet of the legal profession and kept my emotions outside the office door at all costs. I told myself, at least that would help me keep down the muffled screams that were continually building up in the cavernous emptiness inside me. Playing to those indifferent screams, I thought I could ensure they wouldn't push out and splatter all over my unsuspecting clients.

In the weeks that followed, I felt as if I had become wrapped up in a most peculiar shell. Outside the shell, I was the woman-lawyer newly arrived from New York City, who lived alone in a house in the woods at the end of a dirt road with no street lights, in the company of a dog. People would wave to us wherever we appeared and, if the dog was asleep on the seat next to me in the car, they would flag me down so they could peek into the Jeep to make sure she wasn't trying to miss a day of work. We would laugh and chat carelessly, me smiling all the while as if they were shooting cameras at my face, and people would offer her biscuits wherever we went.

Inside the shell was where the empty space was. In a whip of a moment there had been a complete clearing out of all the things that had been my former life. It seemed Art had taken everything with him; the intense action that had been in that space had stopped, just stopped and then vanished way too fast for me to grab and hold onto anything before it was all gone. I hadn't had time to prepare, to switch gears, to figure out another way I would have to live, by myself. I hadn't expected to live. I was stunned to find myself alone, suspended in the eerie, empty silence. It was so heavy I heard myself as if I was speaking and breathing from the bottom of an ocean so dense it made looking around me sluggish and cumbersome, and even moving was a nearly impossible task.

I was desperate to hold on to whatever scraps Art might have left behind that might still needed me, and when I looked, the secret was the only thing left. I told myself it was safe with me, no one would ever know I was carrying it, and I would never tell. I would protect it as if it were Art. It wasn't my secret to tell anyway. I had no right to tell, because Art had forgotten to tell me what he wanted me to do with it.

It would be fine with me, I decided, if everyone would think whatever they wanted to as long as they left me out of it. I was pretty sure no one could figure out I had such a secret by looking at me, and I told myself the new people I would meet never knew him, so they had no claim to his private information. If I never told anybody, no one else would ever have to know what really happened to him, or to me. It could all end right there with whatever decision I made about what to tell and what not to tell.

Besides, it seemed like a no-brainer—why would I tell anyone? Who would hire a lawyer who had moved to town after she lost her husband to the greatest political disease of the century? Keeping it seemed like the something I could still do for us both, protect his good name and keep myself safe against whatever it was I was afraid of, at the same time. Thinking about it, I patted my heart, as if to be sure the secret was still there, where we would both be safe.

Watching myself acting outside my shell, I marveled to see how I could still so easily fool everyone all the time. I wondered why no one seemed to notice the chaos that rumbled and threatened me on the inside, yet I was soon enough grateful for the hiding place the shell provided. Once I got used to pulling the weight of my invisible bulk, I counted on the safety of that shell. It kept all the people on the outside separate and apart from me.

In time, I could imagine some of the people must have heard I had a husband and law partner who died, but I knew I could count on most people being too polite to ask me about that. If anyone did, I always responded quickly as I had rehearsed it: *heart attack*. It was the familiar I counted on, not to provoke any follow-up questions. All I had to do was say those two words and then each of us could move away from the uncomfortable subject of Art's death as quickly as possible. To the extent it could be said I had a plan for the rest of my life, it was surely to keep everything just that way, hidden well behind the shell I pushed out into the world every day and retreated back into whenever I was alone.

The secret takes on a life of its own

Perhaps I should have known things couldn't stay that way, but I was caught off guard when the secret started to force me to choke it up. This occurred at the time I was busy clinging to the popular wisdom that time was going to heal all my wounds as if it were my magical life raft. Soon enough, I would have to accept that, in the same way time would refuse to make my feelings go away, it would also refuse to diffuse the power of the secret. I learned, then, that time's real job was something other than healing altogether. As it went by, time seemed to drop in my lap more and ever more new truths to deal with before I could even hope to inhabit that empty space inside me again.

I got good and angry at that. Art had it easy by comparison. He got to die out of all the debris AIDS left behind, while I was still carrying it around. I was slogging through endless days and nights of pretending I was a regular person who cared one whit about having a house and a dog and a new business to grow. It was maddeningly unfair, but I didn't seem able to be in control of anything and I deeply resented that. Now on top of everything else, time seemed to be telling me I had been holding on to a secret that was determined to leak out on its own power—the very power it would force me to learn I had given it by promising I would not tell in the first place. Where was the fairness in that?

From the safe distance of where I am now, I can see some secrets are not meant to be secrets at all, no matter how much we might be driven by our fear to pretend they must be. I had been so afraid of the secret I was holding I couldn't even ask myself what exactly it was I was afraid of. What did I think would happen to me if people knew my husband died of AIDS? What could they do to Art? What could anyone do that could be worse than what had already happened?

Of course, I could imagine answers that served to keep me locked in with the secret, and because I could, I did imagine them. After all, our brains are designed to help us anticipate fearful things so we can prepare to protect ourselves as soon as possible, even in advance, and our brains can't tell the difference between things that are real and harmful and merely our imaginations gone wild.

I was far from naïve. I knew people were afraid of the very word *AIDS*, and I knew fear could keep them from hiring me in the small hamlet in which I lived, or worse. By then, there had been so many terrible stories reported in the media, of people hurt and discriminated against by their families and neighbors and governmental agencies alike. Sometimes in the darkest nights on my unlit dirt road I could see my fear running rampant. I could imagine people storming my house and running me out of town. I counted myself lucky, then, that I had been wise enough to arm myself in advance. I could not be challenged nor named and marked as unfit by anyone else's fearful anger as long as no one knew what they might have to be angry about.

What I never imagined was that the cost of keeping the secret could be greater than the protection my fear afforded me. My fear was born of the AIDS epidemic, and from that first night it had been powerful enough to keep me from ever asking too many questions whose answers I might not want to know. Without the spell cast by my fear of the secret, I might have asked fear if it was preventing me from even thinking of something I could do to help myself. Perhaps I would have thought to ask if I was willing to risk trusting people who approached me in honest friendship, who would have been able to bear my telling of a terrible truth. I never even considered that telling might have lightened my burden. Instead, I continued to keep my fear close, wrapped tightly in the silence that held it, with everyone else on the outside as I watched from where I was deeply buried inside myself.

I told no one about the secret until the night I met with the group of women and men who gave me Rule Number 1, almost three years after Art's death. That telling had made me uncomfortable, but I had quickly determined I had to trust those strangers with the secret because they had been so kind and loving toward me. I owed them the truth, at least.

It wasn't until I joined the Caregivers' Group, whose members had each lost someone they loved to AIDS, that telling forced me to take out the imaginary box of feelings I had marked *"Later"* and packed away in the back of my closet, tightly sealed. There, in that room where I knew I could trust everyone to keep my secrets as I would keep theirs, I finally allowed myself to unwrap all the hidden truths I had packed into that box.

It was because there I could, finally, trust I was able to talk freely about anything on my mind without being judged or scorned, or worse. I was able to admit all my confusions and conflicts and report my terrible fears and the sorrow of watching Art waste away over three years. I wept over the life I had come through with these others at the table, and I knew it would be okay with them if I struggled as long as I had to in order to find the words that would say my long-denied feelings. Over time, I came to trust that, for however long it would take, I would be able to remain right there, telling all there was inside me to tell about what had happened to me.

I learned I couldn't pick and choose among my feelings to tell about some while I left others untouched. I learned telling has no beginning and no end, and it comes with its own rules; each telling leads to another and no single piece of telling, by itself, is sufficient to clarify the matter, even if I might hope some things will not matter enough to be told. Bits of the secret surfaced in every telling, in every conversation, even though I worked hard to avoid it. Why shouldn't I tell these people who cared for me, that I was left holding the secret I couldn't release?

Sometimes, I imagined the secret as an agile boxer who was slowly closing off all the open avenues I might flee down to get away from it, one after another, until I would have to meet it fully, head on, and I could only hope I would be allowed to meet it in a ring of my own choosing. Other times, I watched the secret as I talked, saw it building up from the deep emptiness inside me like a long, ominous wave of something I couldn't bear to look at. I was afraid it was going to keep on coming even if it had to explode me into a million tiny pieces when it got there. Yet, I was also curious about what would actually happen when it did push its way out. What would it take down with it?

One telling, re-told...

One day the secret got away from me and told a story of its own. I admitted to the Group I had revealed it once, while he was alive.

I had taken to counting our life in summers, but I am not superstitious. Art and I met in a summer and two summers later, after we started making plans to get married, he was diagnosed with the disease. Two years after that we were in a summer again when the drug he had been taking stopped working. By that time, I had been reading everything I could find about my deadly enemy, and I knew the drug typically lost its efficacy after a year and a half, so I had been waiting, and watching, for it to fail. I knew what was happening as soon as Art started losing weight and strength quickly, right on schedule. It was summer, and he wasn't going out at all. No one knew how drastically he had changed because no one saw him but me.

When I talked with his doctor about the drug losing its effectiveness at the end of one visit that summer, he told me, "There is nothing else I can give him. There just isn't anything else out there." I asked about getting him on a trial for a new drug I had researched. I was sure the doctor would be able to make that happen before the old drug stopped working altogether.

"I'm not an AIDS specialist," the doctor answered sadly, only a heart doctor who had been on call the night Art had been admitted to the emergency room with pneumonia. There were a lot of doctors in New York City that summer, and not one of them had started out as a specialist on hiv, so that hadn't bothered me. I was alarmed by his obvious reluctance to put Art in a trial for a drug that had not yet been approved. In 1990, that was a relatively unfamiliar medical concept.

The doctor and I never did become the team I had once imagined, and this conversation was just between the two of us, outside of Art's hearing. For the most part, he knew me as the silent partner unless I had questions or had to answer any.

Still, I was a very changed woman from the one who had despaired about being left out. I demanded he act quickly. As he hesitated, something snapped inside me. I jumped up and started waving my arms around with all the suppressed intensity that had long before taken up permanent residence inside me:

> *"Don't sit there behind your beautiful desk and tell me there's nothing else you can give Art to save his life. There are drug stores everywhere in this country, and shelves filled with cures for everything. If there is nothing else, then get yourself out there and find something, or invent something. It cannot be okay that there is nothing you can do to help Art stay alive."*

I was aware I was railing at Art's doctor, the only person besides me who was doing anything to try and keep him alive, but that didn't matter. I wanted Art in the trial, and when I was done with my tirade, I gave the doctor all the proof he would need to convince whoever he had to that Art qualified for participation.

Once the trial started, I added *courier* to my list of new credentials, and for me it carried all the drama and intrigue of a spy novel. I would get the call I was waiting for—*"your package is in,"* the disembodied voice would say—and I would walk my excess energy down to another part of the city, to the dimly lit office of a doctor I didn't know and never met, whose assistant would hand over to me a white cardboard box that looked and felt as if it held a beautiful top-of-the-line man's dress shirt. Wordlessly, I would take it and, tucking it carefully under my arm, I would hail a cab to take me home with my precious package as fast as possible.

In a matter of weeks, Art started to gain weight and feel his strength return. His doctor was thrilled, telling me the drug was a *miracle*. I was happy enough with the results to thank him for making it happen as if it had been his idea all along.

After a few months, though, the gains turned to losses, and I became frightened of what must surely be coming next. One night, I cautiously explained to Art that I needed to tell my parents about his illness because we might need their help, and I asked him please to accept that. Very carefully, I did not tell him I was already certain *I* needed my parents to know what was happening. We were out of options. Art was going to die, and I was terrified.

The fears between us were palpable. He wept and pleaded as he tried to stop me, saying my parents would hate him when they found out he was infected, and I argued back that couldn't happen. I was sure I knew how they would react to such news, just as they always had. They loved him. In my family, if someone got sick or hurt, we pulled together, to help and show our love. My parents had always responded to the people they loved in just that way, and I was confident he had nothing to fear from them. When each of us was done telling the other what we believed to be true, I told him I could not give him this, not this one time. I needed my parents to know for my sake.

Even so, as I sat on the train to their home a few nights later—after Art and I had spoken only minimal words to each other in the days in between—I had a moment when I had to ask myself if I was doing the right thing. How could I be sure my parents, like many other people, wouldn't be so afraid of AIDS they would be unable to stand by him? How could such a thing as that, so unlike them, happen just because it was *this* disease? I tried to reassure myself it would not happen any other way. Then I tried to trust it.

We sat at their dining room table, the meeting place in my parents' home, and I told them, first, Art and I had decided to get married in a couple of weeks. After we chatted about that, I said, *"I also have to tell you Art is very ill and I don't know how much longer he is going to live."* I waited until I was sure they had absorbed what I said, and then I told them the short version of how we had gotten to this point:

"I need you to know this now because I'm going to need your help. I'm here against Art's wishes. He is afraid you won't want to have anything to do with him anymore if you know he has AIDS. We have not told anyone else, and I must ask you not to tell anyone. He doesn't want anyone to know."

I didn't start to cry until they started answering me, just as I knew they would.

When I got home, Art surprised me by asking anxiously what they said, and I told him about their part of our conversation. He seemed unconvinced but resigned.

A few days later they showed up at our door, gifts in hand and ready to work. They held Art and told him they loved him, saying, *"That's the only thing that matters between us."* He might need their help and love, and that's what they were there for. They delivered on their promise—even becoming AIDS activists themselves in the years after his death, always referencing how much they had loved him, their dearest son-in-law—and I was so grateful to see how Art flourished under a new kind of parental love he had never gotten before.

One day, we three were waiting for him as he walked painfully toward us down a long corridor to where we were standing. I felt the strong presence of three of us where, always before, there had only been me holding my breath, as if I could give him my strength for his journey—and then there were hugs and arms to lean on at the end of it. As we walked to the car, Art turned to my mother and I heard him say, *"Gee, Rho, why weren't you my mother all along?"*

...and then the secret told itself....and me

The actual end of keeping the secret started innocently. Instead of crashing down on me like a high wave as I had feared, it let me ride it for a long time before it delivered me, upright, onto a dry shoreline. One night, Anne, the facilitator of the Caregiver's Group, called to ask a favor of me.

"*I'm calling because there is an AIDS awareness conference at the college tomorrow, and a panel has been scheduled for four people to tell their stories of living with the virus.*" One person had gotten too sick to go and had cancelled, and Anne asked if I would be willing to talk about my experience in her place. Before she even got through explaining I was under no obligation to do so, I spurted out, "*Yes.*" I hadn't even taken the secret into consideration, but there was plenty of time left over through the long night of no-sleep that followed for me to wonder whatever it was that made me so sure I did the right thing.

The next morning, I walked into a lecture hall at New Paltz, filled, stadium-style, with almost 250 people. In very nearly the middle of those bleachers, I saw Anne and some of the members of the Group, my anchors. I chose to speak last on the panel out of respect for what I imagined the other three people, who were living with the virus, would have to tell.

I waited quietly, except for my pounding heart, as they spoke about what their lives were like since they learned they had been infected. Listening to them brought back so much from my own memories that I wanted to cry for them, for myself and for all of the young people sitting in that room. All of us were affected by the presence of the virus that had forced its way into our world. It was, as it has always been for me since, impossible not to be moved to watch and hear the telling of such stories as these. I have never been a person who can be dispassionate about the suffering of others, yet their telling revealed just how much our experiences mirrored each other, and I felt powerfully a part of them. I could only wonder how I could possibly have anything worthy of adding when they were done.

Then it was my turn, and I was standing at the lectern with a microphone, facing what looked like an arena full of expectant faces. They seemed to be cascading down from the ceiling to the floor on three sides around me, with no spaces between them. I had no idea what I was going to say. I looked at my Group smiling at me and, hoping not to cry, I shivered through a haltingly slow deep breath, to try and calm myself.

It was the secret, straight away, that showed up to tell them. "*I guess now I know what it must feel like to come out of the closet,*" I said.

"I feel as if I'm coming out of a closet right now as I stand here in front of you to tell you my husband Art died of AIDS three years ago." Then, impulsively, I turned to look behind me at the three people who had just spoken. I thanked them for the courage they had shown by telling us their stories. Everyone in the room acknowledged them with loving applause, and then I did cry.

I know they stopped applauding after that, but I have no idea what I said or how long I spoke, only that, afterward, the secret was out. The next thing I was aware of was applause for me and then, the panel completed, many people running down from their seats to shake my hand and wait in a line to talk with me. Everyone wanted to tell me how brave I was—*I* was brave. *I* was stunned. One woman asked if she could call me some time, and she held me in her arms as she wept. Then she told me her son, a student at another college, had just been diagnosed and nobody knew. She said I had given her courage to help him deal with that, to be able to tell people.

Later in the day, I was introduced to a health teacher at the middle school in my town. He said my story was important to tell young people, and he invited me to come and speak to his students, as well as to tell students in the high school. I accepted gratefully, as I would each invitation I received for years after that. I told my story over and over again, in all sorts of ways and to many different kinds of groups. While I could only hope each telling offered meaning for those generous enough to listen, I could feel for certain each telling brought a little more of me back into my life. What I didn't know—couldn't have known—was that it was also changing forever the balance of what would matter to me for the rest of my life.

High school health teachers often invited me to spend a day speaking to each of their eight section-classes sequentially. Sometimes I couldn't remember if I had just said what I was about to say or if I had actually said it in the hour before. I would laugh with the students about that. I found them, always, thoughtful and attentive, and most kind. Afterward, I would receive a great gift: a thick envelope filled with thank-you letters, each with its writer's own personal message to me. Every letter touched the part of me that needed healing, bringing fresh air to replace the heavy, stale emptiness that had been weighting me down inside. It seemed ironic they would thank me, when I knew it was I who would never forget the love and support they so generously gave.

My talks with the students became an important truth that telling had to teach me. In our communities filled with the common experiences of humans, telling is much more than the fear we hold onto when we allow it to isolate us from each other. Telling is more than its simple dictionary definition, much greater than the sum of its parts. It is an offer of hope and help brought in on the air that carries our common words. It can be a thank-you for allowing me to tell you of my personal experience and your acknowledgment that I am not alone nor rendered invisible by the extraordinary events I may have lived through.

I found it easy to tell these young strangers about Art and our life together. Looking through their eyes as they listened, I could see for the first time how my story was also theirs, as it was everyone's. I saw how listening to another person's story can be provocative, and I understood how telling—and listening—are both acts of love. Rather than keeping me locked in my fearful isolation, telling was making it possible for me to see how connected we all are to one another. Telling is not anything to be treated lightly, neither by tellers nor listeners.

Finally, I felt brave enough to start to tell the secret to the people who I could not have told before. I travelled to Vermont to tell my sister and her family, and we wept together as I explained the promise that had kept me unable to talk about it before. She told me how she had felt when she happened to call to chat one morning a few days before Art died, and I had told her, for the first time, he was gravely ill and I thought he was going to die. She had responded with panic, shrieking when I could not tell her what was wrong and shouting I must get other opinions, talk with other doctors. She had offered to talk with friends of hers, doctors and other medical professionals who might be able to advise me. But she had not been told the truth. I had not allowed my parents to tell anyone, and I had been impatient, too frantic in my own concerns and, finally, trapped into being dishonest with her. I knew I was hurting her, but my own need was greater. Coldly, I had said, *"Please, just trust me; there are things you cannot know"* and *"I'm sorry,"* before I hung up and shut her out—when I most needed her to stand alongside me.

One night, several months after I started speaking in the schools, I was sitting at the center of a long restaurant table filled with people I had recently met in my town. The woman who sat directly across from me suddenly turned to me and asked, *"How did your husband die?"* Startled, I took a deep breath and squeezed my hands in my lap. *"AIDS,"* I said. *"He died of the AIDS virus."*

It seemed that everyone stopped talking then, and I felt all the eyes and ears at the table suddenly on my face. No one said a word. I tried not to look as if I was challenging anyone, nor as if I was embarrassed. I remember I was very concerned to have a *neutral* look on my face, but I needn't have thought about it so much. The beat skipped and the woman took her eyes off me, saying nothing. She turned back to the others and started to talk about her teenagers and how fraught their lives were with dangers we had never known when we were growing up. I wondered if I had met her children in their health classes, if she was thinking in that long moment, *"oh, so this must be that woman they spoke of"*. I had mixed feelings but the group soon returned to normal, and I was content to have been just another piece of conversation at the dinner table.

As I continued to tell, some people surprised me by crying on my behalf, while others surprised me by falling away and disappearing from my life. I tried not to keep a count, just to keep on going for my own sake. Not everyone could embrace my news, or me, and I was grateful enough that no one tried to use what I had to say to hurt my feelings. Every telling made it easier to breathe into the empty silence inside, filling me until I could feel myself fully returned into my own body. Slowly, I began to look ahead to a time when I could accept what had happened to me as a simple truth rather than a terrible judgment against my loving. Telling had become my guide, holding my arm as I walked myself back into my life.

One day, I was in the familiar surroundings of a high school I had visited many times. As always, I had asked to speak on a Friday, when I could specifically address young people who were looking forward to a weekend filled with fun and romance.

"How did your husband get AIDS?" a bright young man asked me. It was the first time I had been asked that question, and I had not anticipated it. I was not prepared to respond.

I took the slow deep breath I had taught myself would calm my body down as I tried to find what there was inside me to answer him. *"I hope I will not offend you by saying I don't feel comfortable telling you that."* I explained it wasn't my information, and it mattered very much to me to respect Art's privacy. I said Art had not wanted anyone to know because he had been ashamed of having gotten infected with the virus, and I had promised to keep his secret for him. I expected that would be the end of the matter.

He demanded more. *"Don't you think you have an obligation to tell us what he did to get it, so we can know what not to do?"*

Even as I felt a pang of hurt by the sharp carelessness implied in his question, I knew he had put me on more solid ground by challenging me as he did. We had spent the first part of my presentation reviewing what most students had heard many times in the age of AIDS: the routes of transmission and the ways we can protect ourselves against becoming infected. Knowing that, I knew how I wanted to answer him:

> *"I'm here because I believe I have an obligation to tell you everything I know about what you need to know to protect yourself. And I'm willing to talk about anything that involves my experience beyond that. But, if you're asking if I have an obligation to tell you someone else's private information—which they might not want you to know—then, no. I think I have a greater obligation to protect the other person's confidential information."*

He glared at me while I waited to hear his further response. Then, choosing not to say anything else, he allowed me to move on to the next question. Although I was relieved, I was also terribly sad to think I had failed to give him what he had asked of me. Had I failed him?

For many years after that exchange, I continued to feel defensive about what I saw as a dilemma I could not resolve. I talked with my friends who also worked in prevention education, and I asked how they might have responded.

"*Confidentiality is the law,*" they all said, and some of them were angry I had been challenged at all, even that the teacher had not stepped in to support my position. While I appreciated what they said—and even though I knew I had answered the young man honestly—our interaction had sparked a growing need in me to be as certain as I could that I had answered his question in the best way I could and not merely run away from it.

My conversations have always been about who we are as humans together. I ask that we examine, each of us for ourselves, the balance between taking good care of ourselves and settling the question of how much risk we are willing to engage in order to have what we want in our lives. For me, that has always been one of the great questions.

As I continued to share my stories and listen to the stories of others, I became curious about something else I found in telling. The more we talked, the more we became connected to each other. It was as if the process of telling itself was making us care about each other, even when I was certain I would not see most of those people a second time. The good feelings were extraordinary, as loving as any I have known.

Connection knows no fear of "telling"

Our connections can break down the suspicion and competition that makes enemies of natural allies. When we realize ourselves as part of a whole, we can look at each other fearlessly. We can see that each of us is unique and know that we are not in competition for a limited number of life's rewards. Knowing our uniqueness, we could find ourselves eager to hear what the others have to tell, accepting the ways we are different without any need to demand some tell more for our sakes, whether they want to or not.

Every one of the rest of us could be your first and most natural ally. We can take comfort from each other even as we offer comfort to one another. We can feel good through our connections—as nature intends—and we can see how sameness creates and supports ample space to hold so many extraordinary individuals.

Our brains have evolved in a way that actually affords us a whole variety of tools with which we can connect with one another, without having to think about it. Telling is one of the ways. It makes us feel good, it is good for us and it may be even more than that: it may be vital to our survival.

We have something called mirror neurons. They are the nerves in our brains that are hard at work every time we communicate eye-to-eye with one or more people, with or without words. It's a fact: we all meet one or more *"others"* from outside and within their skin.

Why would we have such a thing as mirror neurons that get activated, not only by our own actions by our observations of other people's actions at the same time as yours? For one thing, mirror neurons might enable us to learn from someone else's experience something that could be valuable for us to know without our actually having to experience what the other person did. Wasn't that one of the things I was trying to accomplish by telling my story to other people? This is just good sense if you connect it to our brains not distinguishing between actual, positive feelings and ones we imagine.

As an example, think about the look of disgust. It's a necessary emotion in a world in which survival is a fundamental goal. It is believed we first experienced disgust to keep us from eating spoiled food that could be harmful. Without refrigeration in the jungle, how else would our forebears have known they should avoid eating animal meat before they were all wiped out by food poisoning?

Today, disgust continues to be one of our most powerful emotions, and we can catch it from one another just by seeing the look of it on someone else's face. Try making the look of disgust on your face to see how powerful it feels to you, even in simulation; then try showing it to someone else to get their response. We comprehend the emotions or feelings of other people even when they are pretending the expressions of those emotions and feelings on their faces. Try it. Try to mimic someone's expression and see if you can feel what you thought they were expressing. This is human nature, and it has its own good reasons for being. When someone shares their emotions and feelings, we want to acknowledge and even help them. You are more likely to rush to another person's defense, as they are to yours, if one of you sees a look of hurt or sad, or threatened, and you also want to feel happy if they are happy. When two of us share these feelings, we are both more inclined to have an investment in each other's wellbeing. Certainly we see just this sense of connection bringing people together to help one another generously when there is a natural, or unnatural, disaster.

It works something like this. When two or more of us are communicating, our mirror neurons begin, automatically, to align with each other until they are operating in parallel. This is called *"looping"*, and looping is what enables your feelings, thoughts and actions to get *"in sync"* with another person's feelings, thoughts and actions. If it could, your brain would tell you it's bonding you and the other person.

This mirroring helps you read the other person's intentions without you being aware it's happening. You will also understand the social implications of what they are saying and doing. Those are important clues that enable you to anticipate what will happen next in the conversation, so you will be prepared and know how to react. If I am talking, your eyes might start to fill with tears for me even an instant before I begin to sob, because you are completely connected to what I am telling you, without your having to think about it. You would be anticipating my tears and feeling my sadness as if it was your own—which is exactly the way you would feel it, automatically. You will be inclined and prepared to support me with your reactions to what I am saying and doing. I, in my turn, would feel and do no less for you. When we are invested in each other's wellbeing, we are more likely to help each other.

Perhaps one alternative to living in your fear might be to create safe places in which we can have conversations about who we are and dream of becoming. There, in the safety of our communities, we can agree to bear witness for one another and share our wisdom, so each of us can realize what is simply true for us. We can practice fearlessness with one another, and we can reinforce fearlessness for those *"others"* who are striving to achieve it for themselves.

In short, we can empower each other to take comfort in the sameness that humans share. That can free us to run our own lives on our own terms, even as we enjoy the security of knowing we are part of something bigger. The comfort of connection can be as a solid block for our foundation, expanding rather than restricting us.

If we think about our brains, we can easily imagine why such connections might have been selected by nature as a way to encourage us to support one another. After all, we are living and working closely together to keep our communities and the humans in them thriving. As a matter of biological fact, connecting us is one great way for our highly sophisticated brains to work together to ensure the survival of our species; by linking us together, nature ensures we want to, and can, enjoy the work of keeping ourselves and each other alive. Telling one another about ourselves, and sharing our experiences, then, is a primary way we save our species.

Connection is a fundamental truth about humans. Our central nervous systems have evolved in response to the social structures our forebears invented as far back as when they started creating communities. It is easy to think of our own social interactions as intense, complex and even confusing, yet we have brains—our biological computers—that can routinely do more calculations per second than any digital computer ever invented. Looking at evolution is nature's way of attempting to keep up with the enormous changes we humans have generated over eons of time. We can readily see we have, in fact, arrived ready and well-prepared to keep up with ourselves.

While none of us is aware of what our brains are doing, we certainly can feel when we have become connected to another person. That feeling is powerful, and we enjoy those connections. That's not a coincidence: one particular reason connection makes us feel good is because it creates empathy. Empathy is the feeling of two people knowing how the other feels, as well as knowing they are being seen.

This may surprise you, but empathy can also cause you to react when you're alone, when you're reading or watching a movie or a television show, even a commercial—good news for those of us who are astounded to feel our eyes well up at a cheesy sales pitch on television: that was precisely the goal of that well-thought-out pitch. Empathy can even cause you to react to one or more complete strangers you might have in your sights on the other side of a room.

I conducted an unintentional unscientific experiment about empathy one afternoon at my gym, while I was passing the time on a treadmill. Without even being consciously aware of it, I was idly staring at a man across the room who was talking on his cell phone while he straddled his treadmill. Suddenly, he—*and I*—swept up the pinky fingers on our right hands in the same motion at the same moment; my reverie was broken and I just had to laugh. You may have had the same experience without noticing it happened to you: the expression on your face may have changed, perhaps one or both eyebrows raised up or your lips moved, seemingly inexplicably but, in fact, by an automatic prompt from your brain. If that's ever happened, you were responding to what your eyes were *"picking up"* from some other person, even though you were not consciously engaged with that person.

Perhaps it is ironic, then, that there are those among us who prefer to think of empathy as merely an annoying reflection of human weakness. In the presence of an expression of empathy, they may scoff at what they perceive as a flaw in character, something we should diligently guard against lest it runs rampant over our lives and leaves us open to accusations of being soft. Have you ever heard anyone expressing such a sentiment? Am I alone in wondering why some of us seem to want to discredit the very things about us that make us the most human: *our emotions?* At the very least, empathy, another human tool, makes us feel good, naturally, so why deny it?

Knowing empathy is one of a number of biologically-based survival strategies, and that it operates automatically within you, frees you from having to think about it, in the same way understanding, even vaguely, how intuition frees you to trust those messages and that voice in your head. Empathy, like all your other responses to what you perceive, is simply doing what it has evolved to do to meet the needs of the human you are.

Imagine yourself having no empathy, no ability to *read* other people, never experiencing the chance to infer something important about someone from their actions. Without these extraordinary abilities, every action would seem to be random, and life would be as chaos. As it is, you have many fewer things to worry about in your busy life because your neurons just continue to do what they do best. They set you free to do the hard work of thinking about yourself.

While we're at it, have you ever been tempted to think of all those other people out there as competition and not much else? Do you ever wish you could make the world see you as the unique person you know yourself to be? Do you worry there may just be too many of us around for you to distinguish yourself from the mass of others?

Everywhere we look there are countless others, and we all seem to be engaged in what we ironically call the *"race"* to make our lives the best and the most, even if we have no idea of what that is. Are we in a race with one another, and is a race merely the predictable result of there being so many humans on earth? Is that what drives us to distinguish ourselves from all the others, until we're colliding like punch-drunk atoms in our frenzy to resist our brains' best efforts to connect us?

Could we, at the heart of it, be made uncomfortable, not by our differences but by a *sameness* that feels like a threat to our individuality? If so, could we possibly invent another way to think about our *sameness* that wouldn't feel competitive? In reality, each of us is unique, a one-of-a-kind human. If we looked, would we find our *fears* behind our resistance to the bonding and good feelings nature affords us? Could fear have gotten itself mixed up in our natural curiosity? Are we fearful that, if we tell others too much about who we are, we could give them an advantage in the *race?*

You may remember the fear we nurture with our own thinking brains. It's the feeling we also use to limit ourselves, to hold ourselves back or keep us in check. Perhaps this fear also underlies our questions about whether we deserve to be distinguished from everyone else. What if we were to step up to the challenge, dare to talk to one other person and, then, another and *"others"* after that, allowing our brains to connect us together until we feel good all the time? Would we be able to realize our potentials both individually and together?

Holding on to the secret I inherited from Art kept me in isolation for years, at a great cost to my own wellbeing. When telling came to force me out, it found me as a person who kept her thoughts, and many of her most personal questions to herself. I was self-convinced that was the only way I could protect myself in a world in which I feared revealing the secret I carried. As long as I told no one, I could believe I would never have to risk discovering that *"others"* might disappoint and even hurt me.

Perhaps I had simply forgotten *not telling* the secret would cut me off from those others who are most like me, my own kind and my best natural resources. By not telling, I deprived myself of knowing what they might have had to tell me about what they learned before me, even as I deprived *"others"* who might need to know what I knew, after me. More importantly, not telling because I was afraid of some imaginary consequences deprived me of the very same good feelings I needed so badly.

When I was finally all done telling, I saw that telling itself had turned me into a person who would no longer be satisfied to live in the silence of isolation and invisibility. I know now that, by allowing ourselves to communicate with one another about things that arise from our experiences, we not only better serve ourselves but also help the world in which we spend our lives, our common ground. Surely each of us has at least one thing we alone can add to the communal wisdom of human experience.

8

Raising Healthy Voices

"Descartes did not quite get it right in stating, 'I think, therefore I am'; he would have been more on the mark if he had said, 'I feel, therefore I am.'" (See Dacher Keltner, Bibliography)

The little red-haired boy who sat several seats to my right in the circle we made with his fifth-grade classmates asked me, tentatively, "Did you get infected, too?"

"No, I didn't," I answered him, gently, noticing with curiosity that my face was trying to recreate the same earnest look he had on his. "I don't know why I didn't, but I didn't."

He looked down and away and I could see he wasn't finished, so I waited. He was thinking hard about something, and the rest of us were silent, as if we were holding our breath to leave space for his concentration.

Suddenly his whole body brightened and he bolted straight up. "I know," he said, looking at me again. "You didn't get sick so you could come here and tell us how to save us."

He was beaming at me, obviously proud of what he had been able to figure out. For my part, I wanted to walk right over to where he sat, lift him up in my arms and hold him. I wanted to weep into his little shoulder for the impact of his words. His generous spirit lifted me along with himself, and I could feel, as his teacher and friends nodded happily in agreement as I thanked him for saying such a lovely thing, that we were all sharing the same good feeling. I knew it was the feeling of connection. By then, it had become the pot of gold I always found waiting for me at the end of every telling.

For a long time, I didn't know what to call that feeling, and I could think of no one I could ask if they knew what it was that seems to hold people together. I only knew I could count on the feeling being there, over and over again, in every room in which I was privileged to speak. Sometimes I could feel it building until the room nearly vibrated with it. At other times, I would only notice it must have crept in while I was completely engaged. Always, it made me feel I was in the place I most wanted to be, with just that group of people, talking about who we are and what matters to us. This time, I was certain the little red-haired boy's profoundly loving consideration of me had brought the precious feeling of connection, and we all had a share in it. I had started to understand the most wonderful truth of what many years of telling my stories had given me: these connections that form between people are real, even if they are invisible and temporary.

When I first started telling, I had neither expectations nor aspirations for any outcomes that might flow from what I had to say. I knew only too well we all make our own decisions about how we will act, and we do so on the basis of our individual needs and motivations. I made the decision to talk about what happened to me because it was all I had to offer to inspire and encourage other people to keep themselves safe from the AIDS virus. That seemed the most important thing I could be doing with my life. It was a mission for me, a new purpose, and I had thought that, even if the only contribution I could make was to provide food for thought, I would be well-satisfied to have had that opportunity. I knew I would be walking unfamiliar terrain, and the feelings of connection I found along the way seemed a precious reward for my commitment to show up every time.

Even so, showing up at unfamiliar places to tell strangers my personal stories was a surprising turn of events in my life. As the savvy, street-smart city-girl I once was, I had long before convinced myself I would succeed at not looking bad in the world if I practiced holding back, so I had resisted a natural inclination to offer too much information about myself to anyone. For many years, I was the sophisticated cynic who scoffed about people who joined groups in which they shared what I imagined were the most personal facts of their lives, either in the name of therapy or in some self-help *'60s* revelatory word-concerts I was convinced had no value for me. I could not have known what I was missing. Nor could I have even imagined the definition of a modern, sophisticated human depends on just such connections as I had assiduously avoided with my prejudice and bias.

Over time, as I've said, my telling transformed me. The message it gave led me to what I know now: even the simplest talking between people, at every opportunity, gives us a unique access to feelings we humans need to support our wellbeing. It is just that simple. Perhaps it is because so many of us have stopped talking directly with one another that young people have been driven to create dramatic new forms of communication with their technologies, strangers motivated to find others to bond with, perhaps without even knowing what drives them to seek it. If so, then they are surely the wiser, for those of us who deny the existence, much less the benefits of connecting with *others* surely deprive themselves of both the joy and the extraordinary chance to support both their own and the wellbeing of our species at the same time.

I am certain the feeling of connection is one of the most powerful things we humans can create, so powerful it can overcome our natural fears of people we do not know. I have seen it there between the perfect stranger I was at the start—an anonymous speaker from across the country who had come with a story to tell—and the *others*, who came so generously to listen. Through hundreds of conversations with groups, people of different sizes, ages and backgrounds, I have watched as the feeling has overridden even those deep-seated, natural avoidance triggers we typically arm ourselves with in the guise of self-protection.

One night, thinking about that feeling, I found an old memory in my mind's eye. It was about a young man I saw one night, many years before, while I was standing in a long line of weary people waiting for a bus that would take us the rest of the way home from work. I was barely out of my teens, and because I was pretty far back in the line, I could see in the dwindling light of dusk that most of the people ahead of me were much older. We waited a long, chilly time for the bus to arrive, and when it finally pulled up to the curb the young man, who was not waiting in line but in a storefront entrance where, perhaps, he had been keeping warm nearby, soundlessly appeared. He walked directly up to the front of the line and got himself onto the bus before anyone else.

Although I could easily see he had not pushed anyone aside, nor did he or anyone else seem to say anything, I was anticipating people's annoyed reactions, including my own, as we competed for the few empty seats. Instead, I found myself suddenly standing as if I were in the young man's shoes.

From my shifted perspective, I knew he hadn't been disrespectful, and he hadn't been aggressive. He had been trying to make us notice him. I was sure of it. He looked as unexceptional as the rest of us, as we must have appeared to him, and to one another. I could almost feel him feeling invisible, and I knew he felt that way much of the time, longing to be seen.

Instead of annoyed, I suddenly felt empathy. I *saw* him, and I felt how he might have felt. How many times had I known just that same frustration, an almost palpable aching for other people to have a reason to notice *me*, to see that *I* was there among them, and I was worthy of their attention? What despair I had felt at those times, to think there was nothing distinctive about me, as if for no reason I could think of I had somehow been relegated to go unnoticed, to live my entire life without having any power to impact other people's lives.

As I finally boarded the bus, my mind's eye saw me sitting next to him and starting up a conversation. I imagined myself telling him I had noticed him, and I had been thinking about him as the line moved forward, maybe even that I applauded the way he had gotten everyone's attention for an instant, without offending anyone. He had broken into our private reveries before allowing us to return to the safety of our own minds. I wanted to tell him I, too, had often wished I could do something like that, even just one thing to get other people to notice, to make myself feel, for once, I had been seen by the *others*. I didn't do any of that, of course, because as a young person myself—I was only a few years older than he—I was much more invested in looking good in front of strangers and not *making waves* or a *spectacle* of myself. I would never have taken a chance as big as initiating a conversation with a stranger, as I would never have had the courage to do what he did; I would have never done anything that called any attention to me. Nor would I have ever thought that doing so could satisfy any longing I had to be noticed, or heard. It never occurred to me that, if I had we might have made some kind of connection before we parted, or it might have felt good to both of us to know we had shared something of ourselves, strangers who would never see each other again.

Rather, I told myself, I could surely only have a conversation like that in the privacy of my own mind. As soon as I started to think so, my mind raced to fill up with all the reasons I needed to reassure myself conversation between us was impossible. In the safety of my imagination, the young man now said harsh things to me when I tried to make conversation with him, and I was glad I had not taken the risk. When I managed to pull myself back from the brink of connection by justifying my decision not to talk with anyone, I tried to put him out of my mind altogether. Yet, I thought about him all the way home that night, and the image of him, as well as the extent to which I felt powerfully connected to him in spite of myself, never quite went out of my mind.

These days, as an older woman, I am likely to strike up a conversation with the people around me, on the subways and buses, and on supermarket lines. I easily compliment a piece of beautiful jewelry or a scarf, or a handsome tie without any agenda other than feeling good about a brief connection with another person. Sometimes, on a crowded, rush-hour subway car, I'll look around at all the people avoiding each other's eyes, and, in my mind, I wish them all a very happy day, just for the fun of it.

Have you ever had a moment when you felt inexplicably drawn to a stranger? How did it feel? What did you decide to do about it? What did you think about? Did you ever wonder afterward how you might have felt if you had made another choice and acted differently on your feeling?

The rest of the story

What I could not have known, before I started *telling*, is that connection itself has survived because it proves to be an optimal way to enhance and strengthen the common bonds between us. Nature may have determined long ago that connection was way too important for our thinking brains to fret about: connection has been hard-wired directly into our brains. Indeed, it is one of a variety of distinctive and often surprising behaviors that seem both to spring from and to trigger our emotions. While that may seem to be an extraordinarily gracious means to an end, in nature it is merely one of many ways we have evolved to ensure our species will survive. To put it simply, evolution has filled us with things we normally say and do, and feel with one another, that were all designed to invest us in each other's lives.

Even when we might not appreciate what the purpose of such an individual investment might be, connection will occur. So, it is lucky for us we do not have to appreciate it, nor to think about how it happens. Connection occurs between us automatically. Regardless of what we think is going on between us, or how we feel about it, and what we believe we might prefer to choose instead, connection is the trigger that makes us care about the wellbeing of *others* so we and our communities—which encompass the world of humans—may thrive.

Learning about how our lives might occur to our brains, I have begun to think of each one of us as a completely self-contained system, perfect in our construction. With a little of our own attention, we can keep functioning in a fine and carefully-tuned biological balance that maintains a desirable quality of life. That biological balance has been called *homeostasis,* and it is an extraordinary ability we all have. It enables our bodies to sense when something is out of balance so we can react quickly, either consciously (by eating) or unconsciously (by falling asleep), to restore the balance that is our wellbeing. So critical is this physiological balance that our homeostasis is maintained without our awareness. It continues to operate today as it has since our very first days, when it maintained the homeostasis of the first, tiniest living single-cell life-form that existed on earth, long before humans ever appeared.

Recently, one neurophysiologist has proposed homeostasis itself has evolved into something more than the maintenance of optimal bodily functioning. According to Dr. Antonio Damasio's theory, as we started to live together in community our thinking brains became ever more sophisticated in order to meet our emerging needs. He gives equal weight to two kinds of homeostasis that he speculates operate within our bodies. Just as our physiological balance is maintained by our unconscious regulation of our biological systems (of which every breath we take is a perfect example), so is a societal and cultural balance maintained by our conscious regulation. Where they part company is here: the first continues its original purpose of maintaining our bodies' physiological wellbeing, automatically.

By comparison, the second homeostasis is not automatic. It relies on us to carry out its mission. Of course, as always where our consciousness is required, we shall have to pay attention and play our part deliberately if this newer homeostatic balance is to be maintained. We'll have to act, and we'll probably have to stop every so often to evaluate how well we are maintaining the wellbeing of our society.

This more recent homeostasis asks us if we are being effective stewards, and whether we are fostering refinement. It can easily seem, today, that many of the world's people are immersed in societies in which they lack confidence and would hesitate to answer these questions with a positive expression.

Is this merely a matter of not reaching our potential, or is there more to it than that? Could we find and agree on those things and ways we might logically assume will engender the precious state of the state's wellbeing? What would it take?

Damasio suggests it would require, at the start, that we humans will be at the ready with our emotions and feelings. Indeed, the very reason we are able to be aware of all the things we know as belonging to us and no one else—things like our bodies and minds—is because these things, which he believes signify both a profound and tangible presence, as well as a pivotal moment in biological evolution. This shift transformed our unconscious minds into conscious ones, and consciousness is precisely what I have in my mind when I suggest the ability to live our lives deliberately is by far the most powerful state of mind we can reach. In a deliberate life, each of us would participate consciously in the very processes of being alive; it would not be enough for us merely to go along, whether we did so by choice or under the misperception we lack the power to do anything else.

In order to utilize our consciousness to live deliberate lives, we'll need to be able to see how central feelings and emotions are to our present-day selves, and begin to appreciate all the ways nature has ingrained connection in us. In the early years of humans on earth, there were what science calls *basic* emotions. These continue to operate as they always have throughout history: automatically. You probably won't even realize you have had a basic emotion until after it subsides: it will prompt you, immediately, to take action without engaging your thought processes at all (for instance, fear will force you to freeze or stay to fight, or flee; disgust will ensure you will not eat that spoiled food). They have to force you in order to keep you safe, and they will not risk your having to think something through before deciding what to do. If you are truly in danger, you will likely be saved by your very own self—so you can trust you will come to a complete halt when you run out into traffic and hear that sudden loud truck horn.

You also know that's very different from the way your feelings operate, because you know all about your feelings. You know they're filled with intensity, and passion, and they can seem to be moving you all over the place at the same time. By comparison, you may appreciate not having to think about your emotions. You know they have important roles to play, but if you don't need to think about them, why should you?

Well, you might have been able to think that way centuries ago, but your emotions have also evolved. Like everything else that changed about humans as we moved along our way to the present, new emotions developed, with an impressive complexity all of their own. Some of the things that flow from your emotions today can be the very things about yourself that make you the most uncomfortable, even leave you wondering, at times, why it is you might feel like the last person to know what is going on with you. It is understandable to think that emotions might sometimes lead to irrational feelings, ones that seem to undermine your freedom, entire make-up and your equanimity, as well as your very rationality itself.

Despite how they might feel, emotions are deeply embedded in your life and will likely remain so for the rest of your days. They assist in handling the crucial situations that arise—you know what yours are, and sometimes, you feel like your brain cannot always help. Each emotion offers you a unique adventure and provides guidance that has historically been effective in managing the challenges of human life—so important that it has become a fundamental, automatic part of your nervous system.

It almost sounds as if your evolved emotions are still operating pretty much as emotions always have, and many of them do. They're still sending you prompts to act on. So, what is different?

Today, what triggers both the prompts and the actions those prompts suggest make your emotions dramatically different from our ancient, basic emotions, and that's only logical. Your evolved emotions have to be more sophisticated than those early one's prehistoric humans experienced, because they have to support your complex life. So, although they can still cause your heart to race and your skin to break out in a sweat, they are less likely to force you to act automatically in a predetermined way.

Instead, your newer, evolved emotions will pass through your thinking brain on their way to being acted upon. It's likely they meant to take a turn from your feelings—more evidence your feelings are working very well, just as they are supposed to—and you know what that means: Your brain will be calling on you to decide what action you will take in response to the situations your sophisticated emotions will reveal. Your emotions will always send you just the right intuition when you want to do the right thing, like when you need fairness, kindness, virtue, and certainly harm. These will be the standards your evolved emotions will be concerned with meeting as you participate in your world.

Powerful moral guides

Emotions are often described as strong moral guides. But, wait. Don't we usually think of morality as having its basis in our thoughtful deliberations, in the judgments, choices and conscious decisions we can make at any time?

Precisely. One of the ways we know ourselves to be moral is we think about morality. For our brains, though, morality only becomes something to think about *after* our emotions prompt us to think about it.

You could say we are moral beings because we have evolved, because whenever we are called upon to use our thinking brains, something about that process is working well. At the risk of repeating myself, that's because, when we rely on our emotions as powerful moral guides, we enhance both our own wellbeing and that of our society.

Does having a preference for morality mean we always choose to act morally, all the time? You might be inclined to answer it is obvious that not everyone does, and certainly there would be more than enough evidence to support your opinion. That is one big difference between our old, basic emotions and our evolved emotions. When we get an emotional prompt today, we get to think about how we will respond to it.

Although it may not be obvious, we are all being moved toward moral action; there is important evidence that evolution values moral action above the other possible choices. In fact, evolution has stacked the deck in favor of morality by providing us with two distinct methods for making moral judgments. This bias toward nature's preference appears to be a defining feature of our emotions today.

The first method for reaching more judgments involves reasoning, which we recognize as thinking. When we consider how to act in morally-charged situations, we must evaluate all factors.

The second way we reach moral judgments is much more like a variation on the theme of our old, basic, automatic, emotional prompts; it's pretty straightforward. Emotions always show up in our facial expressions. Think of it as an added push to do the right thing, or, at least, to give you second thoughts if you might be inclined not to.

You can experience the way this one works yourself. Remember disgust, that powerful, basic emotion? It makes for an easy experiment. Think about whatever is the most disgusting thing you can imagine and, when you have it clearly in your mind, run to a mirror. You'll probably find your version of the look of disgust right there on your face.

Of course, any emotion that shows up automatically on your face will also show up on the face of any other person, especially one who may be trying to convince you to do something he or she actually knows is not moral. You might want to keep in mind you have an extraordinary ability to recognize deception *instinctively*—instinct, by the way, is another one of those aspects of being human that you do not have to learn. It acts as a powerful motivation or impulse, and because it is so powerful, it makes evident that which you will see in the other person's face: he knows he is offering less than the sum of the words he would have you believe. You will even see it in his face without being consciously aware of seeing it. You will know it instinctively. If there's a hard part to all of this, it must surely be that you have to learn to trust what your eyes are seeing.

This extraordinary ability of yours, to know at a glance when a person's intention does not match the words he is speaking, is there so that, when someone is trying to convince you he is trustworthy when he is not, you will be less likely to be misled by his words. In fact, in order to be misled, you will actually have to talk yourself out of knowing the truth your eyes are revealing to you.

Your emotions are your preemptive alert for dishonesty and your ability to be suspicious can be thought of as a variation on the theme of connection. You wouldn't want to connect with a person you could not trust, would you? Your brain knows that, so it instinctively and relentlessly assesses everyone you meet to determine their trustworthiness. You don't have to give it another thought. Your brain's assessment is ongoing, without your awareness. All you have to do is trust your instincts.

Are you starting to see a pattern here? You may want to spend a little time thinking about how much you trust yourself. You have a full panoply of emotions telling you how important it is.

The purpose of emotions in our lives is to help and support us as we attempt to live together in ever-more complex communities—the very same purpose emotions have had since the very first time two people came together to share their resources. I like to think of that first time as the dawning of connection between humans.

Even more than supporting the commitments you make, your emotions make it possible for you to distinguish which commitments you *want* to make. It is unlikely, for instance, you will want to make a commitment to whatever it was you thought about that put that look of disgust on your face.

As you undoubtedly know from your own experience, words, by themselves, can be unreliable in helping you recognize people you can trust, so it's a good thing your emotions evolved to ensure you would have another way to know what you need to know in suspicion-arousing situations. Unlike language, emotions don't rely on words. They give you plenty of opportunities to get really clear about what they are trying to tell you. All those things are working on your behalf to get you to the *right* decision. Just pay attention, and trust you can rely on yourself.

What would happen if your attention wandered off? *Mother Nature* would attempt to bring you back into your *right* mind. It's been said all conversations travel along two roads simultaneously, a rational road made of words, and another, that underlies the conversation. One way or the other, nothing will escape you as long as you remember you can count on your natural abilities, your senses, to tell and show you what you need to know.

We constantly reveal our feelings through spontaneous facial expressions, gestures, eye contact, and similar cues.

If you're starting to realize the importance connection plays in your life, maybe you can now begin to allow it. It is this synchrony and resonance you are striving for, even unconsciously, in all your conversations, because they are the clues you are communicating with a person you can trust. When we allow these aspects of ourselves to do their jobs as they are intended, the benefits of connection can be there for us at the end of all our conversations. That is the way it's supposed to work. That is the way we are supposed to *allow* it to work.

You could say your emotions have evolved to impact you at the intuitive level in order to encourage you to act in your own best interests, because it is in your best interests to maintain your homeostasis, your wellbeing. Yet, there in the valley between getting an emotional prompt and contemplating an action to take, your creative thinking brain is also likely to be conjuring up all sorts of other possibilities for you to choose from. Some of these other possibilities might be created by your worst fears, so perhaps it would be helpful to remind yourself emotions don't undermine ethical behavior. You have a hard-wired moral preference, but you may also want to keep in mind that, sometimes, you might choose to ignore your emotional prompts. Like your inner voice, emotions will not force you to act in your best interests. You always have free will. You alone get to decide, consciously, whether and how to act on the message. That's why trusting yourself to take good care of yourself is so important.

Reading this, you might be thinking that using *reason* to subvert what you know instinctively must surely be like moving in a universe gone mad. Why would you restrict yourself by choosing to live solely within your rational mind when so much more than that is available to you? What benefit would be had in ignoring the input of emotions and feelings that arise in you over and over again for the very specific purpose of helping you live well? Your emotions are hard-wired into you to be a guidance system, meant to sustain you in situations when it really matters that you take moral actions. Why would you undermine your best self?

Why indeed? As you well know, to say emotions are *"wired into our nervous systems"* is to emphasize their importance in evolution's scheme to keep whatever works for human survival. Think of yourself joking it was a good thing your head was attached this morning or you might have forgotten to bring it with you.

Emotions are attached. They're not stored on an external hard drive you have to remember to bring along.

Nor did evolution stop at *hard-wiring*. It went further, giving you a whole network of activities, responses and characteristics, a great variety of emotional paths you can take to connect with everyone else. Even as they may surprise you, you are intimately familiar with these aspects of being you. You may not typically think of such things as laughter, dance, teasing or embarrassment as important supporting players in your emotional life, yet they are all there to enable and support connections between humans. For all the years of human existence so far, they have performed their jobs without your even realizing they have such a purpose. You may think you do some of them for fun, or you may have no idea why you have to be plagued by others of them, but one of the answers is clear. They cause you to become invested in other people's wellbeing. They motivate you to rely on *others* for help and support, as well as to turn to, and be turned to by *others* in friendship and love. There is something here for everyone, a way each of us can connect with one or more *others*. Let's start with laughter, perhaps the most serious response of them all.

Laughter

Who doesn't enjoy a good laugh? We say laughter makes us feel good, and laughter is contagious. When I was a teenager, I listened, along with a group of friends, to a recording of one man laughing. That's all he did, without music and without any apparent triggers or prompts. He just laughed through the whole recording, and his laughter got more and more explosive as he went along. As we started listening, it seemed weird and a little uncomfortable. Someone might have let out a polite giggle, and someone else a stray guffaw, but before long, we were seriously invested in full-out, tears-in-the-eyes howling laughter right along with him, and we kept laughing long after he stopped. We never knew what made him laugh, but we surely knew we laughed long and hard over nothing more than the sheer contagion of his laughter.

Contagion is a good attribute in an emotion. We laugh when we hear others laugh because our mirror neurons are triggered to respond in kind. You may remember your mirror neurons build loops between you and *others* as you interact, and loops create empathy, the feeling of involvement, connection. Laughter is "crucial for communal living.*" He calls it a "gateway to the realm of human imagination," an "opening

---

*   Dacher Keltner, *Born to be Good*

to the world of pretense," and play. Laughter "suggests that alternative possibilities to reality exist."

Yes. Although if you would prefer a more intellectual explanation, you can think of laughter as something that "acknowledges mutually beneficial interactions" and "communicates appreciation and shared understanding."

Have you ever seen two people start out arguing and end up laughing together? Their laughter likely started just in the nick of time. It made them much more likely to think up creative solutions to their disagreement, because it invested them in finding a resolution to what was keeping them apart. Then, as they shared their good feelings with one another, the laughter continued to bring them even closer together.

In fact, laughter is believed to have been connecting people in just that way for some four million years. It is now "believed that laughter emerged before language in human evolution." We laugh, and that makes us feel great, and it is not a coincidence. Feeling good is the icing on a fun and funny laugh that has a serious evolutionary purpose. Our laughter is meant to create connection between us.

Dance

Another good example of something you might never have thought of as adding to your emotional power is dance. You could say people have been inventing dances since the beginning of time, because dance dates back as far as we do, both as ritual and as an expression of sheer joy.

As I'm sure you know, some dances are just moving to sounds—drums or music—while others come to us with complicated steps and rhythms—*rules* if you will—for how to do them *right*. Perhaps you are someone who has gotten trapped in the rules of a dance. Maybe you have even been made to believe you cannot dance because you cannot keep to those certain rigid requirements some rational thinking brain created.

This would be a good time to re-mind yourself the place of dance is secure in a conversation about emotions and feelings. It's a great evolutionary tool for generating connection among us. Forget about the so-called rules of a particular dance. Get out there and just shake your head if that's all that will move to the music you hear.

Naturally—as in, by nature—we love to dance. We are meant to, and we even enjoy watching each other dance. It makes us feel happy to let ourselves go to the sound of a drumbeat, either in fact or through watching others, and we love to be transported by rhythms that make it impossible for us to keep still or keep from smiling. Dance is an exceptional, glorious, survival skill. Additionally, consider this: "To dance is to have trust."

Smile

If you're still determined that you cannot dance, you might try smiling to create your connections. Did you know there are 19 different smiles your face can make, but only one will actually make you feel good? It's the only smile that cannot be controlled, or at least, it can only be controlled with some considerable manipulation of your facial muscles. The other 18 smiles, which are surely sending some kinds of messages, are not the one message nature intended for smiles: social commitment. A genuine smile not only unites people and enhances their well-being but also strengthens their bonds.

You might be surprised to know how the message of a real smile compares to the message you get when someone bares their teeth at you. We tend to think of bared teeth as a sign of anger, even rage. Yet other primates, who once reflected fear and submissiveness with bared teeth, have, in their more recent social iterations, actually used teeth-baring to promote affectionate cooperation and affiliation. Today, they show their teeth to "make amends, as well as to soothe.*"

Might that not also sound like a smile you've gotten from someone who was trying to appease you?

While we're on the subject of mouths, kisses are said to be derived from primates who passed food directly from their mouth to the mouth of another, nurturing and, perhaps, showing love.[15] This may be a good

---

[15] *Keltner*, p. 85

time to remind yourself evolution is dispassionate and nonjudgmental. It simply takes what works and spreads it around so it can have a chance to work for everyone.

Of course, connection can also come about through a few methods you might never have thought of. One of them can feel anything but good, while the other seems to have gotten itself all caught up with a family member whose reputation would be anything but desirable as a healthy source of connection.

Embarrassment

Embarrassment doesn't feel good. Let's say you just broke the silence in your big office with a profane outburst you usually only use when you're home alone. Suddenly, there is silence in the big room, as everyone jumps up from their seats. They're staring at you from over the tops of their cubicles. Your face starts to feel hot and, dreadfully, you know it's turning red. You wish you could just disappear—die of embarrassment—before you will ever have to face any of them again.

Disappearing would actually be the worst thing you could do about your embarrassment. In fact, embarrassment provides an extraordinary opportunity for connection. If you left now, you'd miss the unique benefits of embarrassment; it prompts a "gesture that unites people." Your embarrassment has triggered in others "simple acts of forgiveness and reconciliation, which are essential to prevent a cutthroat environment."

Everyone who witnesses your obvious embarrassment knows how you feel just by looking at you. Your red face is silently signaling to them you are aware of your mistake, and you are reassuring them it *was* just an honest mistake. If you could take a deep breath, look around you, and calm yourself down, you might see they are actually softening their reactions to you. Your embarrassment is speaking powerfully to them. It's sending a mighty message that you are someone who cares about the rules of your social interactions, and you are committed to the moral order of the community you share with them. You wouldn't want to miss all that, would you?

Teasing

Teasing, on the other hand—which has nothing in common with bullying, even though teasing might make you uncomfortable—actually evolved with the best of good intentions, to enable you to navigate the complexities of social interactions. Teasing is defined as provocation without aggression. It is intended to provoke emotion in an obvious way to help you achieve a specific purpose: to identify another's commitments by attempting to activate their emotional responses so they will disclose—through their expressions or other means—whether they are dedicated to you.

Teasing achieves its purposes by setting up hierarchies, assessing adherence to social norms, revealing possible romantic interest, and even resolving disputes about work and resources. The teaser aims to convey their message through nonverbal cues that indicate the teasing should not be taken literally but rather in a playful spirit.

How can you be sure if it's teasing, you're getting, and not bullying? I'm no scientist, but I'll guess your mirror neurons will enable you to tell the difference. If you take a close look at the person's face, all you'll have to do is trust your brain to tell you what you need to know. *That is as Nature intended.*

While we're considering what nature intends, if you don't feel good about some teasing you've gotten, even after your teaser has assured you it was all in fun, it may be time to switch gears and remember you can always trust your feelings. Your intellectual sense of fairness, or even fear, may want to give the teaser the benefit of your doubt, but your feelings will have no doubt they have been more than good-naturedly teased. Remind yourself feelings are only trying to tell you the truth, while your thoughts may be saying what they only *want* to be true.

Touching

Touch is another important contributor to generating connections between people. We know touch is widely recognized as having great healing properties, but did you know that, when you are touching or being touched, you are also evoking "trust and generosity." It's perhaps not surprising, then, that touching is often described as the "fundamental language of compassion, love, and gratitude."

Compassion

Since we've arrived at the subject of compassion, this might be a good time to take a second look at that potent emotion. The dictionary defines compassion simply, as a *"deep feeling of sharing the suffering of another in the inclination to give aid or support."*

You wouldn't think a deep feeling of sharing could arouse negative and hostile, even fearful, feelings, would you? Yet, mention compassion to *others,* and you'll trigger just that response in some people.

Do you know anyone who seems to go to great lengths to convince themselves, and more importantly you, that compassion is overblown and overstated? Or, to put it another way, that anyone could think compassion would best be relegated to the same wastebasket into which they'd like to toss their feelings and emotions? We've got so much to learn about ourselves now that our brains have started revealing how they see our lives.

Those who would try to minimize compassion may only be trying to mask their own discomfort or fear that others will think they are soft or weak. They think they need to manage their displays of compassion by controlling this emotion, perhaps by restricting it to something that belongs to the province of parents and children. Or, they might restrict their allowance for compassion to *others,* who they imagine are less fortunate than they: old people, homeless people, poor people, people for whom their compassion can be exercised with a donation to a cause.

There are even those among us who would argue we must learn compassion, but only for purposes of religious practice.

It is important for us to know we do not have to learn compassion, nor do we have to *practice* it. Compassion happens automatically, and whether you want it to or not. It has been hard-wired into our brains, earning its place in our hierarchy of emotions, by proving over time it is a generous contributor to the wellbeing of the human race.

Far from being a trait of the weak, compassion is "active concern for others, rather than merely reflections of them. In fact, it encourages bravery, altruistic actions, often at significant personal cost. Compassion does not turn people into tearful bystanders, moral weaklings, or passive observers, but rather into individuals who willingly take on the suffering of others, even when they are not obligated to do so. How can you be considered weak if you choose to bear the pain of others, especially when you could easily walk away from a stranger without any expectation of helping?

Perhaps if we could stop pretending there is such a thing as being *simply* human, we might be able to see why compassion, like empathy and our feelings and intuition, *cannot* weaken us. On the contrary, as with all our emotions, they only strengthen and empower us.

Here are the cold, hard facts: Nature's interest is all about arming humans with proven technologies that work in behalf of our ability to thrive. That interest is reflected in the aspects and responses of our own nature, which has worked for centuries. Societies in which people act on their feelings of compassion toward one another are believed to be better prepared to thrive.

Once again, you might be recognizing the pattern here. Some aspects of ourselves make some of us uncomfortable. We react to our discomfort by trying to diminish their importance with our words. We might call them soft, weak, as we might label those who exhibit a happy abundance of such responses: *bleeding hearts.* We try to replace them with logic, and reason. In our rush to appear to be in control of our emotions, however, all we succeed in doing is belying our true nature. We are bound to fail.

We are tough we say. So how can we be emotional and compassionate at the same time?

We rationalize our pretenses. *Aren't we supposed to harden ourselves against the constant suffering of others, when we cannot alleviate it?*

We lock ourselves in behind words we pile up against the door marked *simple human characteristics,* and we hope—for that is all we leave ourselves to do—no one will challenge or point out the fundamental errors in our thinking.

Here's how important compassion is from your brain's perspective. It is rooted deep within you, in a network of nerves called the vagus nerve, which you have right there in your chest. When this nerve is activated, it "creates a sensation of spreading warmth in your chest and a lump in your throat."

Even reading that description you can imagine how unnerved the uncomfortable someone might be to think of such a thing taking *root* inside him. Yet, that is just what compassion does. The vagus nerve—from which the roots of compassion flow starts at the top of your spinal cord and travels throughout your body, linking to the muscles of your face, vocalization, your heart, lungs, kidneys, liver, and digestive organs.

You feel compassion with all those body parts, whether you are aware of it or not and whether or not you want to feel it. You feel it because it has been built into your nervous system. Surely, you could choose to ignore its tug, force your mind and body to work hard to deny it, but why would you want to do that out of some misguided notion it makes you look weak and, therefore, undesirable, or worse?

Compassion does nothing of the kind. It is a major response in humans, and we all have it in common; no one can be singled out for shame by weakness because of it. Perhaps it is time to rethink our relationships with those negative words we fearfully use to describe our emotions.

That said, it might interest you to learn your body actually knows you sometimes struggle in your relationship with compassion. Our nervous systems are thought to recognize that we are "constantly at odds" with this powerful emotion, and that we're moving constantly between our fight-or-flight instincts for self-preservation and our inclinations to care. In the end, compassion is born of precisely this challenge.

Sympathy

Like compassion, sympathy has also been encouraged by natural selection. Charles Darwin considered sympathy to be the strongest of our instincts. Indeed, he believed *"those communities which include the greatest number of the most sympathetic members, would flourish best, and rear the greatest number of offspring."*

Kindness

While we're growing our list of powerful *"soft"* responses to life, we are bound to add kindness. You may easily imagine a compassionate society would value kindness, but you may not have heard that, among people surveyed across 37 countries, kindness was the overwhelming choice of the most valuable of all desirable characteristics in a prospective mate.[16]

Our inclination toward kindness extends not only to those we care about but also to strangers. Evidence shows that kindness is so crucial among strangers that evolution placed it directly into our genes, as if it would leave nothing to chance to make this point.

Do you need still more reasons to accept and embrace compassion, sympathy and kindness as premier aspects built right into you to make you *simply* human?

We're all an other

This brings us right back to connection, begging this question: If so many of our biological and neurological impulses are moving us toward connection, why does it seem so hard for us to connect with each other? Why do we find it so difficult to trust our own natural instincts and wisdom?

It is unlikely anyone alive today would fail to notice there is much strife in the world. In many places, people are fighting one another to prove their religious or spiritual practices are somehow superior to those of *others*. In other places, people are fighting to keep privileges and lifestyles they believe are being threatened by *others*, whether the threats are real or perceived. When we listen to the arguments of these

---

[16] *Ketlner*, p. 245

cultural warriors, we can despair that the connections between us are tenuous indeed. Yet, the more passionately we hold on and hold ourselves apart from each other, the more we enable fear and suspicion to build up, increasing and reinforcing the scaffolding around the emotional chasms we all use to separate us. In the big picture of survival, wouldn't we be one another's best natural resources?

One possible reason for our fear and suspicion may be our first reactions to strangers still arise automatically, as they always have, from our earliest brain-parts. Those same prompts that long-ago caused our forebears to run away when danger threatened still come from our basic emotions, which have never stopped working. On top of that—literally—our brains evolved to include a hypervigilant fear-sensor designed to warn us about the seemingly never-ending dangers and threats we confront today. That sensor is called the amygdala, and it senses potential threats in everything, even when our thinking brains will later override those first impressions by determining no threats actually exist.

This means it might only be instinctive that your first reactions are the same fear and suspicion humans have always felt at the sight of an unfamiliar *other* approaching. Keep in mind, though, the appearance of a new *other* in your life can be the start of a new conversation and not the end of an old one. You can choose to discern what your amygdala cannot distinguish. Your modern brain can easily think about your first reaction and then decide, *on second thought,* to take it in another direction.

To say this another way, after you have acknowledged your prehistoric inclination toward fear and suspicion of strangers, and then thought your way through to realizing there is no actual threat to your wellbeing, you can move on into the present and out toward your future. You can share your laughter, perhaps a dance, certainly a smile and any of the other tools you have readily available in your natural toolbox—the very same tools, by the way, the *other* will be bringing to you.

To be fair, it may not be easy for us to *get over* our ingrained fears and suspicions. New York University's Joseph LeDoux, who I was eager to ask about this in light of my Fear Weekend experiment, told me that, once fear makes its presence known, most of us cannot figure out how to get our thoughts to control it very easily. He admitted this is something scientists don't really understand, and we may, for now at least, have to accept the initiation of our fears is not always under our control.

As you well know, fear can be initiated by something outside yourself—something that occurs either to or around you can cause you to react with fear—and it can just as easily come from within you. That is, something like a random thought can occur to your mind and activate your entire system of fear. While this is true, it doesn't have to mean it won't be in your best interests to consider you have more choices and possibilities. Unless your basic emotions force you to act, you can always decide how you want to react where *others* are concerned.

Of course, it may not be your amygdala at all, not even your brain that makes it difficult for you to trust your instincts. It may be the sound of all those external voices trying to convince you to see your life as they would have you see it, that is the real challenge standing between you and enjoying a life of connection with the *others* around you. At the very least, they can certainly confuse you about what is truly in your best interests.

Those may be the voices that would have us believe there isn't enough of whatever is *the best* or the *most desirable* to go around to everyone. Isn't scarcity the standard by which we recognize what we think of as *the best?*

For example, the voices barraging us with endless words designed to convince us the features of beauty are X and not Y may be nothing more than voices promising they can sell us beauty. Perhaps we could excuse them for having a vested interest in convincing us most of us are Y and want to be X. Even so, is there any evidence the features of X are more beautiful just because fewer people have them? Did you ever wish you had blue eyes?

Or, they could be the voices that, since the days of ancient Greece, have been trying to convince us there is no need to be held hostage by such things as our emotions and feelings. No less an expert than the famous behavioral psychologist B.F. Skinner was said to have declared (I expect with tongue in cheek), *"We all know that emotions are useless and bad for our peace of mind,"* and yet, there are all sorts of people trying to convince us of just that today. They would urge we be reasonable and strong, perhaps re-minding us we can trust the facts as they tell them, but it is more likely they are only invested in our not-thinking they are soft, or weak. Are our natural responses to life, and each other, so seditious as to be a threat to our wellbeing? Or does misery, after all, merely seek company to shore itself up?

As I was getting to know my brain and to think of it as the point of action for everything I do and am, I was beginning to wonder. If we understand our brains have evolved to accommodate the great changes in the ways humans have lived on earth, and things like connection and feelings and emotions have been hard-wired into us to meet our needs, why can't we just accept ourselves the way we are? Was something else going on that I didn't—yet—understand or know anything about?

Imagine how an ancestor of yours might have viewed some *other* on the day she was able to put aside her fears and anxiety about strangers for the very first time. Imagine them discovering, together, there could be safety in numbers, and the *other* could be far more useful as an ally than an enemy—perhaps even the *other* really wasn't so scary after all, maybe was even likable. Those brave pioneers were setting you and me on an extraordinary course toward living in today's world.

Just like the young man who put himself on the bus before anyone else, we all want a chance to be seen as a unique individual in the world we have created with our agreements about how to live. When we watch one another closely and envy what we perceive *others* have that we ourselves fear we shall never have, we cannot see one another, not for all the time we spend watching or fighting with each other. We can only assess, not who they are, but, rather, whether we think they are better off than we. How can it be different when we do not try to know one another? We can only make up stories about them, often out of nothing more than our perceptions, and then we determine the only way to deal with the *others* is on the basis of what we have *discovered* about them from our safe distance. In such a world, we are bound to believe we are always at risk of losing or having something taken away from us by someone else.

Are we devolving, reverting back to the very lives it took our prehistoric forebears so long to get out of, just because we resist the changes nature sought in us to ensure our survival as a species?

If there is no evidence that says we cannot change our lives, is that the evidence that we can? Wouldn't it surely be turning the world on its evolutionary head if we continued to live lives we greatly diminish without any evidence that we cannot change them for the better? If we are the creators and owners of language, and if all our creations are made of language, can we not start to set the world upright again by trying something different, by talking together, nurturing the very connections that have proven themselves to be, so far, our best chance for survival?

There were new questions that I was starting to ask myself. What would it take for us to exchange scarcity for a different reality, one in which it is possible to realize abundance that is shared by all?

9

Say It Isn't So

"There is a vitality, a life force, an energy, a quickening that is translated through you into action, and because there is only one of you in all of time, this expression is unique.... if you block it, it will never exist through any other medium and it will be lost. The world will not have it."

Martha Graham*

In the twentieth year after Art died, I found myself pondering this question for the first time: What is truly possible for humans? I wanted to know because something much bigger than me seemed to be pulling me toward it, something that was calling me to change, for good. So much of what had once been familiar felt as if it had been split wide open by the challenges I had confronted, and since there was nothing to *go back to*, I felt bound to be moving forward into some new territory that was calling to me.

I was changed. Sometimes, when I would try to imagine looking at me from the outside, as if I could see what exactly was different, I

---

*   Agnes DeMille, *The Life and Work of Martha Graham*

was struck by how everything still looked the same. I looked the same, and people still related to me as they always had. Even so, I knew the world in my tiny hamlet, where I had expected to spend the rest of my life, had stopped nurturing me. The most important thing now was to find the one thing I could do that would feel as big as what I had come through.

Even thinking *that* was a big change for me. I often thought my education as a fully grown human in this world really began in the minutes after Art appeared in my life. Until then, I had been content to take life as it came, without challenging it, or myself, too much—.

Here's one of the wonderful things love can do for you: It can take you right out of yourself and into a new Self you might have only daydreamed about before. It can also show you where you've been hiding from yourself, as if you have been trying to live *under the radar*, and love—our most joyful feeling of all—can no longer allow you to do that.

I had always tried not to call attention to myself, and to live small, but I had to admit Art always told me he saw something very different when he looked at me. I didn't understand it while he was alive, but now I saw he had always encouraged me to find the exact things that would break me out of the safe little corner in which I stood and into a happiness I barely allowed myself to imagine. From the night I met him, he was always nurturing that kind of happiness in me in every way he could. He once predicted, "one day you're not going to be able to be invisible anymore, and then you're just going to soar. Better get used to it, Dean," he advised, and I can still see him laughing at the look on my face while I scrambled to figure out what he was talking about. He said he looked forward to being there on that day, and he'd be proud just to carry my bags. I laughed because I knew he expected me to laugh, but I never took it seriously. What he was taking for granted was way too big for me ever to take seriously.

Yet, after his illness and my experience in the AIDS epidemic, as well as everything that had come after, I knew I needed to do something I had never done before. How could I live with myself if I did nothing but go on playing it safe? He had done everything he could to make the world bigger for me, and now I saw that, without really knowing it was happening, I had moved far away from my life-long willingness to live a default life. What I wanted—needed—was a deliberate life I could embrace, even love. Perhaps that was simply true for me now, as it has been for so many others whose lives have been transformed by unimaginable events, but I was searching for something I could do to honor everything that had brought me to this moment. I was willing to trust that, while I might not know what it was, something would show itself if I would only pay attention and let it come.

While I was paying attention, I continued my work of talking with others and reading about my brain. That was certainly one big way I had changed: suddenly science held a fascination for me. Why hadn't I ever known how interesting and even exciting it could be to learn about the science of myself? I talked with people about the unscientific experiments I was conducting and what I was learning about how my brain works. I told them how knowing the truths about my brain was changing the way I thought of myself, the way I thought about being human. It had even started me asking, *"what is truly possible for humans?"*

Even as I sometimes feared destiny might pick work that was just too big for the likes of me, I remembered how the painfully shy girl I had once been had carefully imagined a very big life for her fabulous fantasy woman, and I had allowed her to inspire me. More inspiration came from the people with whom I had conversations. They were excited to hear about opportunities to realize their own unique personal power as something that just comes, pre-installed, within each human being. I saw we are extraordinary creatures of the earth, and that made it possible for me to see that, if every one of us could know even a little bit about how their brains operate, we might well be able to realize what the well-worn phrase *human potential* is all about. Around the same time, I also started to write this book, for the simplest of reasons: I wanted to share all I was learning about being human with as many people as I could.

Soon enough, questions started to arise in me. At first, they sounded pretty simplistic, yet I knew the answers would be anything but simple. Are we really as powerful as our brains suggest we can be? If so, why do so few of us get to realize what is possible for our lives? Are we limited only because we imagine we are?

What could we do if we really wanted to do something big? Could we change reality itself if we wanted to, create a new reality in which everyone could realize their natural human potential? Such a thought was intriguing, to say the least. Without even realizing it, I was starting to walk a path toward another unscientific experiment, one that would prove to be my grandest so far.

I never thought much about reality, but now I wanted to know as much as I could. What is it? Is it something hard and fast, unchangeable in a way that enables us to enter it, but only to visit? Or, is it fluid; is something only real because we say it is? Once, in reality, the sun revolved around the earth, and the people of the earth trusted that fundamental truth. Then they discovered the earth revolves around the sun, and *"reality"* changed in an instant. So, what is *reality*?

I discovered there's been an ongoing conversation throughout generations of philosophers and scientists about this very question. Even as the debate has continued just beyond where you and I are busy living our lives, we humans have lived as if we have been cemented into reality. All people are certain that what they see around them is real, and yet, if each of us described our reality to others, wouldn't we be forced to admit what is real to one is hardly ever precisely the same for another? Some people believe they're bound and oppressed by their reality and are powerless to change it, but are we surrounded by *reality*, and are we, really, powerless to break its hold over our lives? Are we bound even to live in a reality that may have become more than we can agree to endure?

The more I thought about it, the more clearly I saw that I only knew one thing about *reality* with any certainty. It is a word. It is a word people invented, in many different languages, and as with all words we invent we have given it meaning. I checked a few dictionaries before I found this definition: Dictionary.com said *reality* is *"the state or quality of being real,"* which didn't explain anything. It cited philosophy defining *reality*, as *"something that exists independently of ideas concerning it."* That was a bit more information, but it still wasn't a good enough working definition. Finally, it added this: *reality* is that which exists *"independently from all other things and from which all other things derive."*

Now I was getting somewhere. What are the things which exist independently of our ideas of them, from which all other things derive? Trees, oceans, sky, snow, even animals and other familiar things that exist in nature came to mind, as did a perfectly formed new human being entering the world and the person I loved the most leaving it no matter how hard I had tried to keep him in it. Of course, you and I exist, differently from these other things, perhaps, but also in nature.

Is nature, then, the only *reality*? Is there anything else, in *reality*? Your clothes are real, aren't they? The chair you're sitting in and your desk or table, aren't they real? You can see and touch them. You can sit in your chair as your computer may be sitting on your desk, and neither of you collapses onto the floor. Wouldn't these qualify as *reality*? I had to presume a philosopher would say no, these things are not reality, because it is clear they are not independent of humans. They did not exist before humans created them—would they cease to exist if we all decided they are not reality?

Maybe I needed to invent a new word-category for things like clothes and desks and chairs, one that would place them somewhere between *reality* and not-really-reality as we define it. If we all agreed, then just by inventing new words to define the new category those things could instantly become *as if* reality. But, while we might, then, feel good about having a category for our things, that wouldn't solve the problem about *reality* at all, would it? We would have some certainty in the matter, but we would still always really know the existence of these things depends entirely on us, so they would not, strictly speaking, be reality.

So, are things real because we say they are? If so, what happens to the things we cannot agree about?

Wordplays can be really confusing, and by now you may be wondering why any of this matters. Actually, it matters a great deal. When we think of things as real, even if they are only *as if* real, we can forget we created them, just "made them up." We can convince ourselves, or be convinced, we are powerless to change them, and then, feeling powerless, we might not even try to challenge them.

In our confusion, we give these word-creations lives of their own, and we live according to what they demand of us as if they were more real than we are.

Yet, if the words we create do not satisfy our definition of reality, how can they be real? See what I mean about wordplays being confusing? Once we create something, it seems to become immutable, and then we keep reinforcing it. So, I wondered, if we call a thing real, so real we can believe we cannot change it, shouldn't we also keep in mind we really know the thing is only real because we have agreed to agree it is real?

Here's another thing. We have invented many complex systems to support our so-called reality, and these systems, too, may only be real because we agree to accept them as such. Yet, we have made some of them the rules by which we agree to live our lives. Others we are simply expected to accept because, historically, those who came before us agreed to abide by them and, presumptively, we do too: nations, governments, politics, economics and the very rules of written laws that constrain us to squeeze our lives into these things. We have built them up on foundations of words and ever more words, as endless a supply of words as we can invent, as if the more words we invent to define a thing the more it will be solidified, convincing us it is real.

I may not be a scientist, but maybe I do have a bit of the philosopher in me. As I wondered about reality, I couldn't help asking: Is there anything we create with words that could have come into existence independently of our imagining it? Is there anything people create that fits the definition of being that *from which all other things derive?* It was time to start asking some hard questions about words themselves.

In the shadows of words

Here is a curious thing about our words. Even though they are so critical in our lives—they are a really important part of how we know ourselves and all the things we put into our world—most of us don't even think about them much of the time. We simply use them as our means of communication, both spoken and written. Even our thoughts come in words. For the most part, they simply appear in our minds when we need them. We pull them up from our memories, and we toss them out in a variety of ways, but words never were and will never be real. They are tools we take for granted. We do not even attempt to remember they only exist in us because we put them there by inventing them and using them. Words themselves can never be independent of us.

Even so, we have given them power. We teach our children their words can hurt or harm, and then we teach them the words of others are not *sticks and stones*. Of course, as we experience them, we realize words can just as easily embrace us and make us feel loved. The metaphysician Florence Scovel Shinn, who you met in chapter 5, was of the opinion that, *"We are dealing with dynamite when we deal with words."* She believed the words a person speaks often can actually cause a chemical change to take place in her body, and the words of our thoughts can be transformed into *"concrete experiences in life."* She cautioned her students to *"watch your words with all diligence"* because *"you are continually reaping the fruits of your words."*

Think about all the words you've heard or read, even those that seem to be running around in your mind, ceaselessly. Notice how easily the wrong word spoken to you can change your mood or inspire you to take action. Words you read can make you feel hopeless or elated, as well as provoke other feelings in you. A compliment can *make your day* while a criticism carelessly *thrown* at you can do quite the opposite. If you read the morning newspaper, you might say you are *taking it all in* as if you were ingesting the words, and you might say they *fill your head*. Conversations often *linger* in your mind as good or bad, helpful or not, welcome or otherwise, even empty or meaningful, but rarely do they feel neutral as you think about words after they have *landed*—or been *dumped on*—you. How do the words that comprise your own judgments of yourself make you feel? Have you ever *eaten your words*? Shinn taught, *"we are continually limiting ourselves by our words,"* and she cautioned, when you *"change your words…you change your world."*

So, yes, our words are powerful, but power is not a word that appears anywhere in the definition of *reality*. A powerful word is no more real than one with no clout at all.

What might we do if we agreed some of our words have become too powerful for our own good? What if we no longer agreed to allow them to define our reality? What if we agreed, instead, we want to strip some of them of their power, even end their hold over us? Would we change them, re-define what humans have invented so far in our world of words? Or would we crouch and cringe in the face of words we believe we have no authority or control to erase from the cosmic blackboard, as if they were, in fact, more real than we ourselves?

Most of us do not think of ourselves as the sculptors of societies. We're involved with our individual lives on a daily basis, and we're not likely to leave those good efforts to imagine—much less demand— some other kind of future words would suit us better. Besides, even if we wanted to effect changes that big, where would we begin? Perhaps the very reason we assume the things we call reality cannot be changed is because we are more comfortable thinking some things are hard and fast, immutable, and take on lives independently of us. At the thought of changing reality, we might well ask, *"How can such as we, mere humans, change something as big as reality with a handful of words?"* You might even ask, *"How can those things* not *be real?"* You can measure and report on them, with numbers and words. They're the bills that come in the mail, the work you love to do if you're *lucky* enough to have work, or the job you dread but cannot live without. They're the time of your life and the bane of your existence. Surely, you would argue, reality is not something a powerless human or two can change by inventing a few new words or transferring imaginary power to some old ones.

Still, to my way of thinking, what do you do when you know you can't go *back* to living the way you lived before something so big happened to you that it changed your mind forever? Certainly, Art's death, as much as his very presence in my life, changed my reality more than once. With nothing familiar to go back to, wouldn't it be merely logical to expect anything that came next would have to be a new thing?

What if we could prove the whole world as we know it was created in just this way, with people discarding old ways and moving into new ones? Not the world of nature, of course; we know that exists independently of us (...or does it?), regardless of how much we may meddle in its life. We're talking about the world of words, the world of, let's say, human nature.

Throughout history, people have made and re-made their worlds, even when there were many among them who did not agree to embrace the new reality. We have created something we call poverty out of the creation we call wealth—how could there be unemployment if we had not created employment?—and we may well have invented scarcity directly out of abundance. With our inventions, we have created peculiar cultures in which some of the people are mere observers of the great wealth of others, while they themselves live in terrible poverty, and where only gaping holes filled with words like inequity and unfairness define their lives. To support this reality of imbalances, we have invented economic systems with a wealth of words, and we have chosen to sit by helplessly as the words run away with us, living far better lives than the people. Why does something called a planned economy operate to produce wealth for some of the people, when it might just as easily operate to enhance the wellbeing of all the people who agree to breathe life into it? We act as if we have to accept a reality of *not enough to go around* because that's what the words tell us we must do in order to enable present economic systems to thrive. Clearly, our systems could not exist independently of us, yet, even as we may decry the offense to our senses of humanity and fair play, we continue to agree to accept their survival may be more important than our own. At the altar of such creations, it is a wonder any of us can be quite *real* to any of the others.

After nature, we humans may be the only undisputed reality in the world we have filled with our own inventions. We exist independently of both that which we have imagined and our creations, and, certainly, we are the things from which many other things derive. Perhaps we alone satisfy the dictionary's definition of reality, so I just have to ask: *"Why do we shore up our own invented realities at the expense of ourselves and our natural allies, other people? Why do we have to pretend we are separate from each other in order to enable today's realities to continue?"*

Brains to the rescue

It seemed to me that, if I was going to choose to contemplate a transformation of reality, my brain would be the first logical place to look for a powerful toolkit with which to work. Perhaps I could start with our natural ability to connect with others. Connection satisfies the definition of *reality* because it is part of both nature and human nature. We know it exists because connection has been seen in our laboratories, lighting up our brains as they *loop* us together in synchrony. As we have seen, connection also exists independently of us; it has been hard-wired into our brains to occur automatically as we engage one another in a variety of surprising ways: laughing, dancing, talking and listening, among the most glorious activities we can find in human nature. Connection may well prove to be that from which all other things derive. Couldn't we use it, then, to transform the wellbeing of our world?

As I wondered about words, I thought it was important to understand what their relationship was with our natural connections to one another. I found much has been written about the very words we long-ago invented to create and support the concepts we live by today. I already knew we think of our words as our *reality*, but I discovered they have also been thought of as really nothing more than a *"a series of disconnected fragments with no inherent meaning beyond what we assign to them.*"*

That was intriguing. It made sense, in an abstract kind of way, since words themselves are not reality. When I stared at the letters we made into words, I could see the bits of lines and parts of circles fused together. I thought about our forebears who were so certain all of reality existed on an earth that was at the center of the solar

---

* Marshall McLuhan and Bruce R. Powers, *The Global Village*, p. 131

system. How did they feel on the morning they learned the earth—and they—were not the center of the universe, but just one more planet in the sky? It might have hurt their egos, but it certainly had no impact whatsoever on either their actual lives or the life of the heavens, where the *new* earth-reality had been real all along. Would we, too, be surprised to find a new reality has been there all along if we could put words together to describe one? Wouldn't we be surprised to find a generous and sustaining reality has been waiting to be noticed all along?

I could easily imagine what I would want a new reality to look like. I would only have to rearrange words that already exist to describe it. I want my new reality to afford all people an opportunity to realize only abundance; and I want peace rather than perpetual states of war; money that is easily available for everyone because—as an economics professor of mine once offered—it makes sense that when you're a government and you need money, you go down into the basement where you keep the presses and just print more. Money, by the way, does not fit our definition of reality, and so it begs a question: Is money, in all its forms, real only because we agree to agree it is real? As I went along, it was fun for me to move the words around to put people's wellbeing at the forefront, and it allowed me to imagine it might not be so hard after all to invent a new reality. Wasn't that just what all societies have been doing since the days the first humans stood upright to walk toward one another?

As I began to compile the details of my new reality, I was certain my latest unscientific experiment was well underway. I could always tell, because I was suddenly finding books about the very subject I was pondering. This time, it was the history of words, and it wasn't long before I was surrounded by books about language, communication, writing and brains. It was there that my research started.

Everything old is new again

A neuroscientist named Stanislas Dehaene explained in his book, *Reading in the Brain,* that humans have always had an instinct to learn, and this instinct caused our brains to evolve into a structure that would accommodate learning.[17] While prehistoric humans may have lacked the brain-power even to think about such a concept as learning, history is filled with evidence of how an instinct to learn might have driven us to be in written communication with each other from our earliest days—beginning with images painted on and carved into cave walls.

Consider this: The oldest cave paintings—long-thought to be the earliest evidence of recorded history—were found in southern France and estimated to be about 33,000 years old. Recently, scientists in Spain found *"red disks, handprints, clublike symbols and geometric patterns on European cave walls"* that they dated as far back as 44,000 years.*[18]

While we might think of their means of communication as primitive, similarities between those early cave drawings and hieroglyphics, and the words and letters that form the world's languages today, have revealed writing styles are much more closely related than we thought. In fact, although our written words describe vastly different lives, the letters that comprise them appear to be as old as human nature itself. Our letters, no less than theirs, have been determined, not by our sophistication, but, rather, by our biology. Nature prescribed the way our eyes were going to see, and what we see today is merely a modern version of those very same hieroglyphics our ancestors scratched in stone.[19]

---

[17] Stanislas Dehaene, *Reading in the Brain: The Science and Evolution of a Human Invention*, p. 144
[18] *The New York Times*, June 24, 2012, *Science* section
[19] Dehaene, *ante*, p. 178
* Archaeologists working in Africa also unearthed a 100,000-year-old workshop of tools and ingredients that were apparently used to mix paint. From what they found, they determined that the *"cave people in South Africa were already learning to find, combine and store substances, skills that reflected advanced technology and social practices as well as the creativity of the self-aware"* (emphasis added). They concluded that the humans who left behind what may have been the first artist's studio *"appeared to have developed an elementary knowledge of chemistry and some understanding of long-term planning earlier than previously thought."*[i] This evidence clearly speaks to early ancestors who were not merely communicating but who also exhibited extraordinary curiosity and interest in learning.

[i] *The New York Times*, October 14, 2011, *Science* section

Our letters, then, are the direct descendants of those ancient writing systems.

For example, today each letter in our Roman alphabet carries a subtle, ancient drawing from four thousand years ago. For instance, an 'm' represents waves, an 'n' symbolizes a snake, an 'l' depicts a goad (a long, pointed stick used to prod animals), a 'k' illustrates a hand with extended fingers, and an 'R' portrays a head. These are simplified drawings, reduced to their fundamental shapes.

This similarity is not a coincidence. From the beginning, our visual systems demanded that, if we wanted to write and read—regardless of when that was—we would have to re-create variations of the same things in nature that the first humans saw.

Okay. So, we are all connected to one another, and to nature, through our eyes and the way they see words. What was next?

The plot thickens

I was pleased to think the demands of our visual systems had directly connected us to ancient humans. For the moment, though, I wasn't quite sure how to put that information to good use.

That is, until I discovered that the journey through our written history may not have been as satisfying for our brains as it was for our eyes. In fact, according to neurosurgeon Leonard Shlain, the invention of the written alphabet not only changed reality—it completely threw the two halves of our brains out of their natural balance. As you might imagine, that caused ripples in nothing less than the social and power structures of the world.

Shlain's hypothesis aroused my curiosity. If it was true, it meant the introduction of the alphabet, and the countless written words it spawned, changed dramatically the relationship between our right and left-brain halves. The resulting imbalance, favoring our left-brain over the right, was, according to Shlain, responsible for the long history of wars and dominance that continue to touch many societies even today, a litany of power lodged in the strong over the weak and in men over women. According to him, the whole story goes something like this.

The progression toward our dependence on written words took a giant leap forward in about 1500 B.C., when the ancient Semitic tribes of the eastern Mediterranean—which included Hebrews, Arabs, Babylonians, Assyrians and Phoenicians—invented the *aleph-beth* by reducing thousands of hieroglyphic images down to 22 letters. With the brand-new, never-appeared-on-the-earth-before aleph-beth, anyone who could memorize letters-into-words could finally be set free to interpret the world for themselves. No one would any longer be constrained to rely on external experts to tell them what was true.

Some seven hundred years later, in about the eighth century B.C., the Phoenicians modified the *aleph-beth* and brought their product to Greece, where it was transformed into the *alphabet* we know.

It happened in Greece

It is important for us to keep in mind that people who could not read and write before reading and writing appeared in reality were not ignorant. Most ancient cultures relied on rich oral traditions, the stories elders told their young about who they were and how they got to be that way. Before the written word, life's answers were found in the stories spoken and sung throughout generations, the ways the world was seen and the ways humans saw themselves in relation to it. Many powerful oral traditions can still be seen and heard in the cultural and religious practices of people who live throughout the world today.

Interestingly, the original *aleph-beth* did not contain any vowels; some scholars have speculated this was not because someone forgot they would be necessary for reading to succeed.[20] They suggest there is evidence the ancients may have left out the vowels deliberately, to protect that which they worshipped.*

---

[20] See especially, David Abram, *ante*, pp. 241*ff*

* Even today, among descendants of the ancient Hebrews a practice continues in which vowel symbols are omitted from the holiest prayer documents, effectively making it impossible for them to be read by anyone other than those considered to be the most learned. To the extent that vowels appear anywhere in Hebrew writing, it is only in those books intended for reading by the general population.

When the *aleph-beth*—an alphabet without vowels—arrived in Sparta, it was received by men who had grown up within oral traditions. Socrates, a renowned philosopher-teacher who was powerfully ensconced in his oral tradition, taught his students through the use of spoken dialogs. However, in the hands of those students or, more correctly, their brains, reality itself would undergo one of its most radical transformations. Socrates's student, Plato, would put the dialogs into a written format, and many, many years later, I would be able to study them in a college course on Greek philosophy.

Plato made the dialogs famous throughout the world, and my education possible, by committing them to writing, but his intention was probably not to celebrate his great teacher. Rather, Plato and his colleagues were about the business of building a new kind of nation. They were wedded to a philosophical dream of an ideal society that would honor all things rational, logical and reasonable. Theirs was a revolution against societies which had been built by the seasons and forms of nature, one that would prove humans were superior to anything nature could come up with. In the old, oral traditions, such a thought that a human was anything other than one more life-form in nature would have been unthinkable.

For the young Greeks, therefore, the arrival of the *aleph-beth* must have seemed like a great gift, just the tool they needed to transform their world. They added vowels to it and re-named it *alphabet,* and then they used it to re-configure *reality.*

As you might imagine, in order to realize their dream of a perfect state, they had to redefine their culture from head to toe, slaughter the ancient, verbal civilization and build a new one on its ruins, a world they would construct out of papers and words. They had to convince the people of Greece that they had just discovered everything they had formerly known as reality had been wrong. It was a daunting task, and reportedly not a very popular one.

Before they were through, the path to the new society would be littered with old words that had lost their meanings, and replaced by a new vocabulary for just about everything. Reality could no longer be thought of as immutable.

Perhaps to ensure humans would forever after be known as the masters of the universe, Plato and his colleagues left no stone unturned in their drive to change public perception. They eventually turned their attention to their beloved gods and goddesses, whose lives were so closely intertwined with the people of the oral tradition. They plucked the deities from the vast skies in which they had previously resided and re-created them as the stories, tales, fables and powerless pages of what we know today as Greek mythology.

Into the future

How was it possible that the perceptions of a nation's people could have been manipulated in such a way as to re-define the beliefs of generations—even the generations of people who would live in the 21st century? What did the Greek populace think happened to what they had always known as reality? How did they reconcile their old with their new reality?

We cannot know what those citizens thought, of course; we can only wonder. If we were to look at our own perception of reality, we might see it resembles what Plato created in more than one way. We are still fighting the battle of the purely rational, logical interpretation of reality against what I'll call the natural, *intuitive* interpretation. Surely these vastly differing perceptions have something to tell us about how the ancient Greek citizens might have struggled with their new world.

However, as you and I look out into our environment from where we live inside our thinking brains, we can see something they must have wondered about. In their new reality, humans (albeit only some) were placed squarely at the center of life as the main event for the first time in history. Nature was no longer to be seen as encompassing them. Humans had their own nature, and you and I can still presume we are something different and apart from what we know as the natural world.

In many ways it is a painful legacy for us, as it must have been for the ancients. Even as we celebrate our individuality, we long for connection whether we can acknowledge that or not. We are proud of our private minds and consciousnesses that are unrelated to the minds of those around us, yet who among us would argue that connection does not ease our feelings of isolation?

Once upon a time...jobs and money

In place of our former relationship with nature, we continue to use the words the ancient Greeks invented, and we've added many of our own to describe our modern creations. These are what we think of as our very own immutable reality. You might be surprised to know one of these is jobs.

Before there were jobs, we did plowing and weaving, the stuff of our survival, steps along the way of our natural lives. The jobs the ancient Greeks created, however, were not about survival, even though in our reality they have surely become an important component of our societies. Jobs were about wealth for a particular class of people, who were clearly distinguished from the others.

When Solon the Lawmaker proclaimed Athenians would *"make goods only for export,*"* his followers introduced foreign slaves into society to do the work, and it has been reported that *"profits soared"* after that. So successful was Solon's invention of jobs that, after it, the governors *"began to entertain the idea of a job as a repetitious assembly-line method of making goods"* for the first time in the history of the world. For the first time, too, a job had lost its connection with survival, except, of course, insofar as it determined whether a slave who did not agree with his, or her, new reality would be allowed to survive.

The ancient Greeks did not create money. Money, both in the form of iron coins and, later, paper bills, is much older than that. It was invented in China, which had been a bartering economy until that system failed sometime in the ninth century, B.C. Europe stopped using money altogether in A.D. 476, when money failed, and people returned to bartering. After that, money did not make its reappearance until the latter part of the 15th century.

What is money, in reality? It is clear from money's history that it has no independent existence beyond the humans who give it meaning.

---

*   *Ibid.*, p. 42

Do we, therefore, only think of it as real because we all agree to accept it as real? If our money were to fail as it has at least twice before in history, would we too revert to the oldest form of economics, barter?

...time, and again

Before they were through, the early Greeks and then the Romans who came after them invented and cemented into place dynamically impactful concepts that would solidify the way people perceived their world. They created *"the historical sense,"* which made it *"possible to carve up and deal with time as a rational control device.*"* In the oral tradition, what we know as time was once known as the cyclical rotation of seasons and agricultural crops. With the invention of the concept of history—which is made up almost entirely of words on pages—time itself was invented, and it was no longer cyclical. It became linear, defined, as now and, perhaps, forever after, as a series of events that are separated by coming, according to their newly minted word concepts, *"before"* and *"after"* each other. Thus, time itself, which once flowed seemingly eternally from one growing season to the next, and the people who lived within it, came to see themselves in a universe of numbers, which relied, for its primary interpretation, on the left brain.

When the alphabet showed up in the Middle Ages, words were just endless strings of letters without any spaces between them, nor any punctuation marks to speak of. People had to read them aloud to make sense of them. Spaces were inserted between the words, and punctuation was thrown in to facilitate the reading, which makes it possible for residents of New York City to read in silence on buses and trains, and in restaurants, without having to *sound out* their words. Just image getting on a crowded subway car during the "rush" hour, where everyone is "sounding out" their words.

My husband Art used to love to remind me the one great thing we humans have in common is what he called our "change alarms."

---

*   *Ibid.*, p. 9

We don't take change lightly, and whenever we're confronted with a big change, these alarms go off in our heads. Yet, history is nothing so much as the story of how humans have been changing everything around them—everything that was previously believed to be hard and fast, unchangeable reality—since we started walking on two feet. Indeed, far from calling it unchangeable, it would be more realistic to say no reality can consider itself safe where humans abound.

In the late 1700s, the world was plunged into what has come to be known as *The Age of Reason,* when nearly everything was processed with the growing numbers of words that increasingly supported a new concept: science. Humans pushed ever onward toward elevating reason, logic and linear thinking—the unique contributions of the left-brain—above whatever belief systems had once been the sources of their certainty and confidence. Even science itself was re-invented, until it could be applied to every aspect of humans' lives, and the inventions of its many iterations continue to dominate many societies to this day. Science pronounces the facts and, as science proves what the facts are, they are enshrined in reality.

It was this reality—the radical switch from being a part of nature to being apart from nature—that Leonard Shlain held responsible for the imbalance between our two brain halves. The images on cave walls and the hieroglyphics our visual systems required to interpret life and ground us in it for eons got lost to our consciousnesses inside the countless numbers of squiggly and straight intersecting lines of alphabet letters, and all that we rational people have used them to create.

The newly literate could not have known how their brains would impact the history of the future—our future, the way you and I would see reality. Yet, in today's brain imaging studies, it has been seen that, when you are reading, your left brain lights up while your right brain remains dark, as if resting. If you stop reading and turn to watching television, your right brain will light up and your left brain will go dark.* What those newly literate societies could not have known was

---

* Of course, as with everything having to do with your brain, this process is not as simple as it sounds. This is only an abbreviated description of what your brain is actually doing. *Ibid.*, Shlain, ante, p. 408

that they were creating a built-in neurological bias for the left-brain's talent for seeing the world through logic, reason, order and compliance.

By the 19th century, this neurological bias had transformed into a social bias, with the right brain considered the "less significant or quieter" counterpart. In fact, "the cultural bias at that time was so strong" that it was "seriously suggested that the right brain had no role in human thinking or activity.*"

Your better half?

The enormity of the impact of Greek society's transformation can scarcely be understated. We, no less than Plato, continued to glorify reason and logic over what we perceive to be the *softer, weaker and gentler* aspects of our human nature. Since we have minimized them, we have set ourselves free to mistrust our feelings, deny our intuitions and avoid connecting with others.

It is not surprising, therefore, that Marshall McLuhan once described western civilization as having a *"mind-set"* that it has held fast to for some 4,000 years, of a *"monolithic linear self-image"* that *"emphasizes the operation of the left hemisphere of the brain and which, in the process, glorifies quantitative reasoning."*[21] He seems prescient in his 1950s predictions about the impact of a newly technologized world he never lived to see, which he described this way:

> *Ever since the collapse of the oral tradition in early Greece…Western civilization has been mesmerized by a picture of the universe as a limited container in which all things are arranged according to the vanishing point, in linear geometric order.*[22]

McLuhan warned more than half a century ago that the *"intensity of this conception* [of a linear geometric order] *is such that it actually leads*

---

[21] *Ibid.*, p. ix
[22] *Ibid.*, p. 131
* McLuhan and Powers, *ante*, p.187

to the abnormal suppression of hearing and touch in some individuals..."[23] Because of linear thinking, he reasoned, *"Western man thinks with only one part of his brain and starves the rest of it.... he has locked himself into a position where only linear conceptualization is acceptable."*[24] Linear thinking would have been unthinkable in the oral traditions of a world determined by nature.

It sounded to me as if the intellect declared war on the right brain, but why? Is there something about our right brains that drives humans to prove evolution was just wrong about two brain halves being better than one? Was the right brain, perhaps, a good idea that just didn't work out over the long haul? Is the left brain capable of managing our complex lives all by itself?

I had to admit, it was looking pretty bleak for the right brain, historically speaking. What if it was true that an imbalance between our two brain halves could have, in some way, triggered the violent history of the world I had thought so little about as a student trying to memorize endless dates of wars? More to the point, what if the present state of the world we live in—filled with its civil and imperial wars and rulers who seem to have little regard for their own citizens' wellbeing—is still obstructing our ability to see a different, peaceful reality also existing alongside it? How could we ever hope to overcome such a legacy if it was perpetuated not by deliberation but by a mere, regrettable shift that took place inside our heads a long time ago, unbeknownst to us, when our ancestors started to read letters and words? I was going to have to know a lot more about how our two brain halves divide up the tasks of our lives if I was going to be able to answer these questions, and so, having enough of history, I reached for my trusty neuroscience books to continue my research.

---

[23] *Ibid.,* p. 36
[24] *Ibid.,* p. 38

Does the right side know what the left side is doing?

It seemed only logical that this dilemma started early on in human evolution, when our brains underwent "a revolutionary development made necessary by our need to start talking to one another: speech had to be accommodated.*" Our one-piece brain split, creating our familiar brain, which is made up of the two halves that lie on top of and across the original structure.

Although the two halves of our brains are not actually physically connected, they are communicating with each other all the time through a vast network of neural fibers that run between them. As I envisioned what that might look like from my frame of reference of science fiction movies, I saw, just below the surface of my skull, a vast network of electrical currents running day and night. Yet, for all that activity I never have to think about what, exactly, is going on in there. I can just rely on each half of my brain sharing with its counterpart its own unique experience of my life, contributing as much balanced information as I need to run it well.

As with most of what our brains do, this sharing by the two brain halves happens automatically. Given that every brain's goal is the survival of its particular human, thinking about the profound complexity of my brain inspired me to a new respect for everything that must be coming together at all hours of the day and night, regardless of how I'm feeling and what I'm thinking or doing. I can rely on my brain to give me as much input as possible, not only to think and plan and carry out all the things I do deliberately, but so much more: whatever it takes to keep me alive.

Dr. Jill Bolte Taylor marveled at just that same complexity as she was recovering from a stroke she experienced one morning, while she was getting ready to go to her job as a brain researcher. In her book, *My Stroke of Insight*, she described how she vacillated from one *"mind"* to the other as the stroke progressed. Reading her description, you might

---
* Shlain, ante, p. 17

think each of your brain halves lives in a completely distinct universe. Yet, for Taylor, it made exquisite sense to have two uniquely efficient minds working together as a single whole. Indeed, she concluded that, *"the more aware I remain about what my brain is saying and how those thoughts feel inside my body, the more I own my power in choosing what I want to spend my time thinking about and how I want to feel."*[25]

The left brain is considered the "analytical, practical, and detail-focused side, with an emphasis on time." When it was preeminent, she was able to recognize she was having a stroke, and to know she urgently needed to do something to help herself before she would lose the capability of functioning. But as she described it, no sooner would she begin the attempt to take action to try and save her life than the domain of "the blissful state of the intuitive and kinesthetic right brain" would come to the fore. Her right brain brought her "a feeling of total contentment and tranquility" which fascinated her as it drew her into its alternate universe. There she experienced a powerful sense of wellbeing so peaceful it was difficult for her to pull herself away from it, to remember she was having a stroke and needed to act quickly to save her normal life functions.

As you were reading that last paragraph, did you find yourself reacting one way and another to the completely different personalities of her brain halves? Were you thinking, if only the right brain would have *minded its own business* and let her left brain do what it had to do, she might have been better off? Did you create a new respect for your own left brain and its rational mastery? Were you feeling biased against her right brain because you thought it was unrealistic, illogical, impractical and even seemed to be lying to her about how dire her situation really was?

You might be surprised to know Taylor herself holds no such grudges of any kind. Rather, her book can be read as a love letter, a celebration of the majesty of her two brain halves—and, by implication, yours—which she described in great detail.

For the right brain no time exists except the present moment, and each instant is full of vivid sensations. The present moment is

---

[25] Jill Bolte Taylor, *My Stroke of Insight: A Brain Scientist's Personal Journey*, p. 154

both timeless and overflowing with potential...when everything and everyone are united as one...our right brain becomes spontaneous, carefree, and creative, letting our artistic impulses flow freely without restraint or criticism.

Indeed, the right brain is "able to think intuitively and unconventionally, and it explores the creative possibilities that each new moment offers."

However, your right brain is not all about timeless enthusiasm. It has an important contribution to make to your whole brain's ability to understand what is going on around you. Indeed, the two halves of your brain work best when they work in a perfect balance. While your left brain has the primary responsibility for speech, reading and writing, its partner on the right must be free to evaluate—to *pick up*—the more subtle cues of language. It is responsible for catching the "vocal inflection, facial expressions, and body movements" and it must pass that information along both accurately and as quickly as possible for you to be able to use what your senses, so finely tuned, are telling you. It will also file its information in your memory so you can call it up again later, whenever you need it.

In order to do this, your right mind has to create "a comprehensive snapshot of what this moment in time looks, sounds, tastes, smells, and feels like...filled with sensations, thoughts, emotions, and frequently, physical reactions." The right mind might notice that one person is taller or wealthier than another, but such observations are made without any judgment. From the perspective of the right mind, everyone is considered an equal part of the human family.

My right mind does not recognize or focus on divisions or artificial distinctions such as race or religion. "In the awareness of my right mind, we are woven together as the universal tapestry of human potential, and life is wonderful as we are all beautiful—just as we are."

The right side of the brain is characterized as "adventurous," "socially skilled," and "celebratory of abundance." It is described as celebrating its freedom within the universe, unburdened by past experiences or worries about the future, and valuing the well-being of all living things. It sees itself as part of a greater whole, recognizing the interconnectedness of all beings and embracing a sense of unity and purpose.

In contrast, the left side of the brain is noted for its focus on details, organization, and maintaining a strict schedule. It processes information methodically, makes decisions based on past experiences, and tends to view things in terms of right or wrong, good or bad. While the left side excels at managing and categorizing information, the right side brings enthusiasm, creativity, and a broad perspective to the table.

There can be a perceived tension between the two hemispheres, with the left side often preferring to maintain control and avoid the open-minded approach of the right side. The left hemisphere is skilled at multitasking, processing information rapidly, and filling in gaps when data is incomplete. It organizes and categorizes experiences, creating a system for recalling and understanding them.

The left brain is also the place where your stream of consciousness originates. It transmits that voice in your head and makes it possible for you to remember who you are and not "lose sight of your life and sense of self." Listening to Taylor's words, we might even imagine the left brain is the home of what we have been calling our very own inner voice, the one that simply tells you what is true for you.

Without having to control consciously or monitor the communications between your two brain halves, you are free to celebrate your left brain's practicality at the same time each half is enjoying the full benefit of its partner's unique perspective on your life, as it unfolds minute-to-minute. When your brain is working at its best, the two halves are perfectly balanced, as they were intended to be. You need have no concern your powerful left brain will restrict you to a life of *linear and methodical* thinking, anymore than you need to worry your right brain's *euphoric nirvana* will sweep you away from your reality.

What that means is you get to decide how you want to act on the combined wisdom of your fully communicating brain halves. You can reserve for yourself the right to choose to act on or against the best advice your brain can give you, advice that is based on what is simply true for you: what you see and how you interpret your life as it is occurring. In short, you get to live your life deliberately, consciously.

Luckily, you and I can only imagine the full extent of impact of an imbalance such as neurosurgeon Leonard Shlain posited taking root in the brains of people who lived long before us. Happily, in our reality, the balance between our two brain halves has at last been restored.

Unlikely hero restores brain's balance

How did the long imbalance that may have sparked humans' history of war and domination reverse itself? That happened in modern time, when reality underwent yet another dramatic change. It started when we invented something we call *technology*. Of course, it also has to do with all the new words we have invented to launch and sustain, once again, that which never existed before in the world.

In the early 1900s, and especially in 1939, the written word finally met its match. First, motion pictures were invented, then television, and our brains—whose halves we may imagine were, if Shlain is correct, barely speaking to each other by that time—had to pull themselves together to be able to utilize these new technologies. Because your left brain is not as adept as your right at interpreting images, the right brain was called back into action, and fast, no matter how much the skeptics may have wished it would simply fade out of evolutionary history.

Although we do so much of our thinking and communicating with words, our brains do not *see* words. You may recall that Dr. Taylor referred to her right mind's "comprehensive tapestry" of every moment, and Dr. Dehaene's advice that our visual systems demand letters consist of shapes that mimic scenes in nature. That's because our brains need images in order to make sense of what they see, so you can translate them into the words you will speak. Scientists call this *mapping*, and mapping, they say, is "crucial for advanced management." Indeed, when the brain creates maps, it updates its own information. That would be You.

The creation of mental maps is a continuous process, even during sleep, as evidenced by dreams. The brain maps every external object or action, including their relationships in time and space, relative to each other and to the central self. You.

It is only after your brain has its maps in place that consciousness "enables you to recognize the images as something or someone."

Television, of course, is all about images. With the advent of television, all you had to do was add your consciousness to the mix and you could interpret the widest range of information any human brain had ever been able to *take in* at that point in history.

You know the rest of this story, about the technological revolution that followed the invention of television. We live in it every day, with our computers and smart phones and the many devices that attend them, which we can no longer live without. These have become so familiar we take them for granted—and that's the way it often is with humans and their brains.

Just as those 18th century readers could not have known how they were changing their brains by their revolution in reading and writing, you cannot feel yourself using your whole brain when you create compositions on the computer. Yet, that is just what you are doing when you're working away at your screen. You are using eye-hand coordination, and you are working with images. You just think you are setting your spirit free.

This interaction prompts you to establish and possibly expand your own boundaries. As you "compose" text on your screen, you are reinforcing the balance between the two hemispheres. Additionally, the absence of physical pages on a computer further discourages linear thinking. Even when you are idly *scrolling* you are relying on your right brain's map-recognition skills—reading scrolled text is said to be much closer to reading Chinese characters—not to mention the great exercise your brain enjoys when you challenge it with your computer interactions.

With our technologies, we have already changed reality from what it was for those who came before us, adding our stories to the vast history of human survival. Television brought us the expansive scope and intricacies of a world beyond our immediate sight, enabling us to become familiar with the existence and lives of others.

Computers and their progeny have taken us even further, making it possible, for the first time, for humans of the world to impact and interact with one another directly across the earth's great breadth in real time. Can we still pretend we are not powerful enough to change reality? Clearly, we have already done so, many times.

Back to the beginning

After my sojourn through history and neuroscience, I came back to the questions with which I began: What is really possible for humans, and can we change reality? I had a much better idea of what reality has looked like as it has changed over the lives of humans on earth, but I still wasn't sure about what is really possible for us. What are the limits—if there are any—to human potential? What could we invent if we were to transform our reality into a new one to leave to those who come after us? What is the best we could come up with?

What we presently call our reality is, clearly, vastly different from what was real at the time people believed the sun revolved around the earth. It may be nothing at all like what it was under the oral traditions of the ancients, and it is not even very much as it was before television was invented in 1939. What is apparent is that, even without a working definition of reality, we humans have spent great portions of our lives reinventing the realities in which we have lived.

Perhaps all those societies that were created before us have brought us to an evolutionary moment, when we can make at least one more extraordinary contribution to the history of humans. What if we, just like the humans who thought the sun revolved around the earth, could explore the unknown as so many others before us have done? Would we be willing to accept that the reality we so adamantly cling to is nothing more than one more possibility for life?

Suppose we got agreement to choose to live without the burdens of words like scarcity and inequality, to toss out or discontinue applying phrases like *not good enough* and *nothing you can do about it* in our lives. Think about some words and phrases you might like to eliminate from your cultural vocabulary, and the new words you might want to replace them with—even new words you yourself might invent. You could have some fun creating your vision of a new reality, building in things that would make your life easier, more pleasurable, beautiful and abundant. You could even decide to return things like psyche, virtue, goodness, justice, temperance and courage to their original place in nature if you wanted to, and then we could agree to decide our forebears had merely made an error by removing them from nature in the first place. We could argue nature must surely have intended all the people of the earth naturally enjoy and share in these precious things equally, and it is simply logical we respect nature's positioning of these things within itself for that enjoyment to be realized.

Since words are our inventions, we could choose ones that would declare no words are better, or more real, moral or reliable than others. We could declare dreams are part of reality, and that's why they seem so real to their dreamers. We could return something we call spirituality to legitimacy instead of keeping it trapped in something we diminish in order to elevate what we prefer to call *hard and fast* logic and reason. What if words like channeling weighed as much as science?

From our vantage point of balance restored to our whole brains, we could re-create the balance within us as a new reality and apply it to everything we see outside ourselves. We could exercise our willpower to make this real, call the imbalances remaining in the world today merely remnants of the ways people were forced to live once, when their brains were out of balance, a passing flaw in human development, a glitch, to be replaced thankfully and at last by a return to the balance nature intended, our new reality. Who is to say with greater authority that these things cannot be decreed so? All we have is the present. Could there ever be a better time than these moments in which we are alive to begin to create the future?

What if the world woke up tomorrow and all its words were gone, swept away in a storm, even out of our memories? What would be revealed? How would our lives appear without the excess of descriptive words we have piled on top of them? Fear words, paucity words, exclusionary words of disconnection, disrespect and bias, and even worse—what if all we saw was filled with joy and abundance, supported, not by words, but by our well-felt connections to one another? The new words we create could become the new images of our wellbeing, supporting what scientists have seen in brains that light up at the sight of a loved one, or the connections mirror neurons make as they are bonding, and our investments in each other take hold between us. What would it be like to live in such a world, to see and know our lives as filled with richness and abundance enough to go around?

How would it feel if, as we set out to change the old words, we discovered all these new ones were there all along in equal measure, that we are not, as a matter of fact, bound to the limited choices we have made so far? Is it possible we do not see such things only because we have agreed to agree they are not there, not parts of our reality?

You may well ask how bringing about such a shift could be accomplished, and I would suggest we have tremendous resources for such a task, the best natural resources there are. Each of us is a perfect *other* for every one of us, and through our connections we can become the power that can change anything. How would we know until we try? How could we fail to try once we know?

Together, the people of the world can undertake what would perhaps be the grandest unscientific experiment there is: the transformation of the world itself, once again. We can do it deliberately, calling upon each other, and we can do it consciously, using the very consciousness that only human beings can call on. It represents a brain process that has shaped our development as a civilization, for better or worse. This form of consciousness is reflected in literature, film, music, and philosophical inquiry.

Moreover, the social responsiveness of the brain highlights the importance of understanding how not only our own moods but also our biology is influenced by the people around us. It emphasizes the need to be aware of how we impact others' emotions and biology. Relationships can be evaluated by considering the effects individuals have on each other.

We can talk with each other, learn to trust both others and ourselves; surely, we have instincts, feelings, intellect, memories, thoughts, intuitions and imaginations with which to meet the real challenges confronting humans today.

Along the way, we may have to learn what humans before us might have once known about empathy, intuition, sympathy, love, even embarrassment. Perhaps we shall even have to learn to free ourselves to dance to the music each of us hears. We can practice these things with one another, and we can reinforce them in ourselves by communicating even with those *others* who only a mouse can bring to our screens. It may take some practice, but, then, history, by definition, gives us nothing so much as time to use as we please.

Would we be pleased to strip away the pretenses we have learned to wear in our word-created reality? Perhaps we might discover nature has even older facts to teach us about our instinct to learn.

As we settle in to our new reality, we would be well-reminded that schools haven't always been the ways people learned; Nature has a lot to say about the way she teaches. Schools have their own agendas, which are mandated to accomplish and support the goals and outcomes of those who created them, perhaps those who, like the ancient Greeks, strive to re-define reality from their own fantasies of a *perfect* society.

Real learning is a by-product of being alive. We can educate ourselves, and one another. We can start by having earnest conversations about the very things we humans have most in common with each other: our brains, and our senses—all of them. We are learning many new things about and from our brains. History has taught us about what humans and nature have created so far, and we can keep learning together until we reflect life itself—inclusive, going vastly beyond any borders humans have been limited by in the past. These are the ways to the future, to our next reality.

Looking over my shoulder

I was about ready to close the door to my unscientific laboratory and head out into the world again, at long last. As an inveterate dreamer, I believed I had chosen the one dream I would most want to make real in my lifetime. The time had come to leave the lab that had held me safe for all the years of my life so far. I carried with me this book, the blueprint for one last unscientific experiment, and I now hand it over to you, dear reader, as my offering for your consideration. What you do with it will determine the outcome of this, our grand experiment.

To treat it well would be to use it as the start of conversations, with people in your communities, your parts of the world, everywhere people have brains and the history they share. Talking together about these things we have most in common as humans—our extraordinary brains—we can invent answers to the questions raised here, about who we are, what our human potential is, and what reality can be. Listening for our inner voices, we can make the kinds of choices and decisions, each of us for our own lives, that will guide us through the maze of today and determine what we shall leave for those who will follow, tomorrow.

For me, the decades of the 90s and first 2000s have proven that, when life gives you a transformative experience, the very least you can do is rise to the occasion and transform your own life. Maybe Art was right; maybe someday soon I—and you—will cease to be invisible, silent partners in our present reality, and start to soar. If I could soar, it would surely be to visit all of you as you sit in your conversation groups, talking about re-inventing a reality in which all people can thrive. If I do soar, it will surely be because you have agreed to hear me out, perhaps to participate in this experiment, having agreed to agree we shall use our collective power to re-create the world in our own image. I can hardly wait to hear how each of you will define your own version of soaring.

Art would have loved it, a challenge as big as the sky itself. One that requires the participation of all the people of the world, altogether.

Appendix A

Exercises for the Brain

The "Clearing Your Head" Exercise

This exercise will help you clear out all those external messages that have built up over time and are cluttering your mind. After you've done it, you can be left with only the sound of your inner voice. Try it in a few private moments; that's all it will take. You can do it as often as you like without experiencing any negative side-effects. It's even more fun if you do it with a few good friends who love to laugh.

Advisory: If it's been awhile since you last heard your voice, or if you've internalized a particular abundance of external expertise, you may have to do this exercise more than once to clear your head.

Sit quietly (or stand in a circle if there are three or more of you). Let your head(s) fill up with all the words you don't want to keep: commercials, warnings, nonsense, even good intentions that just didn't seem to fit you. Do it slowly; you don't have to give yourself a headache. Just breathe easily and relax.

When your head is full, open your eyes. Take in a long, slow, deep, happy breath. Then, blow all those words out onto the floor and imagine them piling up in front of you. Be sure to get them all out.

Now, stomp on them as you walk away. Laugh out loud and whoop it up (this is where it gets to be fun if you're doing this exercise with friends). If you prefer, you can also just step over them, shut the door and get on with your life.

When you can feel it is quiet in your head, you are cleared again to focus on yourself. Feel very, very self-centered. This is your time to think about you. No one will hear the sound of your voice. You need not apologize or be embarrassed about anything.

If you want to, you can have a conversation with your voice about any number of things. Start by asking yourself any question you want answers to. Here are some good ones:

> Do I want to be happy?
> What do I love about me?
> How do I see myself?

You can also be more specific in your questions:

> How do I feel about _____? (Fill in the blank) What do I want to do about it? (You may also want to ask yourself, *"What am I afraid of?"* but not until after you read my Fear Weekend in chapter 4.)
>
> Since I know what I really want to do is _____ (be happy?), what would make me (happy)? If your goal is happiness, you can start slowly and easily be telling your brain you want to be happy. When you're feeling in high spirits, be sure to share that information with your brain (tell it, "This is the way I always want to feel!").

Remember you have nothing to be afraid of by asking yourself any kind of questions. You are the sole asker and the decider, the only one who counts. If you don't know the answer right away, talk with your voice; it will help you think through to your answer. If an answer doesn't sound right to you, trust your voice. Do the exercise to clear your head again. You might discover you have more external experts trapped in there, blocking your own truth.

As you go through your day, give yourself permission to imagine and fantasize how your new default posture will look on you. This is important. Your brain will only know what you tell it!

The Collage Exercise

If you're not a person who relishes having a conversation with yourself, you might try making a collage. This is easy and fun, too, and you may be surprised to learn just what you were thinking that you might not have even known about. (You can also do this exercise with a group of friends.)

Start by asking yourself a question, any question that does not require a yes or no answer. (Here are some samples to help you get started: What will make me happy? What kind of life—or work—or wardrobe—would I like?) You may write it down if you wish, but it is not necessary to do so, as long as you remember it.

Get a large piece of cardboard or other kind of heavy paper and a bunch of magazines. The magazines can be of any kind and age, and any number will do—the more the merrier.

Now, without censoring your mind or your brain, go through the magazines and cut out any picture of any size, any thing(s) you want to. There are no right and wrong answers to this exercise, and you don't have to have any plan in mind—in fact, it's better if you don't.

When you've got a good pile of pictures, lay them out on the board. Move them around freely; try different groupings based solely on how it looks to you. Try to keep your mind free as you work; just lay them out. When you're satisfied with the look of it, glue all the pieces down.

Look at your board. Can you identify a story line, something it's trying to tell you? What are the similarities in the pictures, the colors, the groupings you've created? Does any of it have any relationship with the question you asked? Does it answer your question? Tell yourself—or have each friend tell their own—the story that you have created, starting at a logical point on the board and moving across it until you have spoken of each picture's contribution. Talking it out aloud is often a helpful way to discover what you're thinking.

Turn the board over and date your collage, and try to give it a name (like "I become a fashionista," or "My beautiful life.").

The story behind the collage

Let me tell you a story about my first collage. I was with my friend Susan, and, at her prompt, we each made one. I had been feeling particularly confused about what I wanted to do with the rest of my life after Art died, so my question was, "What kind of life will make me happy/" I was able to keep my mind clear of the temptation to answer the question, and I randomly pulled out what seemed like a great variety of pictures from about eight or more magazines of all kinds (news, fashion, health, yoga, home repair, to name a few; this part took about 40 minutes).

I laid the pictures out with no apparent purpose, and when I began to tell the story, I got excited to realize there was a powerful theme. My voice was telling me—re-minding me—I wanted to leave the rural life I had been living in for many years, to move to New York City, where I had grown up. I wanted to change the work I was doing, and the clothes I was wearing. I wanted color, and theatre, and dancing, and I wanted to meet many people. I wrote this title on the back: "My Beautiful Life." My heart had spoken directly through my voice, and I got the message loud and clear. Within the year, I sold my house, put everything in storage and moved in with my parents while I looked for an apartment.

Bibliography

Abram, David, *The Spell of the Sensuous: Perception and Language in a More-Than-Human World* (New York: Vintage Books, 1997).
Damasio, Antonio, *Self Comes to Mind: Constructing the Conscious Brain* (New York: Pantheon Books, 2010).
Damasio, Antonio, *Looking for Spinoza: Joy, Sorrow, and the Feeling Brain* (Florida: Harcourt, Inc., 2003).
Damasio, Antonio, *The Feeling of What Happens* (Florida: Harcourt, Inc., 1999).
Damasio, Antonio, *Descartes' Error: Emotion, Reason, and the Human Brain* (New York: Penguin Books, 1994).
Dehaene, Stanislas, *Reading in the Brain* (New York: Viking, 2009).
De Mille, Agnes, *Martha: The Life and Work of Martha Graham* (New York: Random House, 1956).
Edelman, Gerald M., *wider than the sky: the phenomenal gift of consciousness* (New Haven: Yale University Press, 2004).
"Smiles When Lying," Paul Ekman, Wallace V. Friesen, and Maureen O'Sullivan, in *What The Face Reveals*, Paul Ekman and Erika Rosenberg, eds., p. 202 (New York: Oxford University Press, 1997).
Gazzaniga, Michael S., *"Organization of the Human Brain,"* Science, Vol. 245, 1 September 1989.
Goleman, Daniel, *Emotional Intelligence: Why it can matter more than IQ* (New York: Bantam Books, 1995).

Goleman, Daniel, *Social Intelligence: The New Science of Human Relationships* (New York, Bantam Books, 2006).

Keltner, Dacher, *Born to Be Good: The Science of a Meaningful Life* (New York: W.W. Norton & Company, Inc., 2009).

LeDoux, Joseph, *The Emotional Brain: The Mysterious Underpinnings of Emotional Life* (New York: Simon & Schuster, 1996).

_____ "Music and the brain, literally," in *Frontiers of Human Neuroscience,* Vol. 5, Article 49, June 2011

Lehrer, Jonah, *Proust Was a Neuroscientist* (New York: Houghton Mifflin Company, 2008).

Levitin, Daniel J., *This is Your Brain on Music* (New York: Penguin Group, 2006).

Lewis, Thomas; Amini, Fari; and Lannon, Richard, *A General Theory of Love* (New York: Vintage Books, 2001).

McLuhan, Marshall and Powers, Bruce R., *The Global Village, Transformations in World Life and Media in the 21st Century* (New York: Oxford University Press, 1989

Payne, Ruby K., PhD., *A Framework for Understanding Poverty* (Texas: **aha!** Process, Inc., 1996).

Ramachandran, V.S., *A Brief Tour of Human Consciousness* (New York: Pi Press, 2004).

Shlain, Leonard, *The Alphabet Versus The Goddess: The Conflict Between Word and Image* (New York: Penguin Group, 1998).

Shinn, Florence Scovel, *The Collected Wisdom of Florence Scovel Shinn* (Radford, VA: Wilder Publications, 2007)

Taylor, Jill Bolte, *My Stroke of Insight* (New York: Viking, 2006).

Whitman, Walt, *Complete Poetry and Selected Prose* (Cambridge: Houghton Mifflin Company, 1959).

www.ingramcontent.com/pod-product-compliance
Lightning Source LLC
LaVergne TN
LVHW091533070526
838199LV00001B/40